T0336337

TURNING SORROW
INTO JOY

A JOURNEY OF FAITH AND PERSEVERANCE

KENT CHRISTMAS

WITH KEN ABRAHAM

Forefront
BOOKS

Turning Sorrow Into Joy: A Journey of Faith and Perseverance

© 2024 by Kent Christmas

All Rights Reserved.

No part of this book shall be reproduced or transmitted in any form or by any means, electronic, mechanical, magnetic, and photographic, including photocopying, recording or by any information storage and retrieval system, without prior written permission of the publisher.

No patent liability is assumed with respect to the use of the information contained herein. Although every precaution has been taken in the preparation of this book, the publisher and author assume no responsibility for errors or omissions. Neither is any liability assumed for damages resulting from the use of the information contained herein.

Unless otherwise indicated, all Scripture quotations are marked NASB are from the New American Standard Bible®, Copyright © 1960, 1962, 1963, 1968, 1971, 1972, 1973, 1975, 1977, 1995 by The Lockman Foundation. Used by permission. (www.Lockman.org)

Scripture quotations marked ESV are from the ESV® Bible (The Holy Bible, English Standard Version®), copyright ©2001 by Crossway, a publishing ministry of Good News Publishers. Used by permission. All rights reserved.

Scripture quotations marked NKJV are from the New King James Version®. ©1982 by Thomas Nelson. Used by permission. All rights reserved.

Published by Forefront Books.
Distributed by Simon & Schuster.

Library of Congress Control Number: 2023922334

ISBN: 978-1-637-63234-5
E-book ISBN: 978-1-637-63235-2

Cover Design by Bruce Gore, Gore Studio, Inc.
Interior Design by Bill Kersey, KerseyGraphics

Contents

CHAPTER 1

I've Got Nothing!

THE SIGHT IN FRONT OF ME WAS AWESOME. Seated alone on an isolated wooden stool located offstage on the large, elevated platform, I peered out and saw more than 130,000 people in the audience. In a few minutes, it would be my turn to address the huge crowd at The Return, a gathering of people from across the country held in September 2020 on the National Mall. Our purpose during the two-day event was to focus on God and "return" our nation to its spiritual foundations through repentance and prayer. The crowd stretched back across the grass for as far as I could see.

I had been praying all day about what God wanted me to say, but with only minutes to go before I was scheduled to stand before the throng of people, I had nothing. I had no prepared speech, no message, no notes, and more important, no sure word from the Lord that I sensed I should speak.

Earlier that day, I had walked along the Potomac River and through some of the streets of Washington, DC, praying and asking God for wisdom, trying to sense His leading. By now, I realized how enormous this event truly was, with multiple thousands gathered on the National Mall and literally millions of people watching online.

And I had nothing.

I had no specific message that God wanted me to share.

That is not a comfortable position for any preacher to be in, but that tension is amplified when you know you are going to be speaking to multitudes of people who are expecting to hear something good. I had arrived in Washington the day before, on Friday; I checked in at my hotel and then went over to the Mall to hear some of the more than ninety speakers who were scheduled to share a message with the crowd that weekend. I was disappointed. Although there was great music and several anointed words, the leaders seemed obsessed with making public apologies regarding the church's supposed failures, both past and present. We apologized to nearly every racial and ethnic group or minority I'd ever heard of and some that were totally foreign to me. I left the Mall frustrated at what I had heard—not a call to repentance that would lead to revival but merely a mishmash of spiritual navel-gazing that made the body of Christ sound almost silly.

Yes, of course, we needed spiritual renewal and revival, but we were still the bride of Christ and the only hope for the world that Jesus offered. So why bludgeon the believers? It made no sense to me.

As I returned to my hotel after Friday night's session of The Return, I wondered, *Why am I even here? Why did I come to Washington?*

On Saturday morning, I walked up near the stage and listened to Anne Graham Lotz, daughter of Billy and Ruth Graham. Anne brought a powerful and anointed message, and I sensed the presence of the Lord. I felt better about what the day might bring. *I almost wish I could get up there and speak right now rather than wait till later,* I thought. But my assigned time was still nearly ten hours away.

That afternoon, as is my custom when visiting cities in which I am to preach, I walked the streets, hoping to catch the "spirit of the city"; more importantly, as I walk I often receive messages from the Lord. Occasionally, I have written down messages the Lord has given me and then later delivered the prophetic word, but most of the time when I get a prophetic word, it is spontaneous and "in the moment," something that God gives me to say right now. I have no idea that it is coming. The prophetic gift functions quite differently than the process of studying, preparing a sermon, and then preaching it.

Often as I am preparing to preach, a message will marinate in my heart and mind all week long, usually intensifying as the speaking opportunity draws nearer. But prophetic words operate differently. I don't plan for them or prepare for them; I don't ruminate about a subject and think, *Oh, yeah, that will be just what the people need. That must be what God wants me to say.* Instead, prophetic words are inspired by the Holy Spirit, and they come almost unexpectedly—even to the person who is delivering the message.

On Saturday evening, I arrived in plenty of time at the greenroom, a tent near the stage where the scheduled speakers could relax, catch a bite to eat, or engage in conversation together before their turn onstage. I recognized several notable ministers, including a number of nationally known Christian leaders, such as Carter Conlon, who now pastored Times Square Church, which David Wilkerson, founder of Teen Challenge, had pioneered in inner-city New York in the 1980s; Tim Hill, general overseer of the Church of God (Cleveland, TN) worldwide; Puerto Rican evangelist and former gang member Nicky Cruz; and many others. They didn't know me, but I recognized them. As a relatively unknown, struggling pastor of a church with fewer than one hundred members, I felt somewhat out of place and didn't really engage anyone in conversation.

I glanced at the television monitors showing the platform and the speaker who was preaching at the time. My impression was that most of the people in the greenroom were not keeping close tabs on what was happening on the stage but were simply enjoying the spiritual atmosphere.

About an hour prior to my designated time to speak, the stage manager summoned me and accompanied me to the large stage. Backstage, on the right-hand side, at least thirty or forty people were milling about, including musicians, stagehands, sound engineers, production managers, and ministers. It was a flurry of activity. I glanced at one of the monitors onstage and noticed that the person speaking was scheduled only a few minutes in front of me.

A female stagehand came to find me among the group, and she guided me behind the staging area to a stool on the opposite side of the platform. "You can sit right here until it is your time," she said.

I sat all by myself on the stool and prayed, but I still wasn't getting any message from God.

It was nearly dark by now, and the crowd had already been on the Mall that day for more than ten hours. Ricky Skaggs, multiple Grammy Award–winning country music artist and a fellow Nashvillian, sang two moving songs that he and hit songwriter Gordon Kennedy had written. He then led the entire audience in singing two old but powerful hymns, "My Hope Is Built on Nothing Less" and "Nothing but the Blood of Jesus," two segments before my designated time to speak. Focusing on Jesus seemed to set a different tone, and then another minister stood to exhort the crowd.

As I sat on the side of the stage and looked out at the massive crowd, I glanced at my phone and noticed that I had received a text message from Phil Cappuccio, founder of Sound of the Trumpet Ministries in northern Virginia. Phil and I had become friends nearly thirty years earlier and had reconnected within the five years or so before The Return. His first wife had died in his arms after a long bout with cancer, and he was now married to a woman who worked in the nation's capital. They lived in the Washington area but were unable to attend The Return, so Phil had contacted me to let me know he was praying for me. Phil shared my commitment to speak only what the Lord instructed, so I knew he would understand my dilemma and would pray earnestly.

I quickly typed out a response to him: "I've got nothing. It's going to be really good or really bad."

The stage manager motioned in my direction, beckoning me to the podium. It was time for me to speak a message, and I still had nothing. But I knew how to pray. I thought, *I'll just stand up and pray for our nation.* I walked to the podium and opened my mouth.

No one, not the people on the Mall that day or the millions who have heard my words since that moment, was more surprised than I was at the message that came out of my mouth.

CHAPTER 2

Christmas Every Day

I **GUESS NOBODY WAS SURPRISED** when I became a preacher. After all, my dad, Charlie Christmas, was an ordained Pentecostal preacher.

Dad's ancestors had traveled from Germany to the United States as immigrants at a time following World War II when people from Germanic backgrounds were not well received and were often regarded with a great deal of suspicion. My ancestors landed in America on Christmas Day, so to escape the German stigma, they changed their surname to Christmas, the happy holiday on which they began their new life in America. They eventually settled in Mullins, South Carolina, where my grandparents farmed the land and raised a family of ten children.

When he came of age, Dad joined the US Army and eventually served as a corporal stationed in California.

My mom, Hazel Wakefield, was raised in Paradise, California. Her ethnic background included a mixture of Scotch, Irish, English, and Dutch, and she came from a reserved family. She tended to be introverted and stern, not easily won over, but she trusted in Jesus at age fifteen during a service in a Baptist church and was later filled with the Holy Spirit. Those experiences changed her life and opened her heart to the world.

She was participating in a street meeting in California along with Pastor Conley, her own local pastor, when she caught the attention of a young military man named Charlie Christmas, a self-avowed pagan. Charlie and his army buddies had been out partying when they came upon the street meeting, and the Holy Ghost grabbed his heart and wouldn't let go. Pastor Conley led Charlie to the Lord. Charlie trusted Jesus as his Savior that night and experienced a radical spiritual conversion. Later, he was filled with the Holy Spirit.

Charlie went back to life in the army, and, as a new believer in Jesus, he was so full of zeal, he sometimes stood up on a table in the mess hall and preached to the troops. Charlie began attending Brother Conley's church, and that's where he got to know my mom, who sang "special music" in the church along with her two sisters.

Shortly after Dad received his honorable discharge from the army in 1953, he and Mom married in a simple wedding ceremony in California. I was born there in June 1954.

Dad wanted to immerse himself in the Bible, so we moved further north and he attended Conqueror's Bible School in Portland, Oregon, to learn how to be a pastor. One of his first ministerial assignments was in McCleary,

Washington, a town of less than two thousand residents, where Simpson, a plywood and door manufacturing plant, was the most prominent employer. The congregation numbered around seventy or eighty people.

The church was a simple, wooden-framed building and had a spartan interior with handmade pews, a gas stove in the back, and an old upright piano, but we had some powerful services. Our family lived in the church parsonage, right next door to the sanctuary, and folks were constantly dropping by, so there wasn't much privacy. Dad served there for about two years.

Soon after that, Dad became a missionary-pastor to the Quinault Nation. We lived in Taholah, Washington, on the reservation populated by American Indians near the Quinault River on the Olympic Peninsula, a triangle of lush land, loaded with redwood cedar, located between the Olympic Mountains and the Pacific Ocean, in one of the most picturesque places in America. The entire perimeter of the reservation—more than sixty miles long—was rimmed by the Pacific Ocean, and the thousands of acres of rich, natural beauty surrounding us appeared the way I imagined the garden of Eden may have looked.

Dad pastored a small church right there on the reservation. The church had a tough history. A roughneck had once barged into the sanctuary during a service and shot twice at the previous pastor. Fortunately, the shooter was either too drunk or not a good shot, because he missed the minister, but the bullet holes remained in the wall behind the pulpit.

My dad was a big man—nearly six feet tall with a muscular build—with a big personality. And when he prayed, I could hear him all over the house. He was an extrovert and a natural leader who loved people. He was also a sportsman who enjoyed hunting and fishing, so living in the wild came naturally for him. Most of the Native Americans on the reservation loved my dad and allowed him to hunt and fish year-round on their land, a rare privilege granted to few Caucasians. I grew up appreciating the outdoors as well, hunting and fishing with Dad, and enjoying an idyllic childhood.

When he became the pastor of the church, about 35 people attended regularly. Dad served there for six years, and by the time he resigned his position, the congregation had grown to about 150 people, which amounted to nearly half the population of the village. Dad had only a rudimentary knowledge of theology, but he loved the Bible and preached passionately from the heart with a fiery presentation. People came to hear him from far and wide, and his influence increased.

Our home was a magnet for people—friends, relatives, acquaintances visiting on vacation, and those just passing through. Some came seeking help, but many merely sought love and compassion from someone who cared, and they were convinced my parents cared. Ministers and other travelers showed up frequently, and our home was teeming with people night and day. Of course, many of Dad's friends showed up during hunting season, crowding the house. At one point, we had twenty-seven people sleeping in our home, which had only one bathroom! Mom cooked and cleaned constantly, trying to keep up with the visitors. She had grown up in the Northwest and was less gregarious and outgoing than Dad. Our dad grew up in the South and believed in "Southern hospitality," so his attitude was "the more the merrier!"

"Y'all come see us. My wife will be happy to cook for you!"

Mom didn't really want all those people in our home and wasn't particularly happy about entertaining folks she barely knew. But Dad was so gregarious and enjoyed having guests, so Mom played along.

• • •

Once a year, around the Fourth of July, the Quinault Nation hosted a five-day festival that drew thousands of people to the reservation for a time of music, food, physical contests, and, of course, alcohol. One of the festival's highlights was a fifty-mile motorized canoe race up the Quinault River to Quinault Lake and back. Most of the participants were Native Americans, but they welcomed and respected my dad and allowed him to join them for the canoe race, even though he was a white man.

The race began at the mouth of the river, right where it flowed into the Pacific Ocean. From there, the participants pointed their boats upstream. Most of the Native Americans ran sleek dugout canoes powered by 25-horsepower motors, but Dad was a skilled carpenter, having honed those talents as a boy on the farm in South Carolina, so he decided to build a flat-bottomed boat out of planks he found in the basement of the church. As he worked on his boat, the Indians often came by scoffing, making fun of him. "Hey, Charlie! Do you really think that swamp boat is going to float?" they asked mockingly. They slapped their knees and laughed uproariously. Dad didn't say much in response. He just kept working on his boat. When he finished, he painted it and mounted a used 25-horsepower motor on the back of it.

On race day, our family gathered at the river along with thousands of other people to watch the spectacle.

The starter fired a pistol, and the race was on! The boats sliced through the cold water. In the early stages of the race, Dad and his swamp boat did pretty well, staying right in the front, along with the leading pack of canoes. Suddenly a sheer pin broke on his boat, and he was instantly dead in the water, slowly drifting backward toward the ocean. Every boat passed him, but Dad remained undeterred. He wouldn't give up. He had carried another sheer pin with him, so he hurriedly went to work trying to repair his boat. He finally got it going again, and he took off after the pack. He caught every one of them, turned his boat around in the lake, and roared back toward the ocean.

I was standing right next to the finish line when the announcer spied the first boats coming down the river toward the finish. Peering through his binoculars as he called the race, he spoke into the microphone, "I see some boats coming! Keep your eyes on the water. Somebody's getting ready to come into sight. Here they come now! I see . . ." The announcer stopped short. He nearly choked on his words as he tried to tell the crowd that a white man in a swamp boat was leading all the Indians in their canoes. My dad crossed the finish line in first place, at least three canoe lengths ahead of the nearest challenger.

I was so proud of my dad, but after that, the festival banned him from competing in any more of their canoe races. If you visit the festival today, however, you will find that most of the boats in the race are flat-bottomed boats, a grudging tribute to my father.

I was only six years of age when our family moved onto the reservation, and although I was unafraid, there were some spooky elements. On the reservation, many of the men developed addictions to drugs and alcohol; spousal abuse and suicide were not uncommon on the reservation. And many people dabbled in a heavy mixture of black magic and other occult practices similar to voodoo. One such group was known as the Shakers (not to be confused with the Christian group by that same name, known for their utopian views that squelched procreation). The Shakers' elders did not appreciate my dad's influence in town and especially around the reservation.

One night, I woke up around 2:00 a.m. to the strange sound of brass bells clinking in front of our house. The Shakers used brass bells and candles in their occult incantations and worship. A large group of them were outside our house chanting curses over my dad and our family. These were real curses, not simply party games.

Mom and Dad peered out the windows from the front room of our house. Dad knew almost everybody in our town, so he recognized most of the Shakers casting curses on our family. He didn't appear frightened or worried, though. He had confidence that Jesus was greater than anything these minions of the devil could throw his way. "Don't worry, son," he said as he wrapped his arm around my shoulder. "They can't hurt us. 'Greater is He who is in us than he who is in the world.' These people are deceived, that's all."

Dad didn't seem to let the craziness get to him. He sensed when the danger was real or when it was simply more alcohol or drug-induced nonsense. One night, around 11:00 p.m., a distraught fellow came to our house huffing and puffing and pounding on the door. Dad let him in and tried to calm him down. I sat right there in the room and my eyes got wide with alarm as the man pulled out a large, machete-style knife. The man looked at Dad and said, "I'm going to kill myself."

"Well, you go ahead," Dad said. "I'm going to bed." Dad walked out of the room and went to bed. The distraught man sheathed his knife and left the house.

Dad didn't go around casting demons out of people. No doubt, he was aware of the supernatural realm and understood a bit about witchcraft and other forms of spiritual warfare, but he didn't dwell a great deal on deliverance from demonic oppression or possession. Besides, he knew most of the Shakers personally from interacting with them daily, so he chose not to confront the weird religious practices on the reservation unless necessary.

Maybe he was secure in the Lord. Or maybe he was too nice. The Shakers and their demonic cohorts certainly fought against Dad in the spirit world. Although I couldn't have imagined such a thing then, within a year or so after the confrontation with the Shakers, my dad would be dead. Indeed, it seemed the Shakers' curses followed all the men in the Christmas family, trying to destroy us before we could accomplish God's purposes for our lives. Our family suffered oppression in various forms, perhaps resulting from those curses, until we discovered the spiritual power to break them in Jesus' name.

CHAPTER 3

Being "Good" Does Not Come Naturally

AFTER A FEW YEARS OF PASTORING AT MCCLEARY, we moved less than ten miles away, southwest down Route 8 to the town of Elma, where Mom and Dad rented a tiny house for fifty dollars a month. Dad built an extra room and another bedroom onto our home in Elma and continued to lead the church in McCleary.

Church attendance was a big part of my early life, not merely because Dad was a pastor but because our entire world revolved around the local church. From childhood, I felt the presence of God in many of the services. I wanted to be there. Our church was a Pentecostal congregation, which meant we were accustomed to enthusiastic services in which people often exercised various gifts of the Spirit, including speaking in tongues—speaking in a language that the person had not previously learned—and the interpretation of tongues, in which another person could explain what we had heard. We also occasionally experienced gifts of healing.

The most frequently manifested gift of the Spirit in our congregation was speaking in tongues, which often occurred when a person "received the Holy Ghost" or, as many believers described the experience, got "baptized with the Holy Ghost" or "filled with the Holy Spirit," just as the early disciples of Jesus were filled on the Day of Pentecost, described in Acts 2. To many people in our circles, receiving the gift of tongues was clear-cut evidence of having been filled with the Holy Ghost.

That's what happened to me.

I was not a bad or rowdy kid, but I had a tendency to get in trouble. And I could be mean! For instance, when I went to first grade, the school bus driver told my mom, "You're going to have to do something with Kent. He sits on the step of the bus and kicks the other kids trying to get onto the bus."

Throughout elementary school, because I was a small kid, I felt as though I had to stand up for myself or else I'd get picked on and bullied. One of the kids who took a dislike to me was named Damon. He was a big boy who threatened me day after day. "If I catch you by yourself," Damon said, "I'm gonna whip you!" I had never done anything to offend Damon (at least, not that I knew of), but he decided he would try to intimidate me, and he succeeded. As soon as the dismissal bell rang after school each day, I'd dart out of the building and run home so Damon couldn't catch me.

One day, Damon found me alone in the school hallway. I saw him coming and realized there was no way I could avoid him or elude him, so I made a decision: I was not going to run away from him anymore.

Damon sauntered right up to my face. He loomed over me and glowered. "Come here, Christmas. I'm gonna whip you!" he hissed.

For the first time, I decided to stand up to him. "Well, I ain't running," I said. "Do what you gotta do."

Damon stepped back. He stared me in the eyes for a few seconds and then he backed down. "Humph," he said. He turned around and walked away and never gave me any trouble again. In fact, we became friends.

He even went with me to church to hear my dad preach. Whether it was my mischievous streak or a desire for revenge, I'm not sure, but as Dad was preaching and Damon sat next to me, I nudged him. "My dad wants you to get up and read that passage from the Bible," I told him. I pointed to some obscure Old Testament passage containing names I could barely pronounce.

Damon was not familiar with church protocol, but he knew we sometimes had testimony time. "Who, me?" he whispered.

"Yes," I said. "Can't you see? He wants you to get up and read from the Bible—out loud."

Damon looked back at me quizzically.

I nodded and motioned with my hands for Damon to get up.

Dad, of course, was in the heat of his sermon and hadn't noticed any of this when, for seemingly no reason, Damon suddenly rose to his feet and started reading aloud the biblical passage I had pointed out to him. The entire congregation turned and looked at him—including my dad.

I cracked up laughing hilariously. I leaned over and lay on the pew so Dad wouldn't see me, but it was too late. Damon suddenly realized that I had pranked him, and he started hitting me right there in the church pew.

Fortunately, the congregation got tickled rather than mad, although Dad later chewed me out for fooling around in church. Though Damon and I took different paths in life, we have remained close friends for more than sixty years.

At school, I picked up every profane word I heard and learned to cuss like the other kids. Although I usually swore under my breath so Mom or Dad didn't hear me, the attitude in my heart was far from holy. Similar to my encouragement of Damon's soliloquy during Dad's sermon, my mischievous nature sometimes came out to play, too, and that often resulted in Mom or Dad having to discipline me.

Although I was not a bad kid, being good did not come naturally for me. I sometimes willingly did things I knew were wrong or didn't do what I knew was right. I was still sensitive, however, to the Holy Spirit. Any message about sin or the judgment of God or the second coming of Christ always stirred me deeply and caused me to worry if I would be ready for the Lord's return.

One Saturday night in 1963, when I was nine, my family and I were at church. I went to the "young people's meeting," and at the close of the service, several people gathered at the front of the sanctuary to pray. I went forward as well.

I got down on my knees in an area all by myself, with nobody near enough to coax or coach me, and with my face tilted toward the floor, I began to pray. "Lord Jesus, please take full control of my life," I said. "I want to be completely Yours."

Suddenly, I felt my tongue begin to move in an odd way and I heard words coming out of my mouth that I did not know or understand. I felt as though I were out of control, yet I had never felt more freedom.

Dad came by as I was praying, and I heard him call out to Mom, "The boy's speaking in tongues!" They seemed surprised that I had received the glorious baptism of the Holy Spirit at such a young age, but they were elated.

This experience produced a radical change in me. It was a genuine transformation. No longer was I trying to be good on my own power. Now, I felt as though Jesus Himself were living in me and I was being good through His strength. The reality of meeting the living, supernatural God and being in His presence left an indelible impression on me. Even the thought that He loved me and wanted to indwell me caused rivers of joy to ripple through me.

People noticed. My mom told someone, "He's a totally different kid!"

• • •

The Native Americans respected my dad because of his keen tracking ability. Dad had an innate gift at being able to track wild animals during hunting expeditions. He had also been a butcher when he lived in South Carolina, so when the Indians asked him to help guide them in tracking some elk, Dad saw an opportunity. "If you will help us track," the Indians said, "we will give you half of whatever we bring home."

It turned out to be a good deal for everyone involved. But it was not always easy or safe.

On one occasion during my grade school years, Dad and I were traveling up Highway 101 in Dad's old pickup truck when he spotted a place where a herd of elk had torn up the ground. "Let's go see if we can find them," Dad said. We got out of the truck and he grabbed his rifle. We then trudged two or three miles through the heavy brush as Dad followed the indentations on the ground. At one point, Dad stopped, hid behind some high brush, and placed his index finger up to his lips. "Son, I can see them lying up there ahead," he whispered. "And I can tell by the tracks that there's a bull elk in this herd."

That was good news and bad news. Bull elk are massive animals.

About that time, Dad spotted a young spike elk, a bull, that had gotten up and started walking toward us. The elk looked to be about four hundred pounds. "I'm going to have to shoot this spike," Dad said, "because he is going to pick up our scent and will scare the herd."

Dad aimed his rifle right at the young bull's head and fired. The elk dropped to the ground, but unfortunately, the shot startled the entire herd, and the animals scattered in various directions.

Dad and I hurried over to the fallen elk, and Dad pulled out a sharp knife and propped his rifle against a tree. He climbed over the animal's shoulders so he could slit the elk's throat and allow him to bleed out more quickly, which was much less painful for the animal and better for us, as the elk meat would taste much better. But just as Dad straddled the animal and grabbed the horns, the elk regained consciousness. The bullet had hit just at the base of the animal's horns and had only stunned it rather than dealing a death blow. The elk reared up with my dad still on the animal's shoulders!

Dad jumped off the elk and grabbed his rifle from where he had propped it against the tree. He quickly aimed the gun at the elk and pulled the trigger, but the gun jammed.

"Dad!" I cried out.

Dad fiddled with the gun, cocked the hammer again, and fired just as the elk was about to bear down on him. This time Dad didn't miss, and the burly animal slumped to the ground in front of me. We dragged that animal out to the truck and took it home. We had plenty of elk meat for the next month or so.

My dad was my hero, and I relished every opportunity to be with him. He took me to peewee football practice and games and Little League baseball games, and he was really present in my life. I often went along with him to the church early on Sunday mornings, before the services, and Dad allowed me to ring the church bell so the villagers knew it was time to gather. I took seriously that responsibility to call people to the Lord's house.

After six years of leading the church on the reservation, Dad resigned his position as pastor. He had traveled through every province and much of the Northwest Territories of Canada, and he loved the people there. He scouted the area and wanted to be a missionary to the Indians in Canada, taking the gospel to people who had not heard it previously. He found a place he thought had great potential and hoped to move there, so he took our entire family on several expeditions into northwestern Canada, exploring and roughing it along the way. We once drove more than six hundred miles on dirt roads through rugged portions of northern British

Columbia to the small town of Bella Coola. We got stuck so deeply in the mud, some local workers had to get a bulldozer to pull our vehicle out of the mess.

Each night, we camped in a tent alongside the road; during the day, we fished in the crystal clear stream nearby for our dinner. Dad loved cooking in the outdoors, so he made most of our meals, and they always tasted delicious.

I enjoyed a wonderful childhood for the first twelve years of my life, with a loving family, living in a naturally beautiful part of the country, hunting and fishing with my dad. I was an outgoing, gregarious, fun-loving kid.

But that was about to change.

CHAPTER 4

My Hero, My Best Friend, My Dad—Gone!

WHILE STILL LIVING IN TAHOLAH, Dad took a job in Moclips, working on a "green chain" at a sawmill, assessing and grading the least blemished lumber as it came off the conveyer belt and sorting the best into various piles. Many of the boards weighed up to a hundred pounds, and not surprisingly, my dad suffered a back injury pulling lumber off the green chain. The doctors told him that he had an injured disc that required surgery. Dad was hospitalized in Aberdeen, about thirty miles from the reservation, for what was supposed to be a simple procedure.

The surgery went well, but the doctor decided to keep Dad immobile in the hospital for a few days to recuperate. Mom and I went to visit him at the hospital, but I didn't stay at Dad's bedside for long. There was a television in the lobby, so I went downstairs and watched it. We didn't own a TV, and I was fascinated by the images on the screen. "I'll just stay here till you come back from seeing Dad," I said to Mom. That was a decision I would regret for the rest of my life. Later that night, we went home without me having really spent any time talking to my dad.

I woke up sometime during the night and heard my mom sobbing in the living room. I shuffled out of my bedroom to discover the room was filled with people from our church, as well as a couple of Dad's pastor friends.

Dad's best friend put his arm around my shoulder and said, "Son, your daddy went to be with Jesus."

I heard his words, but I didn't believe what he'd said. "No!" I cried. Dad had been so strong, so vital, so alive when he'd gone into the hospital. Now, he was . . . *gone?* It couldn't be true!

But it was.

Dad had suffered a blood clot that had traveled from the surgery area to his heart, and he died on December 16, 1966. We already had his Christmas present wrapped and placed under the tree. I was devastated. Dad's passing away when I was only twelve years of age would forever be a pivotal point in my life.

The next few days were a blur as we tried to prepare for Dad's homegoing celebration. It didn't feel like a celebration to me.

When Mom and I went to view him in the casket, the moment I caught a glimpse of him, it felt as though someone had hit me in the face. I turned on my heels and walked out of the building. I didn't want to see my dad like that. I sat in the car until Mom returned. But I didn't cry. Even at

Dad's funeral, I resisted the tears. We buried my dad in the cemetery in Elma on a cold, dreary, rainy day. The weather matched my spirits. Numerous pastors attended the service, and a pastor friend of Dad's preached a strong message. Dad was a veteran, and when the soldiers presented the military salute and played Taps, the sad wail of the trumpet ripped my heart to shreds.

Maybe other people in our small congregation feared the Shakers' curses might fall on them if they came to our family's assistance. Or perhaps they simply were accustomed to maintaining a tough, stoic demeanor in the face of death. I don't know. But oddly enough, nobody in our congregation attempted to care for us as their beloved former pastor's family. Only one man, Donny Hill, the father of my good friend Dean, expressed an interest in me. Mr. Hill saw a young boy who needed some direction. He took me hunting along with Dean and allowed me to stay at their house for long hours. Nobody else from our church empathized with us. Years later, I would reflect on that and realize God allowed that to happen so I would seek Him as my heavenly Father. Today, I am thankful for the experience, but at the time, it seemed as though the church had rejected our family.

Making matters worse, three months prior to our planned move to northern Canada, Dad and Mom had decided to cancel their life insurance policy. Dad had an attitude that he was invincible. "I'm thirty-eight years of age," he said, "and in good health, vigorous in body and mind, so why waste the money on insurance if we can save what we'd spend on the monthly premiums? We could use the extra money anyhow."

When Dad died, Mom received only a small amount of death benefit money from the Veterans Administration and a meager monthly Social Security check; I also received a few dollars every month, but money was tight. We lived on six to seven hundred dollars per month. We could scrape up hardly enough money for rent, food, and clothing, much less any luxuries. So, Mom got a job selling Tupperware products.

Mom was thirty-four years old when Dad died, and his death plunged her into a deep depression. She had been a powerful prayer warrior, but she never fully returned to her former self and never remarried. Instead, she attempted to take on Dad's role and developed into a more intense disciplinarian, almost militaristic in her approach to parenting—especially with me. She did her best, I guess, but she didn't know how to guide me into adulthood. She felt she needed to be extra tough on me "to help me learn how to be a man."

My dad had been my best friend, and I was only twelve years old when he died. Instead of turning outward, in search of a new best friend, I turned inward and became a loner. Our family didn't own a television, so I immersed myself in reading. I got lost in Louis L'Amour books, living vicariously through the characters in those dramatic frontier stories and Western novels. I also devoured Agatha Christie detective stories and books about military history. During lunchtime at school, I kept to myself and read until the bell rang, signaling that it was time to return to class. I didn't sleep well after Dad died, so oftentimes I went outside at night and walked for miles, all by myself.

Mine was a lonely life. Not that I didn't have friends in school. But it is possible to be lonely even in a crowd; it is possible to be screaming on the inside while maintaining a stoic, silent exterior demeanor. That was me.

I got a job delivering newspapers from house to house at five o'clock each morning. I carried a heavy sack loaded with newspapers over my shoulder. I hoped to earn enough money to purchase a bicycle. The paper sold for around seven to ten cents per issue, with the weekend editions selling for slightly more. Out of that price, I purchased the papers, delivered them door-to-door, then collected monthly from my customers and could keep whatever was left over. Profits were slim, usually a few dollars each week. But I earned about twelve dollars a month, enough to purchase a bike from Western Auto "on time," paying seven dollars a month.

My best friend during that time was my dog, Homer, a beagle that Mom allowed me to get as a pup after Dad passed. Homer was my constant companion, sleeping in my bed with me and running along with me as I delivered newspapers early each morning.

Other people must have been impressed with Homer's gregarious personality because he went missing for a few days. I looked all over for him, but he had disappeared. I couldn't find him anywhere, and I worried that something awful had happened to him. Then one day, as I was collecting from my newspaper customers, I knocked on a door and when the homeowner opened it, out ran Homer!

"My dog!" I called out.

Apparently, my customer loved Homer almost as much as I did and had confiscated him as his own, but Homer returned home with me.

Following Dad's death, Mom moved our family to Shelton, another small town nearby. The only benefit of living in Shelton, once known as the Christmas Tree Capital of the World, was that it was different from Elma, where we had been living when Dad died.

The Shelton school was rough, especially on newbies. The second day there, I was standing in the lunch line when a kid popped me on the side of my head, letting "the new kid" know his place. Well, I wasn't going to take that. I popped him right back.

When I went outside, the bully and his buddies were waiting for me. They beat the daylights out of me. The bully caught me with his fist, smashing me right in the mouth so hard that my front tooth cut all the way through my lip.

Somehow the teachers got us separated and hauled us all into the principal's office. The principal demanded that the bully apologize to me, which he did, but rather reluctantly.

I couldn't wait to get out of that school and was so glad when, after two years of living in Shelton, Mom moved us back to McCleary and enrolled me in Elma High School.

I loved to play basketball, and I was a good shooter, but because I was short in stature, a mere five foot six, I never really got a chance to play. "You're too small for the varsity team," I heard from coaches and players alike. The sense of rejection seared my heart. Nevertheless, after that, I practiced for hours and hours and tried out for the team my sophomore year. My eyes were sparkling as I approached the locker room after the deciding workout. I knew that I had done well during the tryouts and was certain I had impressed the coaches, but when the list of names of the new team members was posted on the bulletin board in the locker room, mine wasn't on it.

The expression on my face fell sullen.

"You're just too small, Christmas," the coach said matter-of-factly. "But I'll tell ya what I'll do. I'll let you play on the practice squad, and you can come out with the team and sit on the bench during the games."

"Gee, thanks, Coach," I said, trying to sound excited. I desperately wanted to be part of the team.

Everybody on the team received a uniform. Unfortunately, the school owned only a few matching uniforms for the practice squad, and I didn't receive one of those. My uniform was mismatched, with a jersey and shorts of two different colors in sizes that didn't fit me. I was so humiliated as I ran out onto the court behind the rest of the team. They could have painted the word *reject* on the back of my jersey because that's how I felt.

I joined the cross-country team because I could run like the wind. I won some events and earned my navy blue Elma High School varsity letterman's jacket with cream-colored sleeves, bearing the big *E* on the chest. *Maybe now the other kids will accept me*, I thought.

They didn't.

CHAPTER 5

Experiencing the Supernatural

OUT OF REJECTION AND LONELINESS, I developed a habit of prayer—talking with God at length, not just for a few minutes but for extended periods of time, sometimes hours on end. Initially, I set a goal to spend one hour each day in prayer. Some days, I'd last for only forty-five minutes or so. Other days, I stayed in His presence much longer. In my younger years, I often went to the church at night and prayed in the dark. Years later, I preferred praying while I walked in the woods, a habit I continue to this day.

To me, it wasn't about how much time I spent talking to the Lord or in what posture I prayed. I wanted to know God; I wanted to know His Word and His will, and I somehow knew that the best way I could get to know Him more fully was to spend time in His presence, talking to Him and listening to Him in prayer. I'm now convinced that when we go through tough times in life, they will either drive us from

God or drive us to Him. I'm so glad that, for some reason (I believe that God had His directing hand on me even as a boy), I drew closer to Him.

Some people thought I was cocky. That wasn't true. I protected myself by creating an exterior shell, giving off an air that no one could touch me, that nothing bothered me, so I could keep people from getting into my inner space. One of the ways I protected myself was by steeling my emotions and refusing to cry. No matter what.

Despite my strong exterior appearance, early on I developed a sensitive conscience. I didn't comprehend how that happened or why, but I had strong convictions, and I knew that I didn't want to disappoint the Lord.

I can trace my strong sense of right and wrong to the biblical values I learned as a boy. God gave me a healthy fear of the Lord—not that I was afraid of God, but I had such a reverence toward Him—and that helped keep me on the straight and narrow path. That included a passion for sexual purity, even though I didn't understand completely the intimate link between spiritual passion and purity. All I knew was that the Bible said to not have sex with someone to whom you are not married and to not fool around before you get married. That was enough for me, so I committed myself to maintaining my virginity until marriage.

Back when I was fourteen, some of my friends planned an overnight campout, sleeping under the stars. Sometime after dark, several girls showed up and slipped into their boyfriends' sleeping bags; one girl wanted to slide into my sleeping bag with me. "No," I said. "I can't do that."

"Why not?" she asked.

"Because that's not right," I told her.

In truth, I thought, *What if the Lord returns and I'm here having sex with a girl to whom I am not married? I'd spend eternity in hell!*

I didn't tell her that, though, and she just got mad and left me alone.

My commitment to strong biblical values permeated everything I did. I wasn't without fault, but I tried to do what was right, even if it was my second thought rather than my first. Once, I got in a fight with a guy, and in the middle of it I recalled that God had said, "Blessed are the peacemakers." I got convicted about fighting and once again thought, *What if the Lord comes back while I'm here engaged in fisticuffs? I'm going to hell!* So I stopped returning my opponent's punches. The guy walloped the daylights out of me!

I just didn't want to disappoint the Lord. That same attitude kept me from getting involved in drug or alcohol abuse, pornography, or other things that many of my peers found appealing. I had tasted of the Lord and had seen that He is good, and from the time of my experience of receiving the Holy Ghost as a nine-year-old, He continually sensitized my heart and mind to what was good or evil, right or wrong, holy or profane. I didn't always follow through or act perfectly, but I took His Word seriously, and I knew that I wanted to choose what God said was good, right, and holy, regardless of what anyone else said or thought about me.

I had known from the time I was thirteen or fourteen that God was calling me to be a preacher, but I really didn't want to be in the ministry. I had watched my parents struggling financially and never getting ahead—they were broke all the time—and I didn't see myself following in their footsteps.

I liked building things, so I decided I might want to become a contractor, developing and guiding construction projects. For summer jobs, I sought out work on construction sites, helping to build houses.

In high school, I had enrolled in a class similar to a trade school curriculum, in which we had learned how to build an actual house. A contractor took a group of students on-site and taught us how to do the work correctly. He oversaw the project and made sure the work was done with excellence. When the home was completed, it sold on the open market and drew a good price.

Convinced that my choice of occupation was settled and I was on my way to a lucrative career as a building contractor, at age seventeen I attended a Christian youth convention. The speaker for the event was Kenneth Phillips, a young pastor from Texas, and his messages pierced my heart. I knew that God was speaking to me through the evangelist. I responded to the call and the Spirit of the Lord overwhelmed me in such a powerful way that I fell onto the floor. I wasn't hurt; quite the contrary, I'd never felt better in my life! I was lying on the floor, basking in the presence of the Lord. I'm not certain how long I lay on the floor, maybe an hour or more—it felt like a long time that swept by in a moment—and when I got to my feet, I knew that I was going to be a preacher, not a house builder. "I'll do it, Lord," I said. "If You want me to be a preacher, I'll preach. I'll go wherever You want me to go, and I'll do whatever You want me to do."

I had no plan for how that might happen, but my commitment was genuine. I had not experienced any dreams or visions providing divine direction, nor did I have images of myself preaching to millions of people. But I sensed a call from God, and I was willing to take the next step of obedience—whatever that might be—according to His instructions.

Back home that weekend on Sunday evening, I went to church in McCleary as usual and the pastor called out from the platform, "Brother Kent, why don't you come and lead the testimony service tonight?"

We were traditional Pentecostals, with a more effusive style of worship than many other Christian denominations. In most of our evening services, we had a lively "song service," as they called it, where we sang encouraging hymns and choruses; then we had "testimony service," in which individuals stood to their feet and declared the good things that God had done or was doing in their lives. Then afterward, when our faith was pumping at full throttle, people spoke out various prayer requests and we prayed over each one of them, believing God for miraculous results. If we were still standing after all that, the preacher might have preached a while and then presented another invitation to pray. It was the old-style Pentecostal service in which the clock was irrelevant, and we never really knew what might happen next.

I walked up onto the platform and had barely opened my mouth when a powerful anointing of the Lord came upon me and I started preaching. I was only seventeen, and I had never done anything like this previously, but I preached the house down that night! I had no written notes and few Scriptures in mind when I began, but the Spirit of the Lord provided all that I needed as He opened my mouth and filled it with His message. The words seemed to simply roll out of my mouth with little thought or effort on my part.

People in the congregation shouted out loudly in joy and ecstasy at what they heard. Some people "got happy," others shed tears, but all seemed affected by the message.

I preached for a while and then stopped and let the pastor take over, but the exhilaration I felt was incomparable to anything I'd ever known.

It was truly an amazing experience, and I was as surprised as anyone else in the building that this had happened. But it felt good. And I felt—I hate to admit it—somewhat *proud.* Well, okay, to be honest, I felt *really* proud! I thought, *Wow, I'm the greatest preacher out there!*

The pastor must have been impressed as well, because after the church service that night, he said, "Kent, I want you to preach on Sunday morning."

"Who? Me?"

"Yes, you!" he gushed. "Just preach whatever the Lord lays on your heart."

"Ah, well . . . er, okay!" My face beamed with delight.

I studied all week long, and when the next Sunday rolled around, I was terrified. I got up to preach, and I was awful. I couldn't keep my thoughts together, my voice cracked, and my chest wheezed through my entire sermon. Even reading Scripture was difficult; my chest felt so restricted, and the words seemed to clog up my throat. "And God says," I huffed and puffed, trying to blow the house down.

The house didn't budge.

And nobody shouted with joy that day, except for maybe those dear people who endured till the end and were so glad when the sermon was finally over.

Looking back, I now see that God showed me, "There is an anointing you can have if you sell out to Me." But He was also reminding me the work would not get done under my self-effort. The key was, "'Not by might or by power, but by My Spirit' says the Lord." (Zach. 4:1) Clearly, I could speak with His power and anointing, or I could preach with my own. God allowed me to experience both, and the difference was obvious—to me and to the people who heard me.

CHAPTER 6

Devilish Counterattack

WITHIN THREE MONTHS I had another experience that powerfully influenced my life in a different way. I was driving Mom's station wagon on the main street in McCleary during a snowy winter day. I wasn't driving fast, but as I rounded a turn, the car slid off the road and down into a ditch. Coming to an abrupt stop, I peeled my hands off the steering wheel that I had been grasping so tenaciously. I checked to see if I was injured. I was shaken up, but I wasn't hurt, so I opened the door and climbed out of the car. The station wagon didn't seem badly damaged, but I could tell that it was going to take a strong tow truck to pull it out of that ditch.

I called for a wrecker, and soon a man named Cecil showed up and pulled Mom's vehicle out of the mess. After he finished his work, Cecil and I stood alongside the road in the middle of a snowstorm. He wrote up a receipt and handed it to me. My hand had barely touched the paper to receive the receipt when a large Greyhound bus came around the curve at about forty miles per hour and hit both Cecil and me, full force.

The impact knocked both of us beneath the bus. I slammed behind the front tires, but before the back dual wheels of the bus ran over me, I somehow flew out from under the side of the bus. I landed awkwardly in the snow and later learned that my back was broken, but at the time, I was too dazed to know what had happened. Some onlookers who saw the accident called an ambulance and also contacted my mom. Meanwhile, they covered me with a blanket as I lay there in the snow.

When Mom arrived, she asked, "Where is he?"

"Over there on the ground," someone said.

Mom saw me under the blanket, and she later said that she thought I was dead. Worse yet, the first responders could not find Cecil. They searched high and low until they finally found him wedged against the back dual wheels of the bus. Cecil was dead.

The emergency workers loaded his body into the back of a station wagon. They then lifted me up and slid me in shoulder to shoulder, right next to the dead man. Someone tried to resuscitate Cecil in the back of the station wagon, but there was no response—except from me. I was freaking out when I realized I was lying there next to a dead man.

At the hospital, the doctors confirmed that my back was broken, and they fitted me with a brace. I wore the brace every day for several months, but as awkward as it was attending classes in the brace, I was able to return to high school.

Cecil's wife received a large financial settlement from the bus line's insurance company, but the attorney who handled the case did not seem to have my best interest in mind. "Here's your part," he told me. He handed me a check for about $1,300. I was grateful for any financial help, but that paltry amount of insurance settlement barely paid for my basic medical services. Nevertheless, I was glad to be alive.

Although I didn't fully understand it then, looking back, I now realize that within two months of me answering God's call to preach, the devil tried to kill me. It seemed that the men in the Christmas family were frequent targets for the Enemy's attacks. My grandfather had died at forty-four years of age when a drunk driver hit him head-on in South Carolina. My uncle was riding in the same car, and he miraculously survived. My own father died at only thirty-eight years of age. At times, I wondered if the devil's attacks might take me out before my time as well.

● ● ●

I was excited to graduate from Elma High School in 1972, so my girlfriend, who lived in a nearby town, came for the celebration. I didn't have a car, but one of my good friends had a red Ford Mustang fastback, a real beauty. I asked him, "Can I borrow your car to take my girlfriend to the graduation ceremony?"

"No, I don't think my dad will go for that," he said.

I went to his dad and asked, "Can I rent your son's Mustang just for tonight? I'll take special insurance out on it, or whatever else I need to do."

"No, I don't think that's a good idea," he said.

So, my girlfriend and I traveled to my graduation ceremonies along with my mom in her station wagon.

Perhaps not surprisingly, my girlfriend broke up with me shortly after that.

CHAPTER 7

On My Own ... Again

I MET PATTI WINSLOW, my wife-to-be, at the church in McCleary. Her dad had found the Lord under my dad's ministry, so our families knew each other well. Patti and I had been acquainted for most of our lives by the time I was seventeen, but it was not until then that I really noticed her. Unfortunately, despite my interest, she was too young to date—a mere fourteen years old, three years younger than me. Any relationship I hoped to have would have to wait.

I was barely eighteen when I went off to Conqueror's Bible School in Portland, Oregon, the same school my dad had attended. The school was associated with the United Pentecostal Church, the ultraconservative denomination that had ordained my dad.

I drove to college in my mom's 1965 blue American Rambler. The car had been wrecked and the transmission had been destroyed, so I worked as a housepainter and earned seventy-five dollars, enough to purchase an inexpensive transmission. After replacing the transmission, Mom's car worked well enough to get me to school. To help pay my tuition, I got a job in a machine shop, doing nasty, dirty work such as taking engine blocks apart and boiling the grease off some of the used parts. Then I used a sandblasting machine to shine the finish. When I was done with them, the used parts looked brand-new. It was messy work, but it provided enough income to pay my tuition and to have a few dollars in my pocket for gas and spending money.

One night, some friends and I went out joyriding till about three o'clock in the morning. On the way back to campus, one of my buddies missed a curve and his car skidded off the road and down into a ditch. The police came, and although they didn't press charges, they called the dean.

Nobody was drinking or causing trouble; we had simply had an accident, but the Bible college administration treated us as though we were a bunch of alcoholic hooligans. The next morning in chapel, the leaders rebuked us publicly and then everyone gathered around my friends and me, praying for us as though we needed deliverance. The school put me on probation for six months, and since I hadn't done anything wrong, I didn't respond well to that. In fact, I quit school and went back home to McCleary.

I had not been the professors' pet anyhow. At school, I took all the usual basic ministerial classes, including English, speech, and homiletics. In homiletics, the professor would grade us as we preached sermons in front of the class. That grated on me for some reason. I thought, *If I'm going to preach, I have to preach from my heart, whatever the Lord is saying. I don't want to worry about having impeccable grammar and perfect diction.* While I wanted to speak with excellence, I had already learned the most valuable lesson: that the ministry was not about me—it was about Jesus.

I felt that I couldn't find what I needed to advance the call on my life through Bible school, so I left and committed myself to self-education. I had always been an avid reader, and now I began reading everything I could get my hands on, especially some of the great preachers in church history. I devoured classic books by some of the old saints, such as the great evangelist Charles Finney. I read books on prayer by writers such as E. M. Bounds and Oswald Chambers as well as mystical writers such as Watchmen Nee, Andrew Murray, Smith Wigglesworth, and my favorite, E. W. Kenyon. I was not driven to read modern Christian charismatic leaders' materials so much as the heroes from the past. They wrote in ways that seemed relevant to me, and more than that, they wrote about changed lives, about people who were healed and set free. They told of Jesus healing sick people—people sick in body or sick in their souls. That appealed to me.

I also listened to recordings of Mark Hamby, Kenneth Phillips, Tom Fred Tenney, and other anointed speakers, learning biblical principles from them as well as receiving marvelous spiritual inspiration. Despite my lack of formal theological training, God used my love for reading and my desire for learning to provide me with a broad education for ministry.

When I returned home, I applied for a job at the plywood plant, one of the largest employers in our area. "Naw, we aren't hiring," the plant manager told me.

I went back a few days later and applied again and was met with the same response. I knew other people were being hired at the plant. *What's going on here?* I wondered. I recalled that when I was a sixteen-year-old kid, I tried to get a job in the grocery store in McCleary. They hired box boys all the time, but for some reason, they would not hire me. Now I was bumping into that same resistant attitude again. But I would not give up. I went back repeatedly and applied for a job. I bugged the plant manager thirteen times before he hired me. I was only five foot six and weighed only 132 pounds, and he didn't think I could handle the work physically, so I had to prove to him that I could. Working at the plywood plant turned out to be my first real job as an adult, and it was not an easy one.

The logging company owned a large pond in which the felled trees floated as they were guided onto a conveyor belt that led to a large lathe that peeled the logs and then sliced them into thin veneer sheets of wood. Once a log was trimmed down to a core, it dropped down, and the remains were ground into sawdust.

My job was to physically pick up every log and muscle it into the core chipper. Some of the logs were so large, it took three strong men to pick them up.

Later, I worked as a roofer, a carpet installer, and a truck driver who drove an eighteen-wheeler. I sold office furniture and I logged for a while. I took every preaching opportunity that came my way, too, preaching salvation messages as well as faith and healing messages. All the while I worked every sort of job I could get, hoping to earn enough income that someday Patti and I could get married.

When I turned eighteen, I got another job at the plywood plant, working on a "green chain." I had to be at work by four o'clock in the morning, and I worked ten-hour shifts.

By this time, a young married couple had moved in with Mom and me. Mom wanted me to remodel the garage as an apartment for them, but I was exhausted each night after work as it was. Beyond that, I knew that the husband had some carpentry skills equal to mine or better, and he wasn't working nearly the long hours that I was working.

"Kent, you need to do that for them," Mom nagged.

"No, Mom," I said. "The husband needs to do it, not me. I'm working really hard as it is."

Mom did not respond well to my refusal. "Well, you just need to shut up," she huffed.

I was always respectful to my mom, and I believed God would hold me accountable for treating her right, not to mention that she was a widow, and the Bible clearly instructs Christians to care for widows and orphans (see James 1:27). So, I always tried to honor Mom, even more so after Dad's passing, but her words and her lack of consideration grated on me. I kept my tone of voice under control, but I said firmly, "Mom, I need you to be quiet. Okay?"

She stood up and reared back to slap me in the face, but as she swung her arm in my direction, I caught her hand. "Don't hit me," I said.

Mom was undeterred. "I will not have some snotty-nosed kid in my house telling me what to do!" she yelled. "Leave!"

I could hardly believe Mom's words, but I took her seriously. Nevertheless, her rejection hit me hard. I gathered my few possessions and left home. I rented a room at an extended-stay motel and then later rented a small apartment nearby. I was on my own again.

CHAPTER 8

Livin' on Love

BY THE TIME I HAD RETURNED TO MCCLEARY after only six months in Bible school, Patti was sixteen. She was a sweet, shy, beautiful, blue-eyed blonde, and her parents approved of us "dating." After all, we were among the few Christian teenagers in our town, so we were both fishing in a small pond.

Patti's personality was so innocent that she would blush at anything that hinted at a compliment, yet she also possessed a fun, flirty, flighty side that seemed to crave attention. We were both virgins when we began dating and still virgins when we fell in love, and I asked her to marry me. Her parents were supportive and signed a legal document granting Patti permission to marry me even though she was underage. The pastor who gave me my first preaching opportunity conducted the marriage ceremony.

I was a baby-faced nineteen-year-old and Patti was barely seventeen when we got married in McCleary, in the same church where we had met as children, the same church my dad had pastored, the same church where Patti's dad had been converted, and the same church where I had first preached a sermon. Years later, after the church had built a new sanctuary, I visited and found the old pulpit, the same one my dad had preached from, the one where I was standing the night the Holy Ghost fell on me and I preached my first message. The leaders of the church were willing to sell the old pulpit to me, and I still have it.

Our wedding reception was held in the local VFW (Veterans of Foreign Wars) hall. Thanks to some volunteers from church who provided decorations and food for the reception, our entire wedding cost less than six hundred dollars. We drove north to Vancouver for our brief honeymoon.

For the first part of our marriage, we got up each morning and I went off to work at the White Star plywood plant and Patti went to high school. We set up housekeeping with a bunch of castoff furniture and hand-me-downs, but we were happy. We knew nothing about what a good marriage involved or what it meant to be compatible in a strong, healthy relationship. We were young and in love, as much as we knew of it.

• • •

In addition to being hit by a bus, I experienced multiple incidents shortly after Patti and I married in which it seemed the devil was attempting to kill me. At twenty years of age, while working at the plywood factory, I was on some scaffolding when it collapsed and dumped me onto the conveyer belt, which whisked me directly toward the core chipper. In the nick of time, I was able to roll off, avoiding certain death. Again, I'm convinced that the Enemy was attempting to take me out before my time, and it was only the goodness of God that spared my life.

The millwright at the plywood plant was an older fellow, and he seemed to like me. A millwright is a skilled craftsman who installs or conducts repairs on the equipment and keeps the machinery working at high efficiency. He asked me one day, "Would you like to be an apprentice millwright instead of working on the lumber side making plywood?"

"I sure would," I responded. As a millwright, I learned electrical and mechanical skills. One of my jobs was ripping out and removing defective or worn-out equipment that the plant was no longer going to use.

A few weeks into my apprenticeship, my supervisor approached me with a special assignment. "Take down that electrical panel," the boss told me. I looked at the panel and saw that it was a large, 440-volt panel, a powerful piece of industrial electrical equipment.

The electrician there said, "It's not live. It's unplugged." But he didn't know there was a short in the panel. It tested as though it were dead, but it was not.

I picked up a tool and attempted to unscrew the panel. But the moment that metal tool in my hand touched that powerful source of electricity, the panel lit up and the electrical jolt zapped me full force with 440 volts! The shock knocked me off my feet and propelled me backward through the air. The electricity seared my stomach, my vision blurred, and I hit the ground hard with a thud.

No doubt, the other men around me thought I was dead. For a few moments, I wasn't so sure myself! But once again, God had protected me, and although I was badly shaken up, by the end of the day, I felt fine.

On another occasion, I went down to the lower level of the plant to repair a sump pump. Debris in the form of dust and chips from the lathes above sometimes fell into the pumps and could clog them. I was working on a pump and standing in some water several inches deep when an electrical panel right in front of me blew up. Even a child knows that electricity and water don't mix, so by all logic, I should have been instantly electrocuted.

But once again, I walked away unscathed.

I realized early on that the devil was after me, and apparently, similar to what Satan attempted to do to the man Job, God allowed him to hit me, although He refused to allow the devil to kill me. But the Enemy's efforts sure kept me on my toes.

When plywood is being made, a lathe peels the logs down to a veneer sheet about an eighth of an inch thick, depending on the depth of wood required. The sheets are then laid out in thin veneers with glue sealed in between each until the desired thickness is reached. Then the plywood boards are put into a large press to compress them under high temperatures. The plywood presses are about eighteen feet tall and have two-inch plates with a notch in each corner that makes them easier to handle. Each plate weighs about 1,800 pounds.

I was working on the plywood press one day and had just grabbed hold of one of the corners of the large plate, with my arms wrapped tightly around it, trying to get it into position. While putting the last plate on top, without warning, it slipped, and the press collapsed around me, causing sheets of unfinished plywood to skew off awkwardly in various directions.

Several guys were severely hurt and hospitalized. But miraculously, I was untouched, and I walked away without injury.

I didn't fully realize how the devil worked back then, but I knew I was in a battle. Later, I learned how to war in the Spirit against the plots of the Enemy, taking authority over him in Jesus' name. The devil doesn't give up, but we don't have to take his guff either.

• • •

By the time I was twenty-one, Patti and I started evangelizing full-time, traveling from church to church across the United States wherever anyone would invite us. We carried with us everything we owned, all our earthly possessions, jammed inside a small, orange Datsun B210. We couldn't afford a hotel room, so we usually stayed with the pastors and their families in the towns where we conducted services. We ate most of our meals with them as well. What's for dinner? Whatever the host family is eating. Occasionally, we even stayed in a Sunday school room during the time we were at the church. We had "revival" services every night of the week and several more services on Sunday. I preached every sermon I had. I'd preach three weeks or more and receive a "love offering" of about $125. After an exhausting season of revival services, we returned home and stayed with Patti's parents.

The lifestyle was especially tough on Patti. She was barely seventeen when we married, and, like most teenagers, she probably would have much preferred to be hanging out at the mall and trying on new clothes with her friends than enduring yet another church service. Being a minister's wife is not an easy role at any age, but to be thrust into that position that young was not fair to her.

Nevertheless, I accepted every invitation for me to preach evangelistic services, regardless of the size of the congregation, and Patti usually accompanied me. There were times when I preached only to the pastor, his wife, his children, and Patti—that was the entire audience— and we'd be there in that community for six weeks. The "love offerings" we received were just that—mostly love and not much money.

After a series of services in Pocatello, Idaho, once known as the "Gateway to the Northwest" by pioneers on the Oregon Trail, a local pastor contacted me. "Why don't you move here to Pocatello?" he asked. "I have a small church. You do the preaching because you are good at that, and I'll do the administrative work since I'm good at that. And we can split the tithes contributed by the congregation." We had few other invitations, so we accepted his offer.

Patti and I moved to Pocatello, and I preached to a congregation of about twenty people. I got a job selling office equipment on commission to support Patti and me while I served the church. Within six months, more than one hundred people were attending, but we still had not received our portion of the tithes and offerings. Pocatello is located in "lava country," about five thousand feet above sea level, and the winters can be ferociously cold. The wind chill factor sometimes reached eighty degrees below zero. After the first horrible winter, I told Patti, "We aren't staying here." We packed up and moved back to Patti's parents' home, staying in one of their bedrooms. I worked with my father-in-law in his small sawmill to support us.

It was embarrassing when, after church on Sunday evening, everyone was going out to eat and they wanted us to come along. "No, we can't do that," I said. I knew we didn't have any extra money.

"Oh, come on," my mother-in-law said. "Don't worry. We'll pay for it."

Patti and I went along, but it was humiliating to me not being able to provide for us.

I knew that God had called me to preach. Eventually, Patti's uncle helped us financially and we were able to secure a motor home that made travel easier. We could also live in it, too, as much as necessary.

Patti and I traveled all across the country in the motor home, stopping to preach to small congregations in small churches. We traveled to Steubenville, Ohio, a rather depressed coal town, where I preached every night for three solid weeks to about fifteen people each night. One night, I was so deathly sick and vomiting that I could barely walk. But I got out of bed, put on my suit, and went in the side door of the church after the service had already started. I preached as best I could, then stumbled back out to the motor home and went to bed.

After that, it was back home to Patti's parents' home, since Patty and I had no home of our own, except the one on wheels. I worked with my father-in-law in McCleary long enough for us to afford to make the motor home payment and put some fuel in the fifty-gallon tank, and then we went back out on the evangelistic circuit.

One night I parked the motor home next to my in-laws' garage and ran a power cord from the garage to the motor home so we could have electricity inside without running the motor all night long. I awakened in the middle of the night and noticed that no lights were on and it was cold in the motor home.

That's odd, I thought. *Maybe we blew a circuit or something. I'd better find out.* I got out of bed to check on the heater. I looked out the window, and what I saw sent a chill through me much stronger than the cold. The entire garage was on fire!

"Patti, wake up!" I yelled to her. I ran to the house where Patti's parents were sleeping, and I banged on the door. The flames were already licking at the house, and it was filled with smoke. "Wake up! Wake up!" I yelled as loudly as I could. Finally, I was able to rouse Patti's parents, and they came out of the house wearing nothing but their underwear. They had been fast asleep and may have perished in the home had the power not gone out in our motor home.

I pulled the power cord out of the garage wall and quickly started the motor home and moved it away from the flames. We called for the fire company, but there was nothing else we could do. We gathered out on the road and watched as the house was engulfed in flames and burned to the ground.

The devastating fire was a double blow. Not only were all of Patti's and my possessions—meager as they were—stored in that garage but so were all my dad's possessions that I had saved after his death. My dad's rifles and his tools, papers, books, and some of his sermon notes were all destroyed by the fire. Everything but his Bible that I had kept with me. It was as though the last vestiges of my father's gifts to me were turned to ashes.

• • •

In South Carolina, I preached at a church near Conway. The pastor had known my father well, and several of our extended family members on Dad's side of the family lived nearby in Mullins, a town of about five thousand people in the heart of tobacco country. Many of them came out to hear me preach, even though they were not committed church attenders.

As usual, I preached a strong black-and-white message about sin, with no gray areas. Afterward, Patti and I returned to my aunt's home, where we were staying. My aunt said, "We need you to come over to Grandma's house, next door."

Patti and I accompanied my aunt to Grandma's house, where a large group of our relatives was already gathered. They had positioned a number of chairs in a circle and placed one in the center of the room. Someone said to me, "You sit right there in the center chair. We want to talk to you."

Patti sat down on a couch, and I sat in the middle chair. The family members proceeded to tear into me, excoriating me for preaching against them. "How dare you say those things about us!"

I really did not have specific family members in mind as I preached hard against sin, but apparently, they had seen themselves in the message—or the Holy Spirit had convicted them.

I tried to placate them. "I wasn't really preaching against you," I said. "I was simply preaching the gospel. If the message spoke to you, that's between you and the Lord."

My relatives weren't buying my explanation. They continued to rail against me, warning me never to say such things again.

Patti sat in the room, sobbing and weeping; she was almost hysterical. I felt rejected on every level. When the family meeting was over, we went back to my aunt's home, and after everyone went to bed, I told Patti, "Come on. We're leaving." She didn't need me to ask her twice. We quickly packed our possessions into the car and got out of there. We returned to the state of Washington. I wouldn't go back to South Carolina for more than ten years.

CHAPTER 9

First Church, First Child

THE FIRST REAL PASTORATE OF MY OWN was at a small church in Scatter Creek, Washington, where I began in 1978 as an associate pastor to Rev. Bob Stark. Brother Stark had invited me to preach revival services at his previous church in Lacey, Washington, near Olympia. We became friends, and he was the first man who seemed like a father in the Lord to me.

His new church in Scatter Creek was not located in the best part of town. A stock car racetrack operated directly across the street from the church. I often went to the church at night and prayed for hours, sometimes till daybreak.

One day, the pastor stood up and said, "I'm resigning and I'm turning over the church to Pastor Kent."

That was news to me—and to the congregation! Some of the people were not happy about that and let me know it. But it certainly wasn't my fault. It was, however, now my responsibility to lead the congregation.

Another small church in Olympia was struggling, so we combined our resources, and I became the pastor of both groups. We renovated the sanctuary as much as our skimpy budget allowed, recarpeted the floors, and reupholstered the pews.

Patti and I lived about twenty-five miles from the church. We had only about eighty people in the congregation, and they could not afford to pay a full-time pastor. To help support us, I got a job at a shipyard in Tacoma, Washington, about fifty miles away from our home. For a while, I worked the graveyard shift, from eleven o'clock at night till seven the next morning. I worked seven nights a week, even Saturday night. Then I'd come home, shower, and dress for church. I taught a Sunday school class and then preached. I would try to catch a little sleep on Sunday afternoon before returning to church for the evening service. Then it was back to the shipyard at eleven, where I worked all night till daybreak. It was a wrenching schedule, but the income paid our bills. The church tolerated my inexperience as a preacher, and I tried to serve them well. Most of all, I was hungry for more of God.

After a while, our congregation separated from the strict United Pentecostal Holiness denomination with which we were associated and became an independent congregation. Since we disaffiliated with the denomination, I had to give up my ordination with them as well, which was okay with me. I knew I had been ordained by God, so the imprimatur of the "organized church" didn't really matter to me. I served that church for five years before once again launching out on evangelistic endeavors.

Some relatives pastored a congregation in Moscow, Idaho, a small college town, and they invited us to come for revival services. I liked to pray at night, so late each night while we were there, I went to the church alone to pray.

One night I was praying and binding demons, when something grabbed me by the back of my neck.

"Whooooh!" I cried out.

I thought for sure I was under spiritual attack again.

I wasn't. The tag on the back of my shirt had caught in my hair and was rubbing up against my neck as I prayed more fervently. I felt foolish, but I wasn't about to let one of the devil's demons sneak up on me!

• • •

Although he had resigned, Bob Stark still lived in a three-bedroom house near the church, and he offered me a deal. "I'll take over payments on your motor home," he said, "and you take over payments on my house."

"Okay. That sounds good," I said. Patti and I needed a bit of stability in our lives if we ever hoped to raise a family.

The arrangement worked well until one day, when I got home from work, I found a note on the front door of the house announcing, "You have two weeks to come up with a balloon payment or you will be evicted." That was an enormous amount of money for a struggling pastor and his wife.

Next, I received a call saying, "You are three months behind on your motor home payments. We will be repossessing it."

What?!

Apparently, Pastor Bob had neglected to make the payments.

Pastor Bob possessed many wonderful character traits and incredible personal charisma. I loved him dearly, looked up to him, and admired him for the fatherly role he played in my life. But making wise financial decisions was not his forte.

Fortunately, Patti's uncle helped us resolve the situation by taking back the motor home and assuming the payments, and Patty and I moved out of the house with the impending balloon payment and into an apartment in Olympia.

I still missed my dad terribly. Other than Bob Stark, no other man had thrown an arm around my shoulder after Dad died, so I grew up missing that father-and-son sort of relationship. Maybe that's why I was willing to overlook some of Pastor Bob's failures and flawed wisdom. As I observed some of my peers, I couldn't help but notice that their dads were a big part of their lives, helping them get jobs or working together with them to buy a home.

I didn't have that sort of encouragement, and one day I felt it. I had watched with great interest as my fellow Bible school students succeeded early in their ministries; it was both inspiring yet discouraging. I was glad for them, but I experienced little fruitfulness in the ministry. I worked hard, preached hard, prayed hard, and did all the things a good pastor should do, yet I saw little fruit.

One day I was talking honestly with God, expressing my innermost feelings. "God, I really miss my dad. All these other guys have their dads to encourage them, to help motivate them, and to urge them on when times get tough." As I prayed, I said, "Lord, I just struggle sometimes because I don't have a father . . . I don't really have anybody . . . and I really wish I did."

The Lord responded, "*I will be your Father.*"

From that time on, God the Father became dearer to me and, in many ways, became my best friend. I could tell Him anything, my hopes and dreams as well as my fears. Sometimes I shared with Him my complaints, my pitiful concerns, and He was always patient and kind with me.

I wasn't aware of it then, but these were training days for me, learning to trust the Lord for everything, from having the right messages to preach to providing enough money for food, clothing, and a roof over our heads. I was also learning to obey our heavenly Father's instructions, even if I didn't always understand them or follow through perfectly.

Even Jesus had to learn obedience, Scripture says—obedience that eventually led to suffering and the cross. He didn't begin His ministry with a bunch of bombast and bravado but rather through the trials and temptations in a wilderness experience before He was adequately prepared to begin His earthly ministry and His heavenly reign. I realized that we shouldn't be surprised when God allows us to experience something similar, leading us into the wilderness before we are effective representatives of Him. But I can't say that it was easy.

• • •

Patti and I had been married for five years when our son, Josh, was born in 1978 with no complications in our small-town hospital. At our tiny medical facility, I was not permitted in the birthing room, so I sat nervously in the waiting room while the doctors performed a Caesarian delivery. We were excited to have a baby, and I was overwhelmed with thanksgiving to God—especially when the nurse came out to the waiting room and said, "Mr. Christmas, you have a son!"

Even though we were struggling financially, I felt that it was a joy to have our baby. Every time I looked at our beautiful baby boy—with his perfectly formed tiny fingers and toes; his tufts of soft, fine hair; his cherub-like cheeks—I gave thanks to God for our healthy child. I was delighted to be his dad.

In the hospital, as I gazed into our Joshua's barely opened eyes, it hit me that most of what this little guy was going to learn about life—at least the most important things—he would learn from Patti and me. And while I had absolute confidence that Patti would be a loving, caring mother, I knew the moment I saw Joshua that there were many things that he could learn only by being with me, talking with me, watching and hearing me interact with other people. I took that responsibility seriously and considered our baby boy as my own personal discipling project.

Although I certainly didn't regard myself as an expert on parenting, I had learned much from my dad. I assumed that Joshua would learn best by my example, that my attitudes toward love, marriage, family, and, most of all, faith in God would have a profound influence on shaping his values. What he would see in me would be even more important than what he might hear from his peers—at least, during the formative years of his life—and perhaps even more important than what he might see in other relatives. I wanted him to see good things in me. Above all, I wanted him to see Jesus in me.

And I wanted to be a role model for him. Although both Patti and I were scared to death, I somehow inherently understood that being a father was the most important role of my life. In our day and age, television and movies so often portray dads as inept buffoons, absentee workaholics, or wimpy, overly permissive parents with no ethics, morals, intelligence, or courage. I wanted to be different. I wanted to be the sort of father my son could look at and say, "That's my dad, and that's what it means to be a man. That's what it means to love Jesus."

I realized that I'd probably make some mistakes as a father; most guys do, it seems. But I also believed God would guide Patti and me in our parenting. I was convinced that if we kept doing the right things long enough, Joshua would notice, and sooner or later, our son would learn how to live right.

I loved him dearly. While working at the plywood plant, I often went home at lunchtime simply to hold him for a few minutes. Those were special moments when I could look into his eyes and pray for the great things God would do in and through Josh's life.

While Patti and I were still living in Pastor Bob's house, located about a half hour's drive from the church, I was trying to help a family in which the husband and wife were having marital issues. One night, the husband called our house at about two o'clock in the morning. "My wife and kids left me," he cried into the phone. "They're gone. I don't know where they are. I don't know what to do!" I talked with him for a while, tried to encourage him, and then prayed for him and hung up the phone.

When I went back to bed, I tried to sleep but couldn't. Instead, I felt a strong urge to pray for this family. I like to walk as I pray, and I usually pray aloud. So, I got up and drove twenty-five miles to the church and went inside to pray. I paced back and forth in the dimly lit sanctuary as I prayed and interceded for that family.

I was immersed in prayer when I turned around suddenly and saw a small, shadowy figure in front of a window in the back of the sanctuary. I thought for sure it was a demon. "Oh, Jesus!" I cried out.

It wasn't a demon. The wife and kids who had run away from the man I had been talking with earlier had hidden inside the church and fallen asleep in the nursery. My loud prayer had awakened them. The little girl had slipped into the sanctuary and unwittingly had scared the daylights out of me—the strong man of God.

Sometimes it takes some spiritual maturity to understand that we don't find demons under every rock or hiding behind every tree. But perhaps because of my upbringing around the Shakers and their occult practices on the reservation, in my early years of pastoring, I was hypersensitive to demonic activity—or what I supposed was the devil's shenanigans.

It never even occurred to me that the devil's shenanigans may take a totally different form that would send my life reeling.

CHAPTER 10

Deceived

LIFE WAS SIMPLE; Patti and I didn't have a lot of material possessions, but I pastored our small church and enjoyed helping people. Josh brought tremendous joy to us, and Patty was a wonderful, caring mother; in fact, Josh was her whole world.

We had a scare when Josh was eight. We were at a family reunion in Oregon, and Josh was playing with some kids when he fell off a thirty-foot cliff and landed in a ditch alongside the road. A passing drunk hiker came by and found that Josh's body was already turning blue. Amazingly, the hiker did CPR on Josh and got him back to breathing normally. Someone called 911 and an ambulance transported Josh from the campground to the hospital. He could have died right there, especially with what seemed to be a curse on the men in the Christmas family. I couldn't help thinking that the devil was trying to take Josh out early so he could not accomplish all that God had in store for him in the future.

Josh had a genuine hunger for God, even as a child. He said he always felt the presence of the Lord, so Patti and I were not surprised that he received the Holy Spirit when he was only eight years old. We were a happy little family—or so I thought.

That's when I began hearing rumblings that Patti might be having an affair. In our small town, secrets were few and rumors flew faster than the speed of light. But of course, I didn't believe that my sweet, sheltered, innocent wife could possibly be involved in something sordid.

Even when my mom came to our house and told me that Patty was being unfaithful to me—with Patti sitting right there in the room with us—I refused to believe her. "Patti's having an affair," my mom said.

Patti started crying and denied that she was being unfaithful. I told my mom, "You're wrong. Patti is not having an affair." Looking back, it is easy to recognize now that I simply did not want to believe that our marriage was in trouble. At the time, I continued to make excuses for Patti, grasping at any ray of hope that our life together was okay.

I should have known that something was up when I began having unusual pain in my chest. Even in my younger years, whenever I encountered some form of spiritual warfare, my chest would hurt. It felt heavy; my breathing restricted, as though I were having a heart attack; and I felt a palpable, physical pain. Now, as the blinders slowly lifted off my eyes, I realized that my chest had been hurting for nearly a year and a half. *That can't be good*, I thought.

I came home on a Saturday night, after spending time at our church in prayer, and found a three-page letter written on yellow legal pad paper lying on the bedroom dresser. Josh was in bed, but Patti was gone. In her letter to me, she said, "You deserve better than me. I'm not backslidden, but I've left."

I was devastated by Patti's words, but I felt sure that if I could find her, I could change her mind. I awakened Josh and put him in the car, and we went out searching for Patti. I went to her parents' home, but they did not know where she had gone. I drove around to many of the usual places Patti frequented in our little town. I did not find her, and I knew I had to preach that Sunday morning, so I drove back home. Josh was crying and continued to cry most of the night, until he finally drifted off to sleep. A few hours later, I got up, went to church, and preached a message the Lord had given me, "The Beauty of Serving Jesus." I could barely get the words out of my mouth.

Patti contacted me a couple of days later, and I was able to convince her to come home, but she refused to talk about where she had been. Nor would she discuss the letter she had written. We went to her parents' home instead, and Patti's brother-in-law told me that he thought Patti was having an affair, but I refused to believe it. Patti and I returned home with all sorts of unresolved issues.

Before long, Patti stopped going to church with me. Initially, her absence didn't seem unusual. I normally left for the services early so I could be ready to greet the first folks to arrive. I drove a beat-up old car to church and left the Datsun for Patti and Josh. Sometimes she'd show up late, walking in during the service. But then she stopped coming altogether.

At first, I thought she was simply busy, so I rationalized her absences, but then I realized there may be more to it.

"Why aren't you coming to church?" I asked.

"Oh, you know. Those people are always criticizing me. Sister Mary tells me every week that my skirts are too tight."

Of course, Patti had her reasons for not joining me at church services or during other times when I was at the church. It was later revealed that while I was at the church, she was entertaining another man in our home.

Patti did, however, find the church useful. "Why don't you stay home tonight with Josh," she suggested to me every so often. "I'm going over to the church to pray."

I later discovered that during these times, she was meeting some guy.

One night when Patti left, I thought, *I'm going to follow her.* I hurried Josh out to my old clunker of a car, ready to tail her, but the car wouldn't start. Perhaps God was protecting me.

As the truth became increasingly clear to me, I told our church leaders, "I'm going to take a leave of absence." I didn't need to offer them a reason; I think most of them had guessed long ago what was going on.

Patti suggested that we should spend some time apart. I agreed.

I went to South Carolina and stayed for nearly two months with my grandmother on Dad's side of the family. During that time, I called home frequently, and although Patti took most of my calls and talked to me, I could tell that she was emotionally distant.

My associate pastor at the church called me one day while I was in South Carolina. I assumed that he was simply calling to check on me, to see how I was faring during my sabbatical. I didn't realize that there was much more to his call.

Apparently, his son had been in the park on a Sunday morning, and he had seen my wife with another man. The boy came home and told his dad, "I don't know how to tell you this, but I saw Sister Christmas kissing a man in the park."

When my associate called me, he didn't bring up the subject directly. "How are you doing?" he asked.

I said, "I'm doing all right."

We talked about my health and well-being and when I might feel ready to return; we talked about the church and members of the congregation, including Patti. He hinted at the subject of her unfaithfulness, but he never said anything straightforward about her having an affair.

After a while, he simply said, "I love you, Brother Kent."

"I love you too," I said. And I truly did. This man was not only my coworker; he was one of my closest friends in the world.

And then we hung up.

I put down the phone, thinking, *That was a weird conversation*. Looking back, I realize that my associate suspected what was happening but didn't want to hurt me, especially by informing me of Patti's infidelity over the phone.

• • •

Patti and I had been separated for about two months when, during one of our phone calls, she surprised me by suggesting, "Why don't we make a fresh start someplace?"

I said, "Okay. What do you have in mind?"

"Maybe we could move there, where you are," Patti suggested. "Come on home, and let's talk about it."

I flew home to Washington state, arrived at the airport, retrieved my luggage, and waited for Patti to pick me up. And waited. I glanced at my watch and noticed the time, thinking, *That's odd that Patti is not here yet. I hope everything is okay.* I waited still longer . . . and continued to wait. Patti was more than an hour late picking me up from the airport. When she pulled in, she seemed flustered and made some sort of flimsy excuse about traffic being congested or something, none of which made sense.

"Okay," I said. "Let's just go home."

I didn't want to believe the worst, but I should have.

"Let's just move back to where you were," Patti said, "and we can make a fresh start in South Carolina."

"All right. We'll move," I said. I made some arrangements in South Carolina, resigned my position with the church in Washington, and packed up everything we owned—which wasn't much—in our small car.

About that time, we learned that Brother Bob Stark had moved to Nashville. I contacted Bob and let him know that Patti, Josh, and I were heading eastward and that we might stop by to visit on our way to South Carolina.

As we traveled across the country, every so often, Patti said, "I want to make a phone call. I need to call my mother." We'd stop somewhere, and while Josh and I occupied ourselves, Patti slipped off where she wouldn't be overheard. I didn't think much of it at the time, assuming that she was informing her mom of our progress.

Silly me.

Since we were heading for South Carolina, a stop in Nashville to visit with Brother Stark and his wife was right on the way. They greeted us warmly, and we stayed with them for a few days. We didn't let on that our marriage was in trouble, but it wasn't hard to figure out. Patti seemed distracted and disconnected. One day, Brother Stark and I went out to the golf course, and while we were there, his wife called. "You better get home quickly," she said. "Josh is with me, but Patti just left for the airport and wants to go back to Washington. She left a letter here for you."

We hurried back to the pastor's home, and his wife gave me Patti's letter. I read the words and was devastated. In the letter, she basically said that everything I had heard was true.

CHAPTER 11

Stripped of Everything

AFTER RETURNING TO THE STARKS' HOME and reading Patti's letter, Brother Stark and I raced to the airport. I ran in and found Patti sitting in a waiting area before she boarded her flight. I begged her not to leave.

"I've been seeing a guy . . . ." she said demurely.

I didn't have to ask what she meant. But I did ask, "Well, do you love him?"

"Yeah, but I love you too," she said.

"Well, please don't go," I said. "We'll work it out."

She seemed embarrassed but reluctantly agreed to return to the Starks' home with us. We didn't stay there long. Brother Stark took us to the home of Joel and LaBreeska Hemphill, some ministry friends of his in the Nashville area, where he thought Patti and I might receive some marriage counseling. The Hemphills were better known as gospel music artists, recording albums and performing concerts around the country nearly one hundred days per year, but they had also spent years in the pastoral ministry in Louisiana before moving to Nashville. I had never heard them sing, nor did I know anything about them, but for reasons that I did not know at the time, Pastor Stark thought that the Hemphills might be able to help Patti and me.

The couple welcomed us into their home, and we sat down on a couch in the living room near the staircase leading upstairs. As we talked that afternoon, Patti finally admitted that she had been unfaithful to me—that she had been seeing someone else for more than a year and a half. I was shell-shocked and heartbroken. I had suspected as much, but hearing the words from my wife's mouth smacked me right in the face, and for once, my tears flowed freely. In fact, I was sobbing my eyes out when a beautiful, dark-haired young woman came down the stairs. Joel and LaBreeska curtly introduced Patti and me to their daughter, Carmel, better known as Candy, who was on her way out the door on a date. No doubt, Carmel's first impression of me was not a positive one.

The Hemphills were kind and empathetic with Patti and me. "Why don't you stay with us for a while," LaBreeska suggested. "We'll try to help you."

Patti and I had no firm plan, and any hope that we might establish a fresh start in South Carolina had been dashed, so we were happy to accept the Hemphills' gracious invitation.

That night, I was so broken, I bolted out of the house and rambled down Dickerson Pike in a daze. As I walked, I saw Starlight Nightclub, a rather seedy joint with a less than stellar reputation in Nashville, and the Enemy taunted me, "Why don't you just throw in the towel, go inside, and get drunk?"

I had about $150 in my pocket, and although I had never imbibed alcoholic beverages, I felt sure that $150 worth of booze could do the trick.

It was a beautiful, starlit summer night, and as the Enemy dangled his temptations in front of me, I looked up toward the heavens and spoke to God. "You didn't do this to me, and I won't do this to You," I said, nodding toward the nightclub.

I passed on by.

That night was a tipping point for me. No, God didn't change everything in an instant; He didn't magically bring Patti and me back into alignment. But it was an important juncture for me. I easily could have gone the other way. Instead, I made a conscious decision that I would be faithful to the Lord.

And I meant it.

• • •

Patti and I stayed with Joel and LaBreeska for more than a week, and they talked with us several times about our situation, but nothing seemed to change. Patti's face remained sullen and I remained despondent. The only consolation was that she and the Hemphills' daughter, Candy, seemed to hit it off. They talked freely, laughed together, and established a strong bond of friendship in a relatively short period of time.

Candy introduced her boyfriend to Patti and me, though she was more interested in Patti's opinion of him than mine. Nevertheless, I could tell right off that something was not right about their relationship. I sensed that he was not right for Candy. Later, I made some offhand remarks to one of Candy's friends, and my comments got back to her.

When Candy confronted me, she was as mad as a hornet. "Who do you think you are to make that kind of negative comment about my boyfriend?" she wanted to know. She was convinced that I was speaking out of my own arrogance.

"I'm really sorry I made you mad," I said. "I know that God is going to send you the right man one day. He's going to be a great person, and I'm praying for you."

While Patti and I were staying with the Hemphills, their family frequently held special prayer services in their home, and people came from miles around to participate. Often, as many as fifty or sixty people attended, and Brother Bob Stark led the group. Many of those services were powerfully anointed, and God answered numerous prayers. Other services were merely kooky. But on several occasions, the Holy Ghost moved on Patti, and she cried and fell out in the Spirit.

One night, Patti and I went to a service at the Hemphills' home church in Nashville, when the preacher called me out and began prophesying about us, "reading our mail," accurately describing what was going on in our lives. I was so overcome with the power of the Holy Ghost that I fell to the floor in a trancelike state. It was the only time in my life to that point that I had been "slain in the Spirit." I was so overcome, several friends had to carry me out of the church at the end of the evening. I began laughing uncontrollably as the joy of the Lord overwhelmed me. It was a profound spiritual experience, and Patti witnessed all of it.

I was hopeful that maybe we could make a fresh start after all. But the Enemy had a strong hold on her heart and mind, and she continually went back to allowing the devil's lies to influence her actions. She seemed unable to break the soul ties that compelled her behavior. It's been said that forbidden fruit is the sweetest, and it certainly seems that way—for a while. Immoral sexual affairs are addictive and demonic, taking over every aspect of a person's life, to the point that it often requires supernatural deliverance for a man or woman to be set free from that bondage.

About six weeks into our stay, Patti got up one morning and said to me, "I have a headache. I'm going down to the Circle K [a local gas station and convenience store]. I'm going to get some aspirin."

I didn't suggest that perhaps Candy or LaBreeska might have something for a headache. I simply watched as Patti walked out the door. The convenience store was just a few blocks down the street from the Hemphills' home, so I figured maybe she merely wanted to get out and get some fresh air.

But after a while, Patti still had not returned. She seemed to be taking forever, and I began to get worried. I walked down to the store to check on her, but she was gone.

Patti and the man she was seeing had arranged for her to have a plane ticket with her when she left Washington with Josh and me. Maybe her intentions were not to move to South Carolina after all. Or perhaps she simply wanted *me* to move away. Or maybe she just wanted a backup plan in case our clean start didn't work. I had no clue. Regardless, she had now gone back to her lover, leaving me and leaving our son, Josh, whom she loved more than life itself.

I was devastated.

The temptation to commit suicide loomed largely in my mind. I knew those thoughts were demonic, planted by the devil's cohorts, but on more than one occasion, I held a gun to my head, ready to pull the trigger. What did I have to live for? My wife was gone, my ministry was gone, and I had no money and no real home in which to start over. I had nothing.

But I had an eight-year-old boy.

I knew that I had to take care of Josh. My life may have felt over, but Josh still had a hope and a future. I couldn't walk away from my son.

Still, after my wife left, I was so down and discouraged. One day I was praying and said to God, "I'm such a failure."

A few days later, Brother Bob Stark came to me and said, "Brother Kent, I was praying for you, and the Lord told me to tell you, 'You are not a failure.'"

Bob had no idea that I had been expressing those very thoughts to God. His words lifted my spirits, and I tried to take them to heart.

I attended church services along with some of the Hemphill family and the congregation of Church Triumphant, a few miles from the Hemphills' home.

During one service, the pastor, who had a genuine gift of prophecy, began to speak words over individuals. When he came to me, he said, "The Lord says, 'I broke you and stripped you of everything, but that which remaineth, I am taking from you.'"

Yikes! Who wants to hear something like that? I didn't know how to process his words, but I was about to find out.

I was still staying with the Hemphills, so I enrolled Josh in a school nearby and started looking for a job. We had been there about a month when I went to pick up Josh from school one day, as I did every day after school, but Josh wasn't there. He was gone.

"Where is my son?" I asked his teacher.

"Oh, his mom picked him up today," she said.

"What? No, that's not possible," I said. "She lives in the state of Washington."

"Well, I'm sorry, Mr. Christmas," the teacher said. "I don't know what else to tell you. His mom picked him up already."

I frantically began making phone calls, searching for Josh. It turned out that Patti missed Josh more than she realized, so she and her mother drove twenty-five hundred miles, absconded with our son, and never even discussed it with me. I didn't know what to do, so I called a friend who was a lawyer, explained what had happened, and asked for some advice.

"There's really not much you can do, Kent," he said. "She is his mother, and the two of you have not settled any sort of divorce proceedings. She has as much legal right to have Josh with her as you have."

Hearing his response, I felt even more dejected. I took a job ripping out used equipment at DuPont for seven dollars an hour and threw myself into working eighty hours a week, trying to earn enough money to get a permanent place to live and to pay legal fees for a divorce.

• • •

I have never been drawn to the more eccentric forms of Christian experience—people falling onto the floor in uncontrollable fits of laughter, barking like dogs, or claiming to have had their dental fillings suddenly transformed from amalgam to gold or other more outlandish manifestations. I don't automatically discount such testimonies (although I maintain a healthy skepticism), but I had not personally experienced anything of the sort, nor had I sought to experience anything like that. In the Bible, God sometimes communicated His messages through dreams and visions. I believe that God often speaks to us today through dreams, and I know people who have seen supernatural visions. Not me. At that time, I had never had a dream through which God had spoken to me, nor had I ever had a genuine vision from God. But I've had a few experiences of my own that I cannot explain other than to acknowledge the supernatural power of God.

The Hemphills had a small room upstairs that they designated as a "prayer closet." It was located under a staircase, and it didn't have any lights. No chairs were in the room, so they covered the floor with blankets and a pillow. I would often simply go inside, close the door, and sit or lie on the floor as I prayed.

One day, I entered the darkened prayer closet, closed the door, and began to pray.

I prayed and interceded, and suddenly I saw a light. It was a small, circular light about the size of a softball, with a bluish tint, and then it started moving. It seemed to move and hover above me, then came closer to me. I had been praying with my eyes closed, so at first, I thought it might simply be my eyes readjusting to the dark when I opened them. I rubbed my eyes, shut them, and reopened them. The light was still there. Although I had never before experienced anything like this, I quickly realized this was not something human. I sensed that I was experiencing the presence of God. I was in awe but not fearful.

I had not been preaching anywhere in recent months, but I wondered whether this was some sort of sign; maybe God was clothing me with some special anointing. Whatever it was, the experience impacted me profoundly. It brought to me a fresh revelation and reality of the existence of God.

In the book *Heaven Is for Real*, in which four-year-old Colton Burpo describes his extraordinary trip to heaven while hospitalized for an emergency appendectomy, he pictured the Holy Spirit as a blueish light. I saw something similar.

What I experienced seemed intensely personal, intimate, almost incomprehensible. I had not been expecting anything like that, so it was unexplainable in words. But although I did not know it at the time, seeing that light gave me extra strength to face all that was coming.

The next day, I tried to articulate what I had experienced. I told the group that had gathered at the Hemphills' for a prayer service about the blue light that I had experienced during my prayer time. They seemed interested and enthusiastic, but nobody offered any definitive answers.

Still, I knew God was doing something significant in my life. The experience was overwhelming to me; I could barely talk about it then and still have difficulty describing it all these years later.

• • •

I stayed with the Hemphills for a while longer. During that time, Candy and I had a few serious conversations, although she did not seem interested in me. In fact, she didn't like me at all and she later said that she thought that I was cocky. She had struck up a friendship with Patti, though, and Candy had cried and cried when she found out that Patti had left and returned to Washington. Candy paid no attention to me other than to look at me with disdain as the man who had driven her new friend away. In truth, I wasn't even thinking of Candy in any romantic way; I was still far too banged up emotionally to think she might be interested in me.

Candy's parents, however, were much more concerned and cautious about me. They were not comfortable with the idea of two single adults living under their roof.

"It's time for you to leave," Joel told me one day. "I'm not going to have you sparkin' my daughter."

As a West Coast guy, I wasn't quite sure what "sparkin'" involved, but whatever it was, I hadn't been doing anything of the sort. Still, Joel was having nothing to do with it. He wanted me gone.

I gathered my few possessions and drove away from the Hemphills' home, not exactly certain where I should go. That night, I slept in my car. The next day, I drove to South Carolina and slept on the couch at a friend's home.

The words of the pastor's prophecy came back to mind: "The Lord says, 'I broke you and stripped you of everything, but that which remaineth I am taking from you.'" Within weeks, I had been stripped of everything except Josh, and now he was gone as well. It would be more than a year before I saw my son again and eight years before I saw my former wife.

• • •

For years after my dad's death, I never shed a tear. Now, almost anything that had to do with ministry or marriage brought a flood of tears. At thirty-two years of age, I was broke and had absolutely nothing going for me but my faith in God.

After a few weeks in South Carolina, I returned to Nashville and paid Candy's brother about one hundred dollars a month to stay at his house for a while. I knew I couldn't merely be a freeloader, so I went out looking for work.

I got a job doing menial labor at Mike Rose Foods in Nashville. I was working in the factory one day when I slipped and fell as I stepped up through an unfinished metal doorway. A jagged piece of tin cut a vein in my arm. I looked down and saw that I had a large gash from my wrist all the way across my arm. Blood was gushing everywhere. My coworkers quickly grabbed a towel and wrapped my arm tightly to form a compress, and I was rushed to the emergency room at a nearby hospital. When the nurse in the ER removed the towel, blood squirted out and hit her in the face. The tin had cut a major vein, and had we not been close to a hospital where I could receive treatment, the wound could have been fatal. Instead, the doctor stitched me up and I went home that same day. God had protected me once again.

I heard that my former father-in-law would be traveling to Memphis, so I contacted him and said, "I need to work, so would you be willing to bring my toolbox and my steel-toed work boots with you when you come to Tennessee?" He graciously agreed to do so, and I was glad to retrieve my own tools and boots. Other than that, my most prized possessions—pretty much my only possessions except for some old clothes—were my Bible and my sermon notes accumulated during my years of preaching in evangelistic services and as the pastor of a church.

But God wasn't done stripping me yet.

CHAPTER 12

Surrender

ONE NIGHT AS I PRAYED, I started pouring out my heart to God. "Lord, I feel like an absolute failure." I began to chronicle my list of failures and rejections by other people. "You know I loved to play basketball, but I couldn't make the team because the coaches said that I was too short. I've hated being short. Especially when there's nothing I can do about it. I tried to get a job in a grocery store boxing groceries and they wouldn't even hire me. It seems like I've been plagued with failure all my life, and it really messes with me."

I continued listing my lack of success for the Lord, as though He didn't know anything about it. "And I've never been a success in ministry, neither as an evangelist nor as pastor. As a pastor, our congregation never numbered more than eighty people. I worked the graveyard shift at the shipyards to support myself and my family and still could never get ahead. And now all of this with Patty, losing my marriage, my ministry, my son. . . . I have nothing else to lose."

Or so I thought. But I was wrong.

As I was praying, it was as though the Lord were asking if I really wanted to be successful, not in the eyes of people but in the eyes of heaven, in His estimation of me.

We both knew the answer to that.

But what came next shocked me. "I want you to burn your sermon notes," God said. "Burn all your preaching notes."

"I can't do that," I told the Lord. My notes represented years of studying the Bible, writing out and preparing messages for myself and for God's people. I relied on them not only when I went out as a guest speaker but also as reference material when I developed new sermons for our home congregation. They were my best messages that I had kept with me through the years. In many ways, those sermon notes were *me*; they were the essence of who I was and all that I believed. To burn my notes would be like purging me of everything I had learned about God and His Word; it would be worse than cutting off one of my hands or legs.

But the Lord was insistent. "You have to burn them," He said.

I had no clear idea of why God would ask me to do such a thing; it made no sense to me. I wasn't preaching anywhere; indeed, I had no intention of ever preaching again, so I wasn't depending on those notes.

I had no difficulty understanding God's instructions, but that didn't make following through on His command any easier. I didn't immediately obey. I still hemmed and hawed for several days, with the Lord's clear word in my mind night and day. I had known God a long time and was not bashful about expressing myself to Him. So although I remained respectful, I posed the question: "Why?"

But I knew what I had to do.

One night, I gathered all of my sermon notes and carried them outside. I found some sticks and built a small bonfire near the house where Bob Stark was living, next door to the Hemphills. Finally, I took the sermon notes out and threw them, one sermon at a time, into the flames. I stood back in fear and trembling as I watched the fire lick up hundreds of pages of notes, devouring the last cherished emblems of my former life. Tears welled in my eyes as the best sermons I had ever preached crinkled in the fire. Sparks from the scorched paper wafted up to the sky. Now everything except my Bible was gone.

Again, I asked God as the smoke rose toward heaven, "Why, God? Why are You asking me to do this?"

His answer surprised me even more than the original instructions. "Because there is going to come a day when I put you back in the ministry, and when I do, I am going to fill your mouth with a new sound."

I did not know how to respond to that. As far as I was concerned, any hopes I had were dead. But spiritual death always precedes spiritual resurrection.

In the meantime, on several occasions, it looked as though Patti and I might get back together. I was certainly open to that possibility. I'd forgive her and welcome her back into my life, only to be rejected again. I felt somewhat like the prophet Hosea, who was forsaken by his wife despite his best efforts (see Hosea 2:4–6).

But I loved Patti, and more important, I loved God, so if He wanted us reconciled, I believed that He could put us back together. I tried to stay open to the possibility.

Finally, some pastor friends who loved both Patti and me spoke straightforwardly to me. "You've taken her back several times. You don't need to take her back again. Tell her that you have set your heart toward God, and you are not going to do this anymore."

It was only after their firm word that I was willing to file for divorce later in 1986. I called Patti and told her, "You have made your choice, and I am going to pursue what God has for me."

Even then, it was gut-wrenching. It wasn't simply that I was in the middle of a divorce. That was bad enough. But the divorce attorney took his time. Patti and I had no property, little money, and nothing to contest; we agreed that our son would remain in her custody, so the divorce that could have been completed in a matter of weeks was drawn out for more than nine months.

Divorce was one of the hardest things I had ever experienced, even worse than Dad's death. Divorce feels worse than death because death usually is not a personal rejection. And it provides some sense of finality or completion. Divorce does not.

Moreover, it was difficult emotionally for me. When someone you really love breaks your heart, you don't suddenly stop loving that person. I certainly didn't. Memories of my marriage and thoughts of Patti being with another man haunted me. One night I was tormented with grief, and my sleep was repeatedly interrupted by nightmares. I tried to pray, and God spoke to me lovingly but firmly. "I want you to pray for them."

"Pray for who?"

"For Patti and the man she is with."

"I ain't doin' that" was my knee-jerk response. My righteous indignation rose within, and I said, "I hope they go to hell for what they did!"

"No," God said. "You pray for them."

Have you ever wanted to argue with God, but you know it is a pointless waste of time to debate with Him when He has already told you what He wants you to do? That's where I was.

I finally acquiesced. "Okay," I said, "but I don't mean it."

"Pray."

I did. "Lord, I pray for Patti and her man," I said. "I ask you to forgive them for what they have done. Please don't let them go to hell."

It wasn't a fancy prayer, and it certainly wasn't heartfelt, but I kept at it, day after day, praying for two people whose actions had seared my soul. I prayed basically the same sort of prayers every day, and then after about two weeks, an astounding thing happened: I found that I meant it. I truly prayed for my offenders and asked God to be merciful and gracious and forgiving toward them, just as He had been toward me. And I meant it sincerely.

I don't know for sure what effect my prayers had on Patty and her man. I can tell you what happened as a result in my life. Remember that spiritual oppression I encountered in my dreams?

It was gone.

The day I truly meant my prayers for Patti and her lover, the torment in my heart and mind disappeared. As I released them to God, the devil had to unhand me and let me go. It was as though my unforgiveness were keeping me a prisoner, but the moment I released it and began praying sincerely from my heart for my offenders, the torment was gone. I was free!

I won't say it was easy. It wasn't. Usually, when someone hurts us or offends us, we feel justified in condemning them to hell or worse if we can. "That person hurt me, Lord; I want to call down fire on them and see You zap them!" But we are not justified in doing so—not if we want God to forgive us. That's serious. Jesus said, "If you forgive others for their transgressions, your heavenly Father will also forgive you. But if you do not forgive others, then your Father will not forgive your transgressions" (Matthew 6:14–15 NASB, 1995).

The moment I truly forgave Patti and her friend, I was free—free to live, free to enjoy the blessings of God in my life, free to look up and see the new day and new relationships that God was bringing into existence for me.

After I began to pray sincerely for Patti and her friend, God broke the soul ties, and I had no more bad dreams. Moreover, God loosened me from the past so I could look into the future. I was still banged up emotionally, but for the first time, I began to pray about possibly marrying again. I prayed, "God, if I get married again, this is the kind of lady I want." I made a list of characteristics and told God, "This is what I want in a woman." I'm sure the Lord must have smiled. But I gave Him my list anyhow. I said, "I want her to be pretty with brown hair, to be godly, and to have a strong, consistent prayer life. I've always taken care of my body, so I want her to be healthy and conscious about her body and appearance as well."

Hmm, who does that sound like?

I didn't want to be a preacher, but when God called, I said, "Yes."

My dad, Charlie Christmas, met the Lord in the military. He preached to the troops from tabletops.

My parents pastored a church on the Quinault Nation reservation in the state of Washington.

*Practicing my preaching
poses at two years of age.*

*Dad and me showing off two
elk we brought home.*

*My dad was my hero. His death
when I was twelve devastated me.*

*Dad was an outdoorsman and
instilled a love for nature in me.*

*When Dad began pastoring in Taholah, the church had thirty-five
members; soon, half the village attended regularly.*

*Mom once entertained twenty-seven overnight guests
in this house. I made the four-wheeler myself.*

*I was small in stature, so to avoid being picked
on at school, I kept to myself.*

*I was only five-foot-seven-inches tall when I graduated
from high school; I'm still 5'7" today.*

My high school senior photograph.

At nineteen, I knew little about what a good marriage involved or what it meant to be in a strong, healthy relationship. But my bride-to-be and I were in love as much as we knew of it.

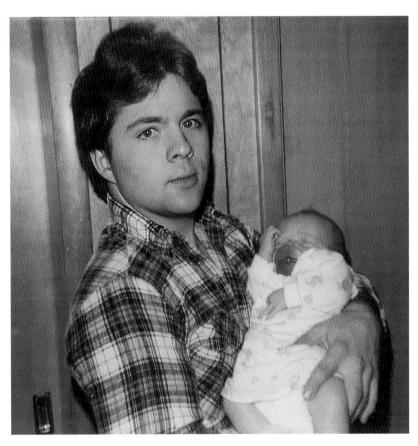

I frequently came home from work during lunch simply to hold Joshua.

Baby Josh brought us so much joy!

Joshua was my wife's whole world.

*When I moved to Nashville, Candy encouraged me to
shave my beard; I've never had one since.*

Young and happy with the woman who believed in me.

Cutting the cake on our wedding day.
We've made a big deal about cake ever since.

Joel and LaBreeska, Candy and me on our wedding
day. Lots of smiles, but tensions ran high.

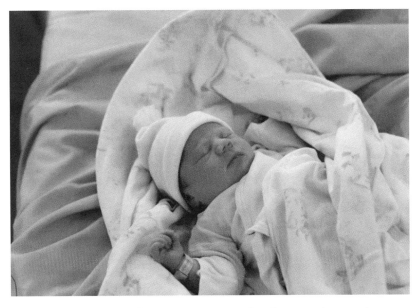

On Candy's and my first anniversary, our daughter, Jasmine, was born.

Jasmine, Daddy's little girl!

We were unsuccessful on the evangelistic circuit. In one church, the pastor introduced me as Jasmine's babysitter.

Our "miracle van." It was a miracle it ran with a blown transmission.

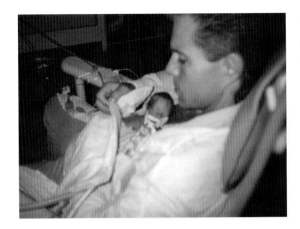

Our "Christmas Miracle," baby Nicholas—he was so tiny at birth!

After living in the hospital for three months, we brought baby Nick home on Christmas day.

When "The 700 Club" invited me to tell about Nicholas's birth, I began speaking prophetically.

*As young parents, we could barely keep the electric
bill paid, but we said, "We are blessed."*

*When the kids were school age, Jasmine took care of
Nick while Candy and I traveled in ministry.*

Sexually accosted as a boy, our son Josh struggled with homosexual feelings early in life before being set free as an adult.

Josh moved to Nashville as a young adult; he shared a love of dogs with Jasmine and Nick.

I believed God was going to bless both my sons, Joshua and Nicholas.

Josh and Jasmine grew really close. Her dream about his death stunned us.

Out of her depression, Candy began feeding homeless people and was healed. Today, The Bridge Ministry feeds thousands of people every week.

Preaching to the homeless; I supported Candy's ministry, but suspected God had more for me to do.

Josh and Nick serving together under the bridge.

CHAPTER 13

Someone Who Believes in Me

CANDY ALWAYS SAID, "I bet on the dark horse," meaning me. I certainly was a dark horse when she and I met. By all common sense, she should never have given me a second look. I was broke, broken, and pitiful, with no real home of my own, and I had a child to care for. Not exactly prime bachelor material!

Candy didn't like me at first and didn't see much potential in me. She was compassionate toward me but not overly friendly. I was quiet and not charismatic, although apparently I seemed self-confident to others, even though I was not. I was a devastated person and cried easily. That may have put her off initially as well.

That didn't surprise me. Rejection was nothing new to me. Some people thought that I had developed a complex as a way of protecting myself. That wasn't it at all. I just felt out of step with so many people, even dedicated Christians, because they seemed obsessed with trivial, transient things—stuff that wouldn't matter ten years from now, let alone things that had eternal value and would be just as relevant a million years from now. Over time, Candy learned that I was serious about praying, that communicating with God was more important to me than anything else in life. Years later, she said, "I put all of my eggs in Kent's basket because I learned that he is a genuine man of prayer." To me, that is one of the greatest compliments she could give me.

Soon after Patti's and my divorce was eventually finalized, she remarried. Although I hadn't been thinking in terms of reconciliation, her remarriage brought a sense of closure about ever being reunited. It was time for me to move forward, but that was easier said than done.

Despite feeling free, thanks to the forgiveness that God had shown me was so essential, I was still emotionally gutted. I attended church services at Church Triumphant, but I had no desire to teach or preach. Nor did the idea of getting married again seem reasonable.

The Hemphill family continued to be kind and gracious toward me—although Joel was much more guarded and kept a close eye on me when it came to being near Candy. But we all attended the same church, so I saw Candy and her family members frequently. Now that Patti had remarried, Candy seemed to take me on as a "project," introducing me to her friends and trying to set me up with dates, even though she and I had gotten off to a rough start in our friendship. In the midst of her matchmaking efforts, Candy began to see me in a different light. She became almost protective of me, especially when it came to me going out with one of her friends.

One night after church, Candy approached me and said, "Brother Christmas." (At that point, she still did not call me by my first name but more often addressed me as Pastor Christmas or Brother Christmas.)

"Hello, Carmel," I said cordially, greeting Candy by her formal name.

She smiled. "Brother Christmas, I came to church tonight with Shelly, but I was wondering if you might be able to drive me home?"

"Yes, of course," I said. "I'll be glad to do that."

We walked outside to my car. Candy slipped comfortably into the passenger side of my old vehicle, and we headed off in the direction of her home. I drove but didn't talk much as we rode along in an awkward silence. Fortunately, the distance was relatively short. The Hemphill family lived high on a hill in a beautiful, antebellum-style brick home, replete with tall, white columns—far out of my league. But as we neared the Hemphills' home, Candy looked at me and said, "Brother Christmas, have you ever thought about kissing me?"

My heart must have leaped to my throat as I tried to form words to answer her. The best I could come up with on the spot was, "Yeah."

Candy was persistent, though. "Well, what do you think?" she asked.

I'm sure my mind was going a million miles an hour. "Well, can I kiss you at the front door when we get to your house?" I asked.

Candy looked back at me and smiled. "Don't ask me," she said. "Just do it."

I pulled into the driveway in front of the Hemphill home, shut the car off, and walked around to open the door for

Candy. She got out and I walked her up to the front door. I put my arms around her, drew her close to me, and kissed her right on the lips.

At that moment, I think we both knew that we were going to be together for the rest of our lives. That was a powerful kiss!

Candy later said, "From then on, it was as though the scales fell off my eyes, and I could see Kent clearly. It was totally a God thing."

From my perspective, I had no desire to date anyone else except Candy—and I never did. Before long, we started talking about marriage.

Marriage? A few months earlier, Candy couldn't stand me. But now we were talking about beating the odds and having a wedding. Strangely enough, it felt right. For the first time in my life, I felt I had found someone who believed in me—even though she had little reason to do so apart from the Lord.

Early on in our relationship, most events we attended were with Candy's friends, not mine. I had few friends in Nashville; Candy had many. She had grown up with them. No doubt, I looked out of place among her friends, but Candy didn't seem to mind—much.

Candy recalls, "When Kent got to Nashville, he had about two pairs of blue jeans, a blue jean jacket, square-toed cowboy boots, and no jewelry. To put it bluntly, he had no polish."

She was right. I had a dark black beard with long, wavy hair, which I cut myself, and I was not a fashionista. I mispronounced words and mostly ignored current events; I didn't care about material things; my car was a wreck. I was a blue-collar worker. I rarely ate out at restaurants, and even when I did, I had little extra money to tip well.

Throughout the time we dated, Candy never saw me without a beard.

One day I told her, "I'm going to shave my beard."

She wasn't sure that was a good idea since she had never seen my unshaven face. "What if I don't like the way you look?" she asked.

"If you don't like it, I'll grow it back."

I shaved my beard and Candy liked the results. I've not sported a beard since.

Candy later said, "I fell in love with his soul." But she has always said that my blue eyes had something to do with it as well.

We became best friends and were a complementary team. I added a bit of routine and discipline to her life, and she added sophistication and polish to mine.

In many ways, the Kent Christmas who Candy met and fell in love with more than thirty-seven years ago would not have been palatable to a modern audience. I was raised in relative poverty, with a mom who was a widow, so that was my norm. Looking back, I now see that God took me to Nashville to get me ready for a broader ministry. My Northwestern roots provided strength and stability. Candy provided the polish I needed in order to have an influence with a broader audience.

Candy also bought an entirely new, stylish wardrobe for me, and her parents were not happy about that. When she first brought clothes home for me, my initial response was, "I'm not wearing that." I thought, *Those are show clothes, calling attention to myself. I don't want to be a showman. I don't want to wear those fashionable clothes.* But eventually, I did.

CHAPTER 14

A Prophet to the Nations—
Who, Me?

CANDY WAS STILL ON THE ROAD WITH THE HEMPHILLS singing gospel music around the country, traveling almost every weekend, so our dating experience was irregular, to say the least. I was so broke that Candy offered to pay for most of our activities. If we went out to eat someplace, she had to pay because I did not have enough money. It was humiliating to me, but I loved her even more for her generous spirit. When she was gone on the road with her family, I ate mostly red beans and rice with a piece of bread. Candy was always gracious. "Baby, I know one day it will be different," she often said.

One night we were watching *King David*, starring Richard Gere as David, which was a big, epic movie at that time. Without me knowing about it, the Lord spoke to Candy about me and said, "He is a prophet to the nations."

I wasn't even teaching a small group Bible study. Indeed, I was still an emotional wreck, crying all the time and sleeping in my car. I had barely enough money to buy food. Oftentimes, when Candy was going out on the road, she would leave a little extra money for me to buy food while she was gone.

And I was going to be a prophet to the nations?

No doubt, she had every reason to wonder, *Lord, are You sure You have the right guy?*

But Candy later told me that the Lord's voice to her was so strong and so loud that it rattled her windows.

She looked at me and asked, "Are you hearing anything?"

"No, I'm not hearing anything. What are you hearing?" I asked.

Candy looked at me sweetly and said, "The Lord just spoke to me and told me that you are a prophet to the nations."

I was stunned. Me? A prophet to the nations? I had no way to confirm that word. I didn't really believe it, yet I dared not deny it either.

She continued sharing the message she had received: "The Lord says to tell you that it is not my ministry that will open doors for you."

It was a puzzling word, yet clear.

At that time, Candy was a well-known gospel music personality. She had been singing with her family since she was thirteen years old. Over the years, millions of people had seen or heard her on radio, on television, and in concerts. She had also recorded three solo albums in addition to those on which she sang with the Hemphills. She had a lot of contacts.

But I was virtually unknown, so the message seemed odd to me. I certainly had no means of establishing a worldwide ministry. Most people in our hometown of Nashville didn't know my name—nor did they care to know it. I had not been preaching since my arrival in Tennessee, so the message Candy received seemed incongruous to me. I simply pondered it in my heart—and would continue to do so for the next thirty-three years.

When Candy and I first met, I was working as a pipe fitter to earn enough money to survive. "I will never preach again," I told her. I wasn't being belligerent or bitter toward God. I was broken and felt disqualified from service as a result of being divorced. I still trusted God and believed His Word, but I had no intention of ever standing behind a pulpit again.

So as my relationship with Candy grew more serious and we began talking about marriage, I reiterated to her, "Now, I want you to know that you are marrying a plumber. I'm not a preacher. If you are looking for a preacher as your husband, you are marrying the wrong guy. Because I'm never going to preach again. Can you live with a pipe fitter?"

Candy didn't argue with me. She simply smiled and said, "Yeah, I sure can," with a twinkle in her eye, as if she knew something that I didn't.

And she did. She knew what God had spoken to her about me.

As Candy and I began making plans to get married, she threw a curveball at me. "You have to ask my dad," she said.

"That is not a good idea," I replied.

But Candy was a traditionalist, and she felt it was important that I ask her father for her hand in marriage and that, hopefully, we might receive the blessing of her father.

I knew that wasn't going to happen. Candy's dad was not in favor of me *dating* his daughter, much less marrying her. He had much higher aspirations for her than marrying a pipe-fitting former pastor. After all, Candy was an integral part of the Hemphills, a well-known, professional gospel music group that regularly toured the country performing in large arenas as well as churches, campgrounds, and state fairgrounds. She was a beautiful and talented singer who had dated a number of famous musicians and other award-winning singers. Because of her talent and beauty, her parents assumed that she would be bringing home a "musical trophy" of a different sort.

Instead, she wanted to marry a broke, divorced former preacher with an eight-year-old boy and child support payments. I was not exactly a trophy in her family's estimation.

Nevertheless, at Candy's request, I met with her dad, and we engaged in an extremely tense discussion. After a short while, I told Joel, "I'm just going to leave. I don't want to say some things I will regret, because I'm going to be your son-in-law."

He asked me to leave town and forbade us from seeing each other. In the meantime, Candy's dad must have hoped that I would simply go away and drop out of his daughter's life.

I didn't.

I did, however, decide to spend some time at my aunt and uncle's house in Gilbert, South Carolina. As emotionally devastated as I was, I enjoyed some powerful times of prayer out in the woods of Gilbert. Two books that ministered to me were *Hinds' Feet on High Places* and *Mountain of Spices*, both by Hannah Hurnard. It was one of the seasons in my life when God was most real to me. I found a depth and an intimacy with God during those hours in the woods that I did not previously know existed.

While I was visiting in Gilbert, my relatives and I went out to a little church one night. About fifty people had gathered in the building. We sat in the back of the sanctuary throughout the service. I had never met the pastor before, but as I was listening intently to him preaching, suddenly the minister stopped. He looked directly at me. "You," he said, "you, that young man sitting right back there!"

Everyone looked toward me. I gazed up at him and shrugged. "Me?"

"Yes, you," he said. "The Lord says to tell you that there is going to be a double portion of His Spirit come upon you; and God is going to raise you up, and you are going to preach around the world."

What? Was this guy out of his mind? I was not even preaching in my hometown. I was divorced and discouraged and disillusioned, and this man was declaring that I was going to preach the gospel around the world?

I was thirty-three, and I had never experienced anything like that before; nobody had ever addressed a positive prophetic word directly to me. I didn't know what to do with it or how to even absorb that word into my heart, mind, and spirit.

But I never forgot it.

• • •

While Candy and I were still a dating couple, we discussed the idea of her moving out of her family's home and into her own apartment. She had lived in her mom and dad's home the first twenty-seven years of her life, not to mention the many days of each year she spent with them on a tour bus, traveling from city to city.

She wanted to rent her own apartment and have a place where she could express her own decorating taste as well as have a bit more privacy. But when it came right down to it, she was reticent to leave the roost.

"Do you want me to help you?" I asked.

"Yes, I wish you would," Candy replied. "I'm having a hard time making the move."

I helped Candy fill out the lease papers, and she rented a small but nice place in Breckenridge Apartments, not far from her family's home. The rent would stretch her budget to the edge, but we felt it would be worth it. When her father found out that Candy had rented an apartment and planned to move out of their home, he was upset with her but even more so with me. No doubt, he assumed I was encouraging her to go out on her own, which I was. Although I respected Candy's parents, I understood that we were both adults and didn't need to be intimidated by anyone else.

Moreover, from our first kiss, Candy and I knew we wanted to be married, so we talked often about our future together. I couldn't wait to formally ask her to be my wife, but I also wanted to be able to give her an engagement ring—a ring I could not yet afford. Truth is, we really couldn't afford to *date*, much less get married. How was I going to buy her an engagement ring?

I worked hard, saved every penny, and prayed, asking for God's wisdom and guidance in getting Candy a ring. I understood that her top priority was not receiving a ring; she was focused on the relationship. But our heavenly Father must have known that this symbol of our covenant was important to me, because within a matter of weeks, a woman at church approached me and said, "I have a little diamond I want to give to you." She knew that Candy and I were in love and wanted to get married. She gave me a beautiful, emerald-cut diamond, about half a carat in weight.

I could hardly believe my ears and eyes; yet I had prayed, and God had provided, so I graciously accepted her gift and thanked her. I took the diamond to Dick Bundy, who owned Bundy's Jewelry Store, and asked, "What can you do with this? I don't have money for an expensive ring, but is there some way you can put this diamond on a tiny band?" The jeweler knew Candy and created a beautiful ring for her. He charged me a rock-bottom price and wished us well. My next goal was to arrange a romantic way to present the ring.

Candy and I often met at Steak and Egg, a small restaurant similar to Waffle House, on Gallatin Road in Madison. That was "our place" since we no longer felt welcome together at her parents' home and I was living in only one bedroom at her brother's home. We couldn't really afford to actually *eat* at Steak and Egg since neither of us had money to spare, so we simply sat there for hours sipping coffee and talking. We got to be on a first-name basis with the friendly, gravel-throated, hardworking waitresses, and they regarded us as "regulars," a dubious distinction, to be sure.

What better place to get engaged, I thought, *than with our special friends?* I bought a dozen roses and attached the diamond ring to one of the flowers in the center of the bouquet, slightly buried and surrounded by the bright red roses. That afternoon, shortly before I met Candy for coffee, I took the roses to Steak and Egg, and one of our favorite waitresses stored them for me in a cooler. "Tonight, after we sit down, I'll wink at you," I told her, "and that will be your signal to bring the roses to our table."

The waitress nodded and smiled. "Okay, I'll be watching," she said. She seemed genuinely excited to be a part of our love story.

It was a slow night at Steak and Egg, and only a few other customers were in the restaurant when Candy and I walked in and waved at the waitresses. I nudged Candy toward the interior of the restaurant to a booth along the side wall, next to the window.

We settled in and ordered our coffee. After a short while, I gave the signal to our waitress; a few moments later, she came out from behind the counter bearing the beautiful display of roses. Candy could hardly believe it! We could barely afford coffee and eggs, and I had bought her a bouquet of roses. She was overwhelmed, and when she saw the ring in the roses, her face lit up in surprise and she started to cry. Before long, tears filled my eyes as well.

I leaned toward her and asked, "Will you marry me, Carmel?"

I think everybody in the restaurant heard her response: "Yes!"

I slid the ring on Candy's finger and it fit perfectly. She has worn it with joy as a symbol of our love for more than thirty-five years. Over the many years of our marriage, I knew she would love to have a special pear-shaped diamond. I saved money for a long time and went back to Dick Bundy, the jeweler who had helped me with Candy's engagement ring several decades earlier. I asked him to help me find something special for Candy that I hoped to give her at Christmas. Dick found a large, perfectly pear-shaped loose stone, and I bought it. "I'll put it in an envelope for you and keep it in my safe until you are ready for it," he said.

About two weeks before Christmas 2022, I heard that Bundy's Jewelry Store had been robbed. Apparently, the thieves had used a jackhammer and had drilled through the ceiling and through a foot of concrete, down into the top of the safe, and had stolen thousands of dollars and all of the jewels and expensive watches that were kept overnight in the large safe.

I went to the store and found Dick Bundy. He could probably tell by the expression on my face why I was there. "Did they get my wife's diamond?" I asked him.

"You're not going to believe this," he said. "Somehow, that little envelope containing your diamond must have slipped behind the shelf, and it is the only piece that was left behind."

I believe that God hid that envelope from the sight of those thieves.

With that original half-carat diamond on her finger, Candy happily announced our engagement to her family members. They were not nearly as excited about the news as we were. It was understandable to me that Candy's family did not regard me as the ideal candidate for her. After all, her father was already a wealthy man, and her two brothers were well on their way to building a thriving business of their own. Me? I had nothing to show for my years in the ministry—nothing tangible, that is. I had little money, no real home of my own, and, worse yet, relatively little that I could point to as evidence of a "successful" ministry. I knew that I had preached good, sound doctrine, but I couldn't prove it with some outward evidence of success. No wonder her family questioned how I was ever going to support Candy.

Right up to the day of her bridal shower, Candy continued to receive conflicting messages from her family and friends. By that time, we had been dating for more than a year, and although we were both convinced we loved each other, Candy still had not received confirmation from the Lord that I was the man to be her husband, that I was "the one." On the morning of her bridal shower, she prayed for two hours straight, walking the floors, speaking in tongues, and begging God to tell her clearly that we were meant for each other, and specifically that I was meant for her.

Candy had trusted her parents' and family members' judgment for the first twenty-seven years of her life, so for her to go against their declared wishes was like severing the umbilical cord.

After praying for more than two hours, she said, "Well, I guess God is not going to tell me." She decided to go ahead and get ready for her bridal shower. Before doing so, she went in the kitchen and opened the refrigerator to get some lemonade. That's when the Lord spoke to her: "Daughter, he is the one."

That word was what she needed to hear, and it would be a reminder to her in the coming years, in the good times and during the tough times. Candy knew that I was the man God had for her and that she was the woman He had for me. When you believe and trust that much, you can make it through any trial.

Years later, Candy would recall, "We had some really hard years, our pastoring was not always successful, but I always went back to that truth: this is the path that God chose for me. Not marrying some famous musician, or multimillionaire businessman. But 'Daughter, he is the one.'"

We didn't know it then, but we would certainly need that sort of assurance.

• • •

As we planned our wedding, Candy's dad, Joel, refused to walk his daughter down the aisle or to actively participate in the ceremony. Nor would Candy's parents help us pay for the wedding. That hurt. We felt our union was worthy of celebrating.

But at the rehearsal, when the pastor asked, "Who giveth this woman to this man in marriage?" Joel answered, "Her mom does."

That was not exactly the best way to begin a marriage. But Candy and I were in love, and we believed that God had brought us together and that He had plans to use our lives together.

It was a hot, sweltering evening, and at the rehearsal dinner, LaBreeska made a point of seating my guests from South Carolina outside in the heat and humidity. Ostensibly, Candy's mom thought my guests might feel more comfortable in a warmer environment. Right!

Later that night, Joel and my mom got into a nasty argument over the wedding. They had some strong feelings in common: my mom did not like Candy, and Joel did not like me. Mom didn't think that Candy was "spiritual" enough for me. She looked askew at Candy because she wore stylish clothes and makeup, unlike Mom's more old-time, Pentecostal friends. Joel, of course, could hardly look at me at all! I later heard that Joel and his family prayed that the wedding would somehow not take place.

Despite the obstacles and objections, Candy and I were married in a beautiful ceremony led by Pastor Bob Stark at Church Triumphant on August 17, 1987. Noted gospel singer Doug Oldham sang at our wedding, as did worship leader David Binion. Candy's brother Trent and his wife, Bethni, rented a limousine for us to have as our wedding departure vehicle.

Although we were now married, Candy's dad still wielded tremendous influence over her. Joel allowed his daughter only one day for our honeymoon before getting back on the tour bus and hitting the road again.

The less-than-favorable expressions by Candy's family about our marriage impacted us. Although I knew she loved me, for the first several years we were married, Candy tended to take her dad's advice over mine. I couldn't really blame her. After all, he was thriving—or so we thought—and I was not.

Sometimes when I suggested that we do something a certain way, Candy would respond, "Well, that's not what my dad said."

I had no argument with that and no rejoinder to combat that logic anyhow, other than saying, "Yes, but you are married to me."

I couldn't force Candy to respect me; I had to earn it. We didn't fight about matters, but I knew that we had to be on the same page spiritually, one in spirit as well as body and mind, before God could use us in the way He intended.

CHAPTER 15

When the Holy Ghost Comes

A SHORT TIME AFTER CANDY AND I WERE MARRIED, the pastor of the church we were attending approached me and said, "Brother Kent, I want you to preach for me on Sunday morning."

My first reaction was to turn him down. After all, I had not preached in quite a while, I had burned all of my sermon notes, and, more importantly, I had felt disqualified from preaching because I had been divorced and was now remarried. But God had been softening my heart, and for some reason, I heard myself saying, "Yeah, I will."

The congregation numbered more than three hundred people at that time, and I was amazed that the pastor would ask me to preach to them. I had rarely ever preached to an audience that large.

I studied and prayed during the week before I was to preach, but I could not discern what direction the Lord wanted me to go. As we were driving to the church prior to the service on Sunday morning, Candy asked me, "Babe, what are you going to preach about today?"

"I don't know," I said. "God hasn't told me."

Candy didn't say anything, but I could see the anxious look on her face. She later said, "I'm sitting there in the passenger side of our car, and I'm already thinking of things that I can say to him on the way home. Things like, 'Oh, Babe, it wasn't that bad. You did great. You're being too hard on yourself. You haven't preached in a long while. It was better than you think. You're just out of practice. Next time, you'll be a lot better.'"

Candy had been around good preaching most of her life. She understood that the most effective ministers knew their messages inside out; some used notes and some did not, but all had the message in mind long before they stepped up to the podium. For me to tell her just a few minutes before we arrived at the church that I had no idea what I was to speak about was disconcerting, to say the least. All the way to the church, she pondered encouraging words she could share with me after my sermon flopped.

We arrived at the church and I still had no clue. All the way through the preliminary part of the service, I waited for God to direct me, but when it came time to preach, I didn't even know where to open my Bible.

But when I stepped up onto the platform, something came over me. I didn't recognize at first what was happening, although I was totally aware of what I was doing. As I began to speak, the words that came out of my mouth shocked even me.

"Thus sayeth the Lord: 'There's sin in the house, and God says repent or in six months the doors of this church will be padlocked."

I dared not look at Candy as I spoke. No doubt, she was terrified by what she heard me say. But I knew the words were not my own.

We left immediately after the service, and the church did not even give me an honorarium for speaking. Who could blame them?

This was the first time, at age thirty-four, that I experienced God speaking through me prophetically. In my Pentecostal circles, we believe in the gifts of the Holy Spirit— all of them. We recognize those that the apostle Paul wrote about in 1 Corinthians 12–14 as well as those listed in Romans 12 and Ephesians 4. But the gifts that we emphasized most frequently were the gift of tongues, in which somebody speaks out publicly in a language that he or she has not learned, and the gift of interpretation, where someone interprets the message that was given in tongues so the rest of the audience can understand. Other, more personal "prayer language" sorts of speaking in tongues were common as well.

The gift of prophecy, however, was not a high priority in our circles, although we did believe in the prophetic gift of forthtelling, which was involved in great preaching. We also believed in predictive prophecy, speaking about circumstances or events that God said were going to take place in the future. Both kinds of prophecy are found in the Bible, although the standards were high. Prophets were judged stringently. If their words about the future did not come to pass, they were considered false prophets, a designation that normally ended their prophetic careers—and often their lives.

Nor was there any guarantee from God to the prophets that their words would be well-received and acted on positively. Quite the contrary, God told some of His major prophets in advance—men such as Isaiah, Jeremiah, and Ezekiel—that the general public and God's own people would reject their messages and them. Being a prophet in biblical times was not the path to popularity and prosperity. It was often just the opposite.

I knew that, and I took the gift of prophecy quite seriously. It was not a spiritual gift that I had sought. It was not something I wanted to mess with, flippantly speaking words into someone else's circumstances that I knew nothing about.

But I could not deny that something supernatural had happened in and through me that morning when I declared that there was sin in the church and that if it wasn't addressed, the church doors would soon be closed. Nor had anyone informed me prior to the service about problems in the church. I knew next to nothing about the inner workings of that church. Although Candy and I had attended there, I had no idea of the duplicity that existed within the leadership, so I, too, was surprised at the words that had come out of my mouth.

What neither Candy nor I knew was that a scandal was percolating below the surface within the congregation, and God was about to blow it wide open. Unfortunately, the church did not act on the word they had heard, and within six months, the doors on the church were indeed padlocked and the building was eventually put up for sale. No one was more shocked and saddened by the events than I was, but I also recognized that God had spoken a firm word through me. It was humbling to know that, and almost frightening, even though I knew His love was unfathomable. I also knew the Scripture warned that not many should become teachers of the Word, "knowing that as such we will incur a stricter judgment" (James 3:1 NASB 1995), because there was a responsibility to teach the Word of God accurately and to live accordingly. To me, to be a vessel through which God might speak prophetically in such a manner seemed to carry even more responsibility.

To this day, I always pray and try to prepare any time I am going to speak, just as Scripture instructs leaders to do, but at times, the Lord seems to circumvent my studies and begins to guide my words in a different direction. Oftentimes, that results in a prophetic message. That is always His prerogative, and I simply try to stay open to the leading of the Holy Ghost.

• • •

Because Candy was on the road so often with her family during the first three months of our marriage, I sometimes accompanied her on the Hemphills' tour bus, traveling with them to concerts. I was glad to do it so Candy and I could have some time together. Oftentimes, the bus would roll back into Nashville at 6:00 a.m. and I would hurry home to change clothes and go off to work as a pipe fitter.

There were no extra bunks on the bus, so whenever I traveled with the family, Candy and I crammed together in her bunk as the bus traveled through the night.

One night, everyone else on the bus was sleeping when God gave me a vision or a dream. I couldn't tell which, because I had never had that sort of experience before, but it really made an impression on me. In the vision, I saw an enormous number of people in a city. It looked as though they were in Bible times, dressed in ragged attire, and walking on dirt roads, but I knew they were people of God.

Walking right along with them and intermingled among them were large, demonic beings with hideous faces, armed with spears and pitchforks. The demons moved freely among God's people and seemed to wound them at will, any time they wanted to do so.

Making matters worse, the people of the Lord knew that they couldn't do anything to thwart the demonic attacks. They were powerless to do anything about it. They didn't make a sound, but I could see tears running down their faces due to their pain and sorrow.

As I watched all of this, suddenly I heard a loud voice and saw an old man coming down the main road into the city. It was a dirt road, and I could hear him in the distance shouting, "The Lion of Judah shall roar again today!"

As the old man drew closer, he didn't address anyone in particular; he simply continued more loudly declaring, "The Lion of Judah shall roar again today!"

In the midst of that, I saw the spirit of fear and intimidation that was on the people of God being lifted off them and going straight up into the sky. I then saw the boldness that had been on the demons go straight up as well, and it switched and came back down. Only now, the power and the boldness came upon the people of God, and the fear and intimidation fell on the demonic beings. They dropped their weapons and began to flee.

I saw the people of God pick up those weapons and begin to destroy the demonic entities.

Just then, I woke up with a jolt. I could feel the hairs on my arms standing on end. I had no idea at the time what this vision might mean, but I knew it was a message of triumph in the midst of seemingly overwhelming odds.

What I did not know was that the old prophet would be me. I was a relatively young man, physically small in stature, with no standing in the world, yet God was showing me that "You are the man in the vision. I am getting ready to go to war." It would be another thirty years, however, before I saw that prophecy come to pass.

CHAPTER 16

A Shaky Start to a New Beginning

I LANDED A BETTER-PAYING JOB, still working as a pipe fitter at Nashville's St. Thomas Hospital, where a large expansion project was underway. Years earlier when I had worked in the Tacoma shipyard, I knew nothing about pipe fitting, reading building blueprints, or the other skills required. But they had hired me and taught me how to do the work with excellence. The work had to be done according to the US Navy's strict government standards, so there was no room for complacency or error. I worked hard and mastered the art of reading the blueprints so well that my employers moved me into the engineering department and sent me out on ships to make certain all of the pipework was fitted perfectly.

When I was hired at St. Thomas in Nashville, I went to a Goodwill store and bought a new pair of steel-toed work shoes and a new blue shirt and pants for my first day on the job. Although I was nearly thirty-six years old, I still had a sort of baby-faced appearance, so I looked much younger than my age. The boss peered at me skeptically and nodded toward another employee. "This guy will be your welder," he said. He guided me to a large, elaborate shutoff system, handed me a set of blueprints, and said, "Finish this."

I studied the prints and the shutoff system and realized that something wasn't right. "They put this in wrong," I told the welder. "This isn't according to the blueprints."

"Yeah, I know," he said with a bit of a smile. "We were testing you to make sure you really know what you are doing."

I worked there for a while and the job gave us a bit of security, enough that we could think about starting a family. Although Candy was barely twenty-eight, she felt that her biological clock was ticking as loudly as Big Ben. She had grown up in Louisiana, where many of her peers had married at seventeen or eighteen years of age and had three or four children by the time they were in their early twenties. Her own parents had married at seventeen, were pastoring a church, and had three children by the time they turned twenty-one. At twenty-eight, Candy felt as though she were behind schedule.

When we told her parents that Candy was pregnant, however, her mom and dad were not happy about the news. No doubt, they knew that our having a baby would greatly impact their lives and their careers—and they were correct.

• • •

On our first anniversary, August 17, 1988, Candy gave birth to our daughter, Jasmine. What a marvelous way to celebrate! Candy had gone into labor the night before, and Jasmine came into the world around two o'clock the next afternoon, healthy, radiant, and with a strong voice. We were thrilled! The same day that Jasmine was born, however, I was laid off work. The project at St. Thomas Hospital was done, and my services were no longer needed. We were already struggling financially, so that lost income exacerbated our stress levels even more.

Candy and I prayed about our next steps, and we both felt that I should hit the evangelistic trail again. Working as a pipe fitter was fine with me, but introducing people to Jesus really cranked my motor.

But where could we start? I had not been greatly successful in previous ministries, so I didn't have a large number of people calling and asking me to come to conduct services in their communities. Candy sent out some letters to potential contacts who might be interested in inviting us to their churches. Few did.

In the meantime, to support us as we got some traction as an evangelistic team, I tried all sorts of alternative careers. I took a job selling life insurance; that didn't work. I joined a multilevel marketing group; that was futile as well. I knew hardly anyone in the Nashville area. How was I going to sell them life insurance or involve them in a multilevel business? I concluded that God did not want me to be successful at anything that would take my focus away from preaching the gospel.

Candy and her family had performed in concerts all over the country, so her family knew a lot of preachers. I didn't have those kinds of connections.

When I got laid off work, Candy said, "Don't worry. I have a lot of contacts from places my family and I have done concerts. I'll call some of the pastors of those churches. I can sing for them and you can preach."

Her suggestion seemed like a good idea at the time—until we tried it.

We made arrangements to speak and perform at one church, and as we approached, we saw in large letters on the marquee, "Candy Hemphill in Concert!" During the evening, Candy sang a number of songs and then said, "I'm going to turn the program over to my husband."

When I got up to preach, a large number of people in the congregation got up and walked out. They had come for the music and were not interested in hearing me preach.

That seemed to be the norm for us. Although I still studied, prepared, and prayed over every message, I grew accustomed to being a voice in the wilderness that few people wanted to hear.

I knew that I had an unusual level of anointing from God to preach, but it opened few doors of opportunity, and I could never seem to break through the ranks in the Pentecostal circles in which I ministered. We had good services but never drew large crowds. Most of the invitations I received to preach were from small congregations, but I always did my best to pray, study, and prepare as though I were speaking to millions of people. Maybe someday I would, but for now I knew I needed to be faithful to the calling God had given me.

Even those larger congregations that invited Candy and me often had no real desire to hear me preach. For instance, Candy received an invitation from a pastor who led a large congregation in Carrollton, Texas. She was excited. "You're going to really like this guy," Candy said. "And he might have you preach for him."

When we went to the church, we met with the pastor in his office before the service, and he barely even spoke to me. When he introduced Candy to do a concert, he told his congregation, "We're so glad to have Candy here to sing for us, and she brought her husband along to babysit."

When we got in the car to return to the airport, the pastor's wife asked us, "Did you guys have an affair?"

"What?" Candy and I asked simultaneously.

"Yes, we heard that your former marriage blew up because of an affair," the preacher's wife said to me. She hinted that rumors had swirled implying that Candy and I had gotten together while I was still married.

We let her know that any rumors of that nature were baseless, since Candy and I had not even met prior to my former wife's infidelity. Still, the comment was disheartening. It was a good reminder to be careful about judging when the facts are unknown.

Please don't misunderstand: God always came through for us; He never failed to take care of us. He didn't always show up according to our plans or our schedule, but He was never late.

For instance, Candy and I made arrangements to travel to Houston, Texas, to pick up some furniture at a discount store because we had so little money and could afford nothing else. We were broke because we had used almost all of our money to purchase the furniture. We drove our old Dodge van that had more than one hundred thousand miles on it and pulled an empty U-Haul trailer so we could bring back the furniture.

In the middle of the night, around three o'clock in the morning, we were going up a hill somewhere when we heard a loud *BOOM!* The van jerked hard, so I pulled over on the edge of the steep incline and put the vehicle in Park. But the gear didn't catch and the van continued to roll backward! I slammed on the emergency brake and the van came to an abrupt stop.

"What was that?" Candy asked. "What happened?"

"I don't know," I said.

"What are we going to do?"

I rubbed my chin as though I were thinking about the answer to her question. But I already knew that there was really only one answer. "Well, I've been preaching about faith," I said, "so we are going to lay hands on this van, pray, and ask God to make it work."

We went outside in the middle of the night, laid our hands on the van, and asked God to heal the transmission. Our prayers must have sounded silly to God, but we were desperate. I prayed, "In the name of Jesus, Lord, please fix this transmission. In the name of Jesus, I command this van to run!" That was it. Nothing fancy, no flowery words, just the prayer of two desperately stranded, broke travelers who didn't even have a cell phone to call for help. So we called on God. After we prayed, I put the van's gear shift in Drive, and we pulled away! We drove all the way to Houston in that van, loaded the furniture, and drove all the way back to Nashville.

After we unloaded the furniture at our home, I returned the trailer and then called Mr. Transmission, an auto shop specializing in transmission repairs. "I need you to look at my transmission," I explained to the mechanic. "I put it in Park, and the van rolled backward on me."

I left the van with him and got a ride back home.

The next day, the mechanic called me and said, "You must know Somebody up above."

"Why do you say that?" I asked.

"Because I pulled the cover off and your transmission is in pieces," he replied. "It looks like a bomb went off in there."

It may not seem like much to anyone else, but Candy and I were convinced that God performed a miracle to fix that transmission long enough to get us safely home. The mechanic installed a used transmission, and we finally sold it after more than a quarter of a million miles! God had taken care of us again. If He could do that, what else might He do for us?

• • •

Sometimes my preaching made Candy nervous.

At a church in Napa Valley, California, the pastor introduced Candy and she sang five songs, but the congregation stared back at her blankly. The people seemed cold and unmoved by her musical presentation. Walking off the platform, she passed me and quipped, "Show 'em what you've got, big boy, because I sure can't move these folks."

We were unaware that the church was having internal issues. I had planned to present a simple message, but the Spirit of Prophecy came over me, and I began to speak straightforwardly to specific people in the audience. To one man I said, "Brother, you have stood with the pastor and held up his hands and fought for unity in this church." To another, however, I said, "You have created division and disunity in this church."

The messages were so pointed, Candy got nervous. She later said, "I thought they were going to run us right out of the church!" While I continued to speak, she walked back to the nursery and got our baby, Jasmine, and went outside to sit in the foyer near the front door, just in case we had to make a quick exit.

The power of God fell, and the church atmosphere turned into a roar. Some people were angry, some were crying, others were wailing, and many were on their knees repenting.

I stood aside and the pastor quickly took to the platform. In a loud, frustrated tone, he lambasted the congregation as if to say, "I told you so."

I stepped back up to the platform and spoke gently and quietly, "Brother, I believe God wants to heal your congregation. Let's just pray."

It turned into a sweet time of healing for that congregation.

But they never invited us back.

CHAPTER 17

How Deep Is Your Love?

EARLY IN 1992, I preached about faith in downtown San Francisco at a church in a beautifully renovated old theater. Seven people in the congregation were dying of AIDS. I fervently prayed for them at the close of the service, but not one of them was healed.

I returned home to where Candy and I were living at the time in an old house, high on a hill next to Joel and LaBreeska. I was so discouraged as I prayed sincerely, "God, it's not enough for people to shout. I want to see people's lives changed."

"Son, it takes faith," I heard the Lord saying gently.

"I have faith," I said boldly.

I'm not certain that our omniscient God says such things as "Oh? Really?" but this may have been one time He did. Because His next question provided the context for a test of my faith.

"Will you give me 50 percent of everything that you make until I tell you to stop?" He asked.

Fifty percent? Candy and I had always given a minimum of 10 percent, the tithe, of every cent we earned, and we usually gave a total of 20 to 25 percent of our income to the Lord's work. But now God was asking me to give a whopping 50 percent? I wanted to say yes, but I knew I couldn't make that kind of commitment without Candy's consent, so I went upstairs and told her what I sensed the Lord saying. "What do you think?" I asked. "Can we do that? Can we give 50 percent of everything we bring in?"

"Well, if that's what the Lord says," Candy agreed, "let's do it."

We prayed and said, "Yes, Lord. We will give You 50 percent of everything we bring in until You tell us to stop."

That was the beginning of a new adventure with God. I was excited. "I believe that in three months' time, we will be totally out of debt," I told my wife, "because of this act of faith."

I was wrong. Within three months, we were more broke than before.

Still, we were not about to renege on our commitment. If I spoke somewhere and received one thousand dollars in the offering, we gave five hundred dollars back to the Lord through our tithes and offerings.

We remained faithful, but we were really struggling. The telephone company turned off our phone service and the electric company turned off our power several times. Our bank sent a notice that they were going to foreclose on our house soon. Still, we remained faithful to our commitment, even though we had little to show for it.

Our experiment in faith seemed more like an experience of futility.

We were invited to minister at a church in Columbus, Ohio, where we had ministered previously. We were glad for the opportunity, but it did not look good as far as helping us financially. After the former three-day series of services, the church presented us with an offering of three hundred dollars, for which we were grateful, but it just wasn't enough to cover our expenses. So as we prepared to go to that same church again, I prayed and asked the Lord for three *thousand* dollars, an outrageously high amount for that small congregation to give. But I wasn't asking the congregation; I was asking God.

I preached Friday and Saturday evenings as well as Sunday morning. The services were powerful, but the crowd was not large. We had one more service scheduled for Sunday night. The church had put us up in a hotel room on the twelfth floor of the Holiday Inn, and on Sunday afternoon, I was studying and getting ready to preach Sunday night. But our own dire financial situation weighed heavily on me.

"God, I am desperate, and I am standing on Your Word," I said. I opened my Bible and placed it on the floor. I then stepped gingerly on top of the Bible, carefully and respectfully so I would not crumple any pages, but I literally stood on the Bible as I prayed. "Okay, God, You said that we could prove You in this, that if we would tithe, You would open up the windows of heaven and pour out blessings. You said that You would rebuke the devourer. You said that You would supply our needs. God, we're getting ready to lose our house."

The Lord knew that we were committed to giving half of whatever we took in, and He also knew that we needed

$1,500 to save our house from foreclosure. So I boldly asked Him for the astounding amount of $3,000, knowing that we would give $1,500 of that amount as part of our vow. It was an act of desperation because if God did not provide, we were going down.

I preached that night to about two hundred people. Afterward, the pastor came to me and said, "Brother Kent, I've been here at this church for forty-two years, and this is the largest offering we have ever received for a guest speaker."

When the offerings for our services were counted that night, the congregation gave us a whopping $6,500 and some change! God did more than we asked. He gave us more than we needed, including the 50 percent that we were going to give back to Him.

Years later, a pastor mockingly told Candy during a lunch, "I once heard of a preacher who literally stood on his Bible."

"Yes, sir," Candy said. "That was my husband. Sometimes you do desperate things when you are desperate."

Truth is, we were desperate quite a lot during that time. My faith usually stayed strong, but there were times when I would get discouraged and the devil knew right when and where to hit me. On one occasion, Candy and I were traveling in our old Dodge van through a storm in the dead of winter when the heater went out. The estimate to get it fixed was around three hundred dollars, but that might as well have been three million to us. We didn't have it.

As we were heading home, a sheet of ice formed on the inside of the windshield. It was almost impossible to see the road. We wrapped our five-year-old daughter, Jasmine, in blankets and Candy hugged her tightly trying to keep her warm. I drove as fast as I dared over the icy roads.

As we drove through the night, the devil taunted me, "Look at you. So you are giving God 50 percent of your income. Where is He now? Look at you. What kind of dad are you? You can't even take care of your own family?"

But I knew the Lord had challenged us to give, so I rebuked the Enemy and kept driving.

About a year and half into our commitment to give 50 percent, Candy and I constantly struggled to make ends meet financially. We diligently attempted to pay our bills but were often late for our mortgage payment, not to mention our water, gas, phone, and electric bills. We sometimes got so far behind that the power company shut off our electricity. We never left any of our creditors holding the bag. We always paid eventually, but we were frequently late, often scraping up just enough pennies to pay our bills at the last minute. Sometimes we didn't even have food in the house and had barely enough money to buy any.

On one occasion, I had only a few dollars in my pocket, and I went to the store to see what food I could buy with that. As I walked down the aisle, I spotted a twenty-dollar bill lying on the ground. I looked around and there was nobody anywhere near who might have lost it. I picked it up, thanked the Lord for it, and bought us some food.

On another occasion, we used our last three dollars to put some gas in the car so we could drive to church. We weren't certain if that was enough to get us back home, but at church that night, a dear widow lady gave us one hundred dollars. God always gave us back much more than we gave to Him.

We had been giving 50 percent of our income to our church for about a year and a half, and although we always had enough to survive, we were close to losing our house. We regularly "feasted" on a block of cheese, black-eyed peas, or beans and rice. We lived right next door to Candy's parents, but they seemed oblivious to our financial need. Mom and Dad Hemphill visited frequently to play with Jasmine, but they didn't offer to help us financially. Candy's dad still didn't fully accept me and remained rather aloof. He expressed no hard feelings toward me; he simply seemed more comfortable in ignoring my existence. Consequently, Candy and I never felt that we could ask her folks for help, even though they may have been willing.

Our house payment was only five hundred dollars, but that seemed like a huge amount of money to us. We never spoke publicly or privately with anyone about our need. Some Christian people play on others' sympathy or charity by asking for prayer about their finances or subtly dropping hints about what they do not have. To us, that smacked of manipulation, or a "poor, poor, pitiful me" attitude, begging in the name of Jesus, so we refused to do it.

Candy and I lived our whole married life seeking and desiring the presence of God without being weird. One day I was praying, and I said to God, "I really want to live in the miraculous and the supernatural."

The Spirit of the Lord spoke to me and said, "You can never live in the supernatural until you've learned to walk in the sacrificial."

That was another reason why we felt that we could not reveal our financial needs to friends or family members. We believed that God was testing us regarding the sacrificial, so if we informed other people about our need, we would be subtly attempting to manipulate them. We knew that God was the source for the miraculous, and He was teaching us that He was also the provision in the midst of the sacrificial.

Whatever you lose to obey the will of God will only be temporary. I've always believed that you will never ultimately lose whatever you give up to do the sacrificial. That has certainly been true for us, but that does not mean that obedience is easy. Far from it.

Once I went to a pastors' conference in Paris Landing. I couldn't afford to stay overnight at the hotel, so I drove to the event in our van. Candy and I were struggling financially again, so when the pastors went to lunch or dinner, I slipped outside and ate lunch meat sandwiches in the van.

One afternoon, I came inside the building and sat down where some other preachers were sitting.

"I want you to come preach for me," a leading pastor said.

"Really? You've never even heard me preach," I said.

The pastor ignored my protest. "That's okay. I've heard and seen enough. I want you to come for three nights."

A few months later, Candy and I went to the pastor's church to conduct evangelistic services. A woman there approached Candy. "I noticed you aren't wearing any jewelry," she said. "I've seen you sing on television a number of times, and you've always worn such lovely jewelry. Is there some reason why you don't wear it in our services?"

"Oh, no," Candy replied. "It's nothing like that. I just didn't feel that I needed any jewelry during these services."

In fact, Candy had pawned her jewelry so we could afford the trip.

CHAPTER 18

You Can't Outgive God

I HAD KEPT CANDY'S PROPHECY, that I was to be a prophet to the nations, hidden in my heart, but I rarely spoke of it, especially since I could never get any traction as a speaker. I was not even preaching in our own church, so how was I to be a voice to the world?

Although we lived biblically-based lifestyles and believed that we were anointed and gifted by God, few significant doors opened for me to speak. I knew enough about the Scriptures to understand that if God didn't open those doors of opportunity, it would be foolish and futile for me to try to break through them. I watched in curious fascination as other ministers we knew enjoyed widespread expansion of their work, while we seemed stuck in obscurity. I was happy for my friends and colleagues, but I couldn't help wondering, *God, what about me? Am I doing something wrong? Is there something more that You require of me?*

I simply didn't know.

We rode a continual roller coaster, receiving something good and then something bad, up and down, bouncing from one experience to the next but never really connecting with the broader Christian community. When we did go out and conduct services where we were invited, people responded well, and lives were changed by the power of God, but then when we returned home, the phone stayed quiet, and no subsequent invitations showed up in the mailbox.

None.

We seemed to be ahead of the times. Many churches— even great, Spirit-filled congregations—leaned toward a calmer, more controlled service structure. They enjoyed all the latest praise and worship music, celebrated a liturgical communion service, and relished brief, noncontroversial, conversational sermons that were easy to hear, digest, and tolerate.

That sort of worship experience was fine for some people, but it simply wasn't for me.

Certainly, some people were concerned that we were "too Pentecostal," as if that were possible. For instance, Candy and I once traveled to Kansas City, where she sang during the service and I preached to about 1,100 people. We enjoyed a marvelous visitation of the Spirit, and many people in the congregation responded and were touched spiritually. Nevertheless, at the close of the service, the pastor stood up in front of the people and almost derisively said, "Well, we've certainly had an old-time Pentecostal service here today, haven't we?" By the tone of his voice, it was obvious that his statement was not a compliment, and he was not endorsing us or pleased at the way the service had unfolded.

On another occasion, I preached at a pastors' conference in Missouri, and we had a great service. Candy later told me that I "preached the paint off the walls." When I finished, I turned the service over to an older preacher, and he stood up and rebuked me in front of the entire conference. "Brother, you've got too much zeal," he said. "You're a novice and you have a lot to learn."

I was crushed. We'd had a marvelous service, and the presence of God was so precious. There was no reason for the older pastor to humiliate me in front of my peers.

I did not open my mouth, but I felt frustrated because I strongly believed that we were on the right track with the Lord, and the message was anointed by His Spirit. I did what I knew I was supposed to do, whether it proved popular or not.

• • •

We continued giving half of our income and were determined to do so until the Lord released us from that promise. When Candy was six months pregnant, I was out jogging one morning and God spoke to me: "You can stop giving 50 percent, and go back to what you were giving previously."

I think the Lord saw that we were going to obey Him, regardless of the percentage He wanted us to give. From the beginning of our commitment, I had looked at the promise in light of the biblical father Abraham, who was willing to give up his son Isaac when the Lord asked him to do so. Of course, God did not take Isaac from Abraham, but the test was a matter of obedience for him—and Abraham passed the test by laying his Isaac on the altar.

My "Isaac" was that 50 percent commitment, when the Lord asked me if I was willing to give it. In making that promise to God, I was laying down everything we owned and trusting Him to provide.

We went back to giving at least 20 percent of our income, 10 percent as tithes and 10 percent as offerings.

I was scheduled to speak at a large church in Concord, California, in the San Francisco Bay area. With Candy being pregnant, we planned to fly across the country so she could be there in time to speak to a women's group on Friday and Saturday, and I would speak to the entire congregation on Sunday morning. We were excited about the possibilities.

We took our five-year-old daughter, Jasmine, along with us and went a few days early because the pastor had arranged another engagement for us at a church in Roseburg, Oregon, prior to our commitment in Concord. "I can't really drive you there," the pastor said, "but you can take the church van. It's not a bad drive."

We appreciated his kindness, but when we got to Concord, we discovered that he had provided us with an old, rickety, fifteen-passenger van with worn-out shocks. Every bump we hit on the road, even small potholes, vibrated the entire van.

As it turned out, Roseburg was more than four hundred bumpy miles from Concord, on a route that took us through the mountains. When we arrived that night, I called the pastor to let him know we were in town. "Oh," he said, "we weren't expecting you until tomorrow night. I'll see you tomorrow." The pastor made no indication that the church might be willing to put us up in a motel or even with a family that night.

"Okay," I said. "We'll see you tomorrow." Between us, Candy and I had a total of about $150. We found a Motel 6 and scraped together enough money to pay for it. That night, Jasmine got extremely sick with a high fever.

We had to rush her to the emergency room at the hospital. They were able to bring down her fever, and late that night her temperature returned to normal. The next evening, I preached in Roseburg.

After the service, we drove all the way back through the mountains in the rickety van. As we drove through the night, I was so discouraged. I looked over to Candy and said, "You know, I feel that if we wrecked in this van right now, nobody would even miss us. We just don't matter." Candy commiserated with me, but neither of us saw any light at the end of that dark tunnel.

Whether it was the jolts and bumps or some other reason, I'll never know, but along the way, Candy began having labor pains. By the time we got back to where we were staying, she was in full-blown labor. She was only at twenty-seven weeks. We were still three full months from her due date. I left Jasmine with the pastor and his wife, and I rushed Candy to the emergency room.

The doctor's face looked pensive, and his voice sounded ominous as he said to Candy and me, "We can't stop this. You are going to have this baby whether we want you to or not, even though the child is not due yet." The doctor paused and his voice softened a bit as he continued. "But I want to warn you; you need to prepare yourself. The baby is probably not going to live, and it is better that he doesn't. Because if he is born at this time, he will be blind; he's very small. He will probably be mentally retarded. He has two hernias and a hole in his heart. I'm sorry. There's nothing we can do."

I stepped outside the ER and stood there in shock in the hallway of the hospital, trying to absorb the message the doctor had given us. While reeling from that information, a woman from the hospital's accounting department approached me. She wanted to know how we were going to pay for the hospital and doctors' services. "Your son has to stay in this hospital until his due date if he lives, and the bill will be around three quarters of a million dollars, so I need to know your insurance information."

I looked back at her through my tears and said, "We don't have any insurance." We barely had enough money to pay our phone bill.

She became quite angry, which I certainly understood, but I wanted to be honest with her. She returned to her office in a huff.

I stood in the hall, crying, and I said, "Lord, I've given You everything."

The Lord spoke to me right there in the hallway, "Because you gave Me your Isaac, your son is going to live." I knew I had heard from the Lord, so I went back into the emergency room and watched as the doctor proceeded to perform an emergency C-section on Candy.

When the doctor pulled the baby boy out of Candy, the child weighed less than two pounds and looked like a tiny rabbit. We named him Nicholas. He was alive, but he struggled to breath on his own, couldn't generate body heat on his own, and couldn't eat or swallow.

The hospital immediately transferred Nicholas to Children's Hospital in Oakland. We didn't know it at the time, but that facility was one of the best in America for treating premature babies, and it had a staff of experts to deal with Baby Nick's multiple medical issues. They hooked him up to all sorts of machines, wires, and tubes and gave him constant care. After a while, the lead doctor came out to talk with me. "We're amazed," he said. "Every time we find something that is critical, it turns around."

"What does that mean?" I asked.

The doctor shrugged. "Well, hernias don't usually heal, but your son's have. He does not have a hole in his heart, as was thought. He seems to be doing okay."

Sure enough, Nick survived the night.

One day turned into another, and each new day found Nick growing stronger.

Once Candy was released from the hospital, she and Jasmine joined me at Children's Hospital. Eventually, the nurses took Nick out of isolation and laid his tiny body on Candy's chest each day, with him still wired to machines, and she sang to him and to the Lord, "Great Is Thy Faithfulness."

Each day, I'd put my hand on Nick and speak God's Word over him. "You are going to live and not die," I said.

And Nicholas kept on living.

In the meantime, Jasmine, our five-year-old little girl, had to remain in the hospital waiting room. That was a traumatic experience for her. Although she didn't understand all that was happening, she knew something was wrong. The doctors had rushed Candy into emergency surgery earlier because of her premature labor, and Jasmine had stayed with a family from the church where we were ministering, folks she didn't even know. Now, she was worried about her baby brother. Worse yet, the section of Children's Hospital where we were located was also the area where the most difficult cases showed up. Almost daily, another infant died, and as grateful as we were for the excellent care Nicholas received, it was also frightening for Jasmine. The waiting room was perpetually crowded with stressed-out or grieving families. As days turned into weeks, and then months, Candy and I took turns alternating between being with Jasmine and being with Nicholas. It was draining for all of us.

We stayed there for more than three months, from October 15 to December 25, and Nicholas never had to have an operation. As we neared the holiday season, Joel Hemphill, Jasmine's grandfather, flew to California and took Jasmine back to Nashville, where she stayed until Candy and I could leave the hospital with Nicholas.

Of course, every day we were there, our hospital bills were skyrocketing. I went to an agency in Oakland to see if there was any financial assistance available to us.

"No, I'm sorry," the person told me. "Since you are not a California resident, there's nothing we can do for you."

I thanked the person and made a trip back to Nashville and went to the social services building close to Jefferson Street Bridge. I stood in line for more than two hours. Finally, a woman called my name and I went in to meet with her.

"What can I do for you?" she asked.

"Well, I understand that sometimes there is a way to get some help with medical bills."

"How much money do you make?" she asked. "What was your income last year?"

"Altogether, I earned about twenty-six thousand dollars last year," I told her. I didn't tell her that our actual income was much less than that since we'd given half of our income to our church.

"Hmm," she said, "that's too much to qualify. You made too much money for our agency to help you."

"Okay, thank you," I replied. I was about to leave when she said, "What sort of medical bills do you have?"

I told her about Nicholas's premature birth and how we were thrilled that he was alive but we owed an enormous amount of money to the hospitals and doctors who had helped save his life.

"Hang on a minute," the woman said. She stared at her computer screen and said, "Well, I can't help you, but I can help your son."

"Really? That's why I came here in the first place," I said.

She began punching numbers on her computer. After about five minutes, she looked up at me. "Okay, that's done."

"What's done?" I asked.

"We just paid your hospital bills," she said.

"What!" I could barely eke out the word. "All of them?" I asked, still stunned.

"Yes, all of them," she replied with a smile. "You don't owe them a penny." She told me that the hospitals in California had reduced our debt to around $250,000, and the state of Tennessee had paid the rest.

Scripture teaches that if you give to God, He will give back to you. The truth is, no matter how much you give, if it is given with the right motives, you will never be able to give more than God gives to you.

Later, when I finally got my feet back on the ground, I did some calculations and figured out that during the previous eighteen months, Candy and I had given more than twenty-five thousand dollars in our tithes. The Lord had used our state to give us back *ten* times the amount we had given to Him.

The hospital released Nicholas on Christmas Day. He weighed slightly more than five pounds when we took him on his first cross-country trip, to our home in Nashville. To us, Nicholas Christmas is our own personal Christmas miracle.

CHAPTER 19

The Great Responsibility

I RECEIVED AN INVITATION TO SPEAK at the dedication of the Rock Church in Virginia Beach, pastored by John Gimenez and his wife, Anne. The other guest speakers were all internationally known ministers, such as Pat Robertson, Kenneth Copeland, and Benny Hinn. I was a virtual unknown compared to them. One of the people who heard me speak of the miracles surrounding Nick's birth in 1993 was Jackie Yockey, the longtime guest coordinator for the Christian Broadcasting Network's flagship program, *The 700 Club*. Jackie later said that she had a dream, and in it, the Lord gave her instructions to invite me to appear on *The 700 Club*.

She wrote a letter to me saying in essence, "We'd like you to come on the program and tell the story of the miracle surrounding the birth of Nicholas."

I wasn't too keen on Christian television at the time, so I read the letter to Candy and, as usual, said, "I ain't doin' that." I threw the letter in the trash.

The 700 Club contacted me again, and then again.

Candy said, "Maybe you should consider that God wants you to give a testimony on that program. Maybe He is opening this door for you."

That put the whole idea into a different context, and the more I thought about it, she was right. I accepted the invitation from Jackie.

I traveled to Virginia Beach in 1994 to be on *The 700 Club*. Upon my arrival, I was ushered into the greenroom, the lounge off set where I met Jackie for the first time. We sat down and she said, "I have some questions that we may use on the set today." Jackie had a series of potential questions about the miracle of Nicholas's birth that the show's host, Pat Robertson, wanted to ask me. I began sharing prophetically with Jackie what I was hearing God saying and what the Lord was doing in our lives, although I didn't really discuss too much about Nicholas. Jackie listened quietly and seemed fascinated. After a while, she looked at me and said, "Forget about these questions. Just go out there and share what is in your heart."

"Okay," I said. "I'll be happy to do that."

When it came time for my segment, Pat Robertson greeted me warmly and began interviewing me. I answered a few of his questions, and a powerful unction of the Lord came through me. The producer of the show stood out in the center of the floor and motioned to Pat, "Keep going," so we continued talking and, although I don't remember much of what I said, apparently it was a powerful message. Jackie, the producer, and the stage manager were all wonderfully complimentary toward me after the program concluded.

Candy and I anticipated that as a result of my positive experience on the Christian Broadcasting Network, I might receive invitations from all across the country to come preach and share what God was saying. That didn't happen.

Maybe one reason why we received so little response was that *The 700 Club* had posted the wrong address on the screen as I was speaking. Rather than our address, they had put up the name of the local church where my wife and I attended, not the name of our ministry.

I appreciated the opportunity to be on the program, but as far as enhancing our ministry, the effects were nil.

At least one unexpected blessing came as a result of my appearance on the show. A few months later, Pat Robertson decided he wanted to do a camp-meeting-style "tent revival" on the campus of Regent University. I was invited to be one of the speakers. Again, the event was a "Who's Who" of charismatic leaders, including James Robison and T. D. Jakes.

I was invited to speak at the CBN prayer breakfast at Founders Inn, the hotel on campus. I was not overly excited to accept the invitation since I assumed there would be only a few dozen people at the breakfast, and I never enjoy trying to preach to folks while they are eating anyhow. To me, the Word of God deserves a high place of honor and shouldn't be something that's squeezed in while people are stuffing their mouths full of food.

But I accepted the invitation nonetheless and was surprised to discover that more than three hundred early risers showed up in the conference room for the prayer breakfast, including CBN's founder, Pat Robertson.

Michael Little, the longtime president of CBN, did not appear pleased that I had been asked to speak at the breakfast. A former military man, Michael ran CBN like a finely tuned machine, and I was a cog that he hadn't counted on. Prior to my walking up to the podium, he spoke emphatically to me, "You have ten minutes," he said. "And don't go over."

"Okay, yes, sir," I said.

I walked up to the podium and laid my watch on it in a conspicuous spot so I would see it and not talk too long. People were still eating breakfast as I began preaching, and suddenly, the Spirit of God filled that room. People started crying. Many stopped eating and were listening intently. I preached a bit more and looked at my watch. *I better wrap this up*, I thought.

About that time, somebody stepped up and placed a note on the podium. The note was from Michael and said, "God is moving; keep preaching."

I preached for another four or five minutes, and I looked at my watch and thought again, *I probably better quit.*

Just then, I saw another note on the podium. It said, "Go as long as you want."

I continued preaching, and it was a special time. When I concluded, the organizers asked me to pray for people who wanted prayer. I began praying over individuals, and I didn't do anything out of the ordinary, but when I touched them, people started "falling out in the Spirit," some falling back in their chairs, others slumping peacefully to the floor, some falling straight backward and being gently eased to the floor as they enjoyed an almost trancelike experience with God. People were falling over like cordwood being split. Pat's popular cohost, Terry Meeuwsen, fell out; so did Pat's son, Tim, and others.

I was as shocked as anyone else in the room. That sort of response was not the norm for me.

Afterward, I was still trying to make sense of what had just happened when Jackie Yockey approached me and said, "We have an afternoon meeting in the tent outside, and Pat usually speaks for it, but he wants you to preach today."

"I'd be happy to do that," I said, trying to maintain my composure.

Inside, I was ecstatic. *Hot dog*, I thought. *I have arrived. I've finally gotten a break. This is really going to launch my ministry to a new level.*

That afternoon, the tent was packed with nearly 2,500 people. A stage had been constructed at the front of the tent, hundreds of chairs lined all the way to the back of the tent, and sawdust covered the floor, reminiscent of the old-time camp meetings of years gone by. I went out and stood on the platform between Pat Robertson and Michael Little. I looked out into the crowd jammed with people whose faces were filled with excitement and anticipation.

I felt confident as I thought, *I have a good word today. I'm going to really preach it.*

Just then, God spoke to me and said, "I want you to prophesy, and this is what I want you to say."

NO! I thought. I knew that Pat Robertson and Michael Little were not big fans of outside prophetic ministries because they had seen the gift of prophecy abused all too frequently. Now, I was here right in front of them, having accrued some measure of their approval and favor through my preaching, and God was saying that He wanted me to prophesy! No, no, no!

"I ain't doin' that," I protested to God.

"If you will not obey and say what I want you to say," the Lord told me, "I will not give you a word anymore."

"Okay," I said in my mind. I knew who was Boss, and it wasn't Pat, but I still expressed my thoughts to God. "But he's going to embarrass me in front of everybody and sit me down."

Pat Robertson introduced me, and I stepped up behind the pulpit and opened my mouth. "Thus saith the Lord," I said. I looked right at Pat and said, "God says you have left your roots. And you need to come back because there is a revival that needs to hit this place . . ."

I went on presenting the message that God gave me. I fully expected at any moment that Pat would get up and say, "Okay, that's enough. Please sit down."

But he didn't.

So I went on.

I noticed a distinguished-looking gentleman sitting in the front row. I walked off the platform down to the man and began prophesying over him. That, in itself, was unusual for me. In most cases, when I have received prophetic words, they have been for the church rather than individuals. But as I spoke over this man, he fell out in the Spirit, right there on the sawdust-covered ground. I later learned that the man was Norm Mintle, one of the executive vice presidents of the Christian Broadcasting Network. Norm and I became friends that day and have remained so over the years.

I also had a prophetic word for Michael Little. When I was done prophesying, I turned the microphone back over to Pat Robertson. Pat stood behind the podium and said, "We have heard from the Lord. We need to get on our knees and repent."

Pat led the way as multitudes of men and women fell to their knees, weeping, repenting, and asking God for cleansing and a fresh touch of His Spirit.

I learned something that day: Regardless of my own thoughts, my greatest responsibility as a minister is to obey the Lord and faithfully present His message. He can take care of the rest.

That evening, James Robison, Texas-based preacher and host of the television program *Life Today*, was scheduled as the keynote speaker, along with Pat Robertson. Once again, Michael Little invited me to speak for about ten minutes before James. My message was encouraging but uneventful.

I had hoped to meet James Robison since we were speaking at the same event. Because my dad had died when I was just a boy, I never really had a father figure in my life, especially as a spiritual leader and a mentor in the Lord whom I could emulate. So as a younger minister, I admired James Robison and looked up to him as a father in the faith, even though he and I had no ministry relationship. I was disappointed when James left the event that night without even saying hello, and yet I understood that he didn't know me or anything about me. Nevertheless, I always thought, *That would be a great guy to have as a friend.*

I was invited back to CBN several times over the years, and I grew to enjoy working with the godly people there. I also met many distinguished and anointed preachers.

On one occasion, Jackie Yockey recommended me as a speaker at a partners' breakfast for High Adventure ministries held on the campus of Regent University. After I was done ministering and praying for people in the audience, an elderly man named Wallace Heflin came over to me.

"Brother Kent, I believe I have a word the Lord wants me to share with you," he said. I had never met Wallace, although I was vaguely aware of his sister, Ruth Heflin, a well-known author and speaker, who stood nearby.

"Okay," I said, almost reluctantly. I was tired after a long day of ministering to others, and I was ready to leave, anxious to head back to my hotel. But Wallace looked sincere.

I stood quietly and motionless as he began to prophesy over me. "The Lord says to tell you that there is promotion coming. And that God is going to do a work in you so quickly; it is going to be almost overnight, and men are going to pull on you from all over. So be careful with whom you align yourself, and guard the gift that God gives to you."

Following that event, Candy and I looked forward eagerly to what God was going to do in and through my life. We were excited, anticipating good things that were soon coming. But the good things didn't happen. Instead, my ministry seemed to dry up, and our life went downhill in several ways. We had to move out of our home and into an apartment to help make ends meet.

I didn't fully understand the message Wallace delivered, but I didn't forget it either. It affected me profoundly, especially during those times when I was tempted to give up. Sometimes at your lowest point, the Lord will come to you and reveal glimpses of your highest achievements, even though you may not see them come to fruition until years in your future.

It would be more than thirty years before I saw the fulfillment of Wallace Heflin's prophecy over me.

CHAPTER 20

Rising Star

CANDY WAS ALWAYS A GREAT MOM. For the first year of our marriage, she had continued traveling with the Hemphills and performing gospel music concerts. After Jasmine's birth, however, it made sense for Candy to be home more often. Instead, her parents urged her to take the baby on the road with them for three or four days each week, while I was home alone or out on the road as an evangelist. Often, my wife and baby and I would be separated for ten days at a time. When we all returned home, Jasmine pulled away and didn't want me to hold her. It was as though our baby didn't recognize me.

Candy continued juggling motherhood with life on the road. That worked for a while, but not for long. She made a tough decision that she wanted to leave the family singing group so she could be home with our baby and me.

By springtime of the following year, Candy had left the Hemphills and joined forces with me doing evangelistic work. When that happened, her brothers also decided to leave the group, all of which made me even more unpopular with Candy's dad.

He called her and asked, "Couldn't you just do one or two concert dates per month, instead of us shutting down completely?"

"No, Dad," Candy said, respectfully but firmly. "I can't do that." She knew that if she didn't quit altogether, it wouldn't be long before her dad would want her back on the road full-time. Candy felt that she had been performing concerts on autopilot, and she didn't want to continue doing that. Jasmine's birth gave her the perfect reason for wanting to leave the family singing group and remain at home.

Occasionally, Candy and I traveled together to do evangelistic work. Although she had been featured often with her family's group, she had not previously done many concerts as a solo artist. She had to learn how to control the platform and perform with confidence on her own.

Later, while Jasmine and Nicholas were preschool age, Candy stayed home and enjoyed her role as mom. She was an excellent mom, too, and loved creating new traditions with the kids. Although we were still struggling financially, we did our best to shield the kids from that stress. We never talked about money in front of them, nor did we say things such as, "We can't afford that." Quite the opposite. Jasmine and Nicholas probably grew up thinking we were rich! We weren't. But we used any extra money we earned to purchase nice clothes for them, and we scraped up enough money each month so they could attend Hendersonville Christian

Academy, a private Christian school in North Nashville. When both of the kids were old enough to attend school, Candy joined me in evangelistic services more often, and that's how we operated for a number of years.

Then, in 1995, Bill and Gloria Gaither contacted Candy's mom and dad about appearing in one of their videos. The Gaithers were preeminent gospel songwriters who had composed such classics as "He Touched Me," "Because He Lives," "Something Beautiful," "The King Is Coming," and hundreds of other songs familiar to Christians around the world. They were flying high in the early 1990s, and, as the new millennium dawned, they were honored as the American Society of Composers, Authors, and Publishers' songwriters of the century! To be associated with them was a boon for any musician.

The Gaithers had pioneered a highly successful video series called *Homecoming*, in which they invited numerous other gospel singers as well as a few country artists to gather in a recording studio and sing some of the old hymns and gospel songs together. They recorded the entire affair on audio and video, and when it was later broadcast on television, it took the world by storm. In the months following, more recordings were made, with better planning and production, and were provided for resale by all the artists involved.

One of the songs Bill wanted to record on a Homecoming video was "Let's Have a Revival," written originally by Candy's dad and performed by the Hemphills, with Candy singing the lead part. To do the recording, her mom and dad needed my wife to help them with the song, so they called us in Nashville at 11:00 p.m., the night before the recording session in Alexandria, Indiana (about an hour and a half north of Indianapolis), and asked Candy to help them out the next day.

We were so excited and thought this might be a way for God to open some new ministry doors for us. Candy and her brother, Joey, left before daylight and drove five hours, all the way from Nashville to Alexandria, the next morning. They arrived just in time to get to the studio and sing along with their mom and dad again.

Next thing we knew, Candy was flying all over the country in a private jet to participate in twenty-five Gaither Homecoming concerts. The popularity of the videos and the concerts skyrocketed even more when the videos aired on national television. Candy was busy!

She recorded a new solo album and even appeared on NBC's flagship morning program, *The Today Show*, where she sang from the new album and told some of the family stories. We thought her performance on network television might result in an avalanche of concert engagements, but that didn't happen. Nothing came of it.

Candy's extra exposure as a singer was a blessing and a curse for us—a blessing because it gave her the opportunity to be back up onstage again in front of large audiences both in concerts and on television, but a curse because it meant that she was gone a lot more from our home. And then there was the competitive nature of the music industry. Although the Christian musicians were ostensibly all part of the family of God, as in any family, tensions sometimes surfaced, especially when it came to who was getting more camera time or guest solo spots. With twenty or more top-notch gospel music favorites onstage at every show, it was always an honor to be featured.

Meanwhile, the kids and I made do and carried on as best we could. I was home more frequently because Candy and I had learned that calling various pastors and event promoters regarding speaking opportunities was not the best idea, so we often went for long periods of time with no speaking engagements on our calendar. Then, perhaps a week or two of services might come through, requiring that I be away from home. Sometimes Candy and I traveled and ministered together, but that was rare.

When we were both away, Jasmine enjoyed playing the role of "mom," and she did a fantastic job of it. She was a bright student at school, and taking responsibility for herself and Nicholas came naturally for her. We even secured a hardship driver's license for her when she was only fourteen years of age so she could drive herself and Nicholas to school.

We functioned like that for more than five years as Candy toured with the Homecoming group and I traveled as an evangelist to various parts of the country. For most of that time, Candy was our main breadwinner, which was hard on my self-esteem. I wanted to protect and provide for my family. But we were both doing our best to use the gifts we had, and God was faithful to help us employ some dedicated babysitters and nannies during that period of our lives. We were living paycheck to paycheck, although most people never would have imagined that. We felt that we were blessed, but that did not necessarily translate into financial blessings.

Still, amazing and unexplainable things sometimes happen when a husband and wife decide to put God first in their lives and obey His instructions. When we were attempting to get a loan to purchase a house in Nashville, I looked at our financial picture and said to my wife, "I don't think we will qualify for a loan, because I'm pretty sure our credit is shot since we've been behind on our payments so many times. But I will go to speak to the folks at the bank."

When I sat down with the banker, he ran our credit report, and to our amazement, our record was clean. "That's A-1 credit," the banker said.

"Really?" I asked, my eyes wide with astonishment. I later quipped, "The Lord must have worked a miracle in that computer, because I don't know any other way that we would have received a good credit report!"

In 1997–1998, while Candy was still on the road singing gospel music and appearing on Gaither Homecoming specials, we purchased a comfortable home near Goodlettsville, Tennessee. We loved that house and lived there for the next twenty-eight years. The best part was that the home was not located right next door to Candy's parents.

Thanks to Candy's appearances in the Gaither events, we had some income we could count on. Nevertheless, we still struggled financially from time to time.

During one of those lean periods, a pastor and his wife brought some well-to-do friends to our home to visit on the very day that the power company turned off our electricity again. Both Candy and I sensed what had happened, but we were too embarrassed to let our guests know that we were so broke we couldn't pay our electric bill. We tried to casually pass it off as though it were nothing.

"I wonder what is wrong with the electric," Candy said. "Maybe the power is out in the whole neighborhood."

"Maybe somebody hit a transformer along the road," I offered with little conviction. I instinctively knew exactly what had happened to the power.

Candy hurriedly lit a number of candles and we created a warm, attractive ambiance in the room. One of our female guests asked Candy, "Well, how have you been doing?"

I could anticipate Candy's answer before she said a word. We had a policy of never asking people for money; nor would we drop subtle hints that our circumstances looked dire. We were trying to live by faith and trust God to provide for us. We weren't going to claim to serve the King of everything and then go around poor-mouthing to people so they would support our ministry.

"We are blessed," Candy replied immediately. I knew she was speaking in faith. She could just have easily replied, "We're broke and we're sitting here in the dark." But she chose instead to believe that we were blessed.

The woman did not look convinced. "Yes, I can see that," she said airily, somewhere between whimsically and sarcastically, as she slowly gazed around the candlelit room.

Because we always sought to be well-groomed and well-dressed, most people didn't realize how broke we really were. Some people thought that we were actually wealthy because they saw Candy singing on various television programs and performing at the Gaither Homecoming concerts. They didn't realize that Candy did those many television appearances for free, and most of the Homecoming concerts were only minimally compensated, so we were frequently financially strapped. In our brokenness and embarrassment, we didn't want to admit that our bank account was nearly empty.

So when people asked, "How are you doing?" our answer was always, "We are blessed." We learned to say, "We are blessed" during this time when we were facing great financial need. You can be blessed whether you are rich or poor financially. If you are blessed spiritually, that doesn't always translate to financial blessing. But sometimes it does.

Candy and I had been married for a number of years and had never prospered financially. In fact, we were once again three months behind on our house payment and were about to lose it when we received an invitation to lunch with two businessmen.

We went to lunch with them, and we didn't mention anything at all about our financial status. In fact, we specifically avoided speaking of our severe financial strain. We believed that God would come through.

After lunch, one of the men asked, "Can you drop by the office for a few minutes?"

"Sure, we'd love to," Candy said. We had no idea why they wanted us to visit, since we'd already spent more than an hour with them at the restaurant. We thought that perhaps they wanted to show us some new facet of their business.

We left the restaurant and drove to their office. We had barely sat down in one of the executive offices when one of the men's assistants came in and handed him an envelope.

The businessman thanked her and handed the envelope to us. "This is to help pay off your house," the businessman said. He handed us a check for $125,000.

We were stunned but overwhelmed with joy. The businessman did not know how much we owed or that we were three months behind on our payments, with the bank threatening foreclosure. But he specifically said, "This is to pay off your home." So that is how we used the money.

I walked in to Nations Bank, smiled at the person behind the window, and said, "I want to pay off our house." The woman looked at me with a surprised expression on her face. "Wow, that must be a nice feeling," she said.

"It sure is," I agreed. I didn't tell her that in the past, her bank had sent repossession notices to our front door. Now, we were paying off the entire loan, with enough money left to give to God 20 percent of the gift we had received.

Paying off the mortgage was a turning point in our faith. The payment helped us see the manifestation of our faith. I preached the Word and believed in its power; the rest was up to God. He knew what we needed. We knew it wasn't because of us and our works, but to this day, we can look back and say, "Look what the Lord did."

The Lord was teaching us that if we trusted Him, walking with Him day by day, He would provide for our needs.

And He did take care of us, even when we didn't know how to care for ourselves. On one occasion, I had accepted a speaking engagement while Candy was on the road with the Gaithers. On the flight home, I began to experience extreme discomfort in my tailbone. I was in such pain, I could barely sit in the seat. Upon my arrival in Nashville, I went to the doctor and discovered that I had a cyst on my tailbone.

The doctor gave me lidocaine and did surgery right there in his office. He removed the cyst, but apparently the drug lowered my blood pressure. When I stood up and stepped out of the room to the discharge area, I collapsed to the floor. My blood pressure had dropped so severely and to such a dangerous level that I passed out. I could have died right there in the doctor's office had I not received immediate care. It took more than two hours to bring me back to normal. The medical team monitored me until my condition stabilized, and I went home to be with the kids that same night.

It was another reminder from God, letting me know, "Don't worry; don't despair; I will take care of you."

CHAPTER 21

Overcoming Depression

DESPITE HER POPULARITY IN GOSPEL MUSIC CIRCLES, by 2000 Candy had become increasingly discouraged and depressed. Ironically, she was singing regularly in front of thousands of people; she felt that her dreams were on the verge of coming true and that the lifelong goals for which her family had groomed her were within her grasp. Yet she was not happy.

"We were raised to be people-pleasers," Candy recalls, "and if you are not 'successful,' you must not be pleasing the people. If someone else is winning the Grammy Awards or the Dove Awards, and you are not, you must not be pleasing people." That attitude had been inculcated in her since childhood. When Candy was only twelve, her aunt had entered her in children's beauty pageants, where everything focused on her appearance and performance. She recorded her first album of gospel music when she was only thirteen. She sang professionally for the next fourteen years, and millions of people knew her name. Nevertheless, she was frustrated that she had not achieved greater fame and fortune in the music world, that her loftiest dreams had eluded her. Now, since being on the show with the Homecoming artists, her goals once again seemed achievable. Yet she grew increasingly upset with herself for merely going through the motions, singing her songs, and smiling "professional" smiles at all her adoring friends and fans.

It wasn't enough to satisfy her soul, and she knew it. And I knew it too.

It was hard for me to watch what was happening to my beautiful, self-assured, talented wife. I recalled one of the first times I witnessed her performing a solo concert during the early days of our relationship. Backed by a full band, she controlled the stage, entertaining and inspiring the audience. She had no trepidation at all. Now that woman was gone, on the verge of an emotional breakdown. Nothing seemed to alleviate her sadness.

With our wheels spinning, we went to our doctor, who, after examining her thoroughly, declared, "Candy, you are severely depressed." He gave her some samples of familiar sedatives and antidepressants and wanted to hospitalize her. She refused. She did, however, leave with several prescriptions.

Candy took the medications for two weeks and then abruptly said, "That's it. No more. I don't want to be dependent on medicine." She chose prayer over prescriptions, recognizing that her depression was a symptom of something deeper, not the cause of her pain.

Things came to a head as we stepped into the twenty-first century. She wrote a letter to the Gaither organization, including with it a letter from her doctor stating that she was severely depressed, and she resigned her role as part of the Homecoming events. In one day, she walked away from her dreams, her music career, her closest friends apart from family members, and everything that she had always regarded as her reasons for living. While this drastic step was probably necessary, it plunged Candy even deeper into depression and despair, not merely for a few weeks or months but for the next two years of our lives.

Deep depression robbed Candy of the joy of daily living. She later described it in her book *On the Other Side*: "All I wanted to do was lie in bed in the dark with the curtains drawn and ache from the depths of my soul. . . . I prayed to die; I embraced the thought of suicide and planned my funeral."[1]

For months, she'd get the kids up and off to school each day, then go back to the bedroom, close the blinds, and crawl into bed, where she would remain until the kids came home. She was despondent, and the Enemy had convinced her that the kids and I would be better off without her.

When I realized that something unusual was going on, I began a new routine of my own. Each afternoon, I quietly slipped into the bedroom, opened the blinds, placed my hands on Candy, and prayed for her. Sometimes I prayed for her healing; at other times, I prayed for her deliverance. I was clueless. There was no logical reason for her depression, so I didn't know how to help her, and I couldn't understand what was happening.

At first, as a person accustomed to hard work with a "pull yourself up by your own bootstraps" attitude, I thought Candy was simply being lazy. *Why does she not want to get out of bed? It is a beautiful day! We have much for which we can be thankful. Why is she so down?* I could not fathom why anyone who had so much going for herself would be unhappy. Why was she not making any effort to get past this? I would have done anything I could do to help, but I didn't know how. We were already doing everything we knew to do from a spiritual standpoint.

We prayed, went to church, read Scripture, and anointed Candy with oil, as the Bible instructs; we did everything we knew to do, but she continued to be down. We visited with a well-known deliverance ministry in Louisiana, thinking that Candy may be suffering from some sort of demonic oppression. Nothing changed.

In fact, it got worse. Candy continued to debilitate physically as well as emotionally. Her weight dropped to below one hundred pounds; her body looked frail and her face appeared sallow. "I wanted God's anointing," Candy later said. "I longed to be filled with the Spirit. I just didn't want to die to my own control and truly let Jesus take over and have His way in me."

I felt that I could deal with most things, but I had no clue how to cope with my wife's depression. For the first time since Candy and I had married, I felt helpless and hopeless. After a while, I thought, *God, is this ever going to change?*

Certainly, people in the public would have thought that Candy and I were a happy couple and our kids were blessed, but inside our home, we knew better.

Candy was a fantastic mother, despite her depression, so the kids didn't pick up on the problem. She smiled when they were present, she made dinner each night, and she was good at maintaining the appearance that everything was wonderful. We hid the truth from the kids as much as possible. Her years on the stage and mine behind a pulpit had taught us how to function in acceptable ways in front of other people. Few people knew what was really going on inside our home. But increasingly, I began looking forward to going back on the road, simply to get away from Candy's depression and unhappiness. It was wearing on me.

• • •

Slowly, Candy came to realize that part of the problem stemmed from the fact that she was absorbed with herself, constantly attempting to insert herself, promote herself, and satisfy herself. But how does anyone break the chains of pride? How can a person deal the death blow to the tyranny of self-interest? Candy knew that only Jesus could do that for her.

She had learned to "pray the Scriptures," using the Lord's own words as the authority for her prayers, so she got busy praying against the seething anger within her. "What things I bind on earth shall be bound in heaven," she prayed. "You devil of heaviness and anger that is tormenting me, I bind you in Jesus' name."

One day she was praying intensely, sitting on the floor in our guest bedroom closet, her usual "prayer closet." She was binding the devil and "working up a sweat," as Candy remembers, when she suddenly stopped. She recalls, "I looked up toward heaven and said, 'Lord, this is not working. What is it?'

"And the Lord spoke to me, 'Your will is fighting My will. When your will submits to My will, and you rest in My will for your life, you will no longer be angry.' I realized that *my* will was winning music awards, and flying on a private plane to concerts, and having fifteen to twenty thousand people applauding me. Worse yet, I was angry with God because He had not allowed me to become the 'star' that I thought I should be, that my parents had planned and groomed me to be."

Candy later said, "I realized that the real problem was not my career; the problem was *me*. I repented—as a Christian—for my rebellion against God's will. That was the day I truly died—not a physical death, as I had thought would end my life of pain, but a spiritual death, where I came to the place where I could honestly say, 'I am crucified with Christ' and 'Lord, not my will but Thy will be done.'" Candy realized a key spiritual truth: if you want to be great in the kingdom of God, you must die to yourself. There is no other way.

Candy wrote of the experience, "There [on the floor] in my prayer closet, ... my desire for a stage and spotlight was crucified, and I became willing to ... take up my cross. It was there that my craving for applause and accolades died, and a grace to embrace the will of God for my life was born.'"[2]

She later observed, "My attitudes and paradigms, my entire life, changed at that moment."

I certainly noticed Candy's improved relationship with God. It spilled over naturally into our marriage and family. She smiled more readily; there seemed to be a calm and genuine joy in her demeanor. In some ways, she seemed more serious. She no longer fretted about being applauded or approved by other people. Now, she seemed much more willing to serve others rather than expecting them to serve her. The tyranny of self-interest in her life had been broken, and her life, love, and goals were reoriented around Jesus.

The heaviness left our home. Joy came back to the house. I no longer got up each morning, looked at Candy, and thought, *Oh, boy, she's not doing too well today*. She no longer went back to bed after getting the kids off to school.

After submitting her will to God and giving up her own control of her life, she seemed happier, as though she were living in the overflow, bubbling with love for our kids, me, other family members, and everyone in our world. It was an amazing change. Candy had given herself to God, and He had given her Himself.

I have often said, "When you give to God something that is significant to you, God will give back to you something that is significant to Him. And what is significant to God is always much greater than what was significant to you."

In retrospect, I can now see that, similar to the spiritual death I encountered following divorce, for Candy to serve in ministry alongside me, she, too, had to "die to herself." Otherwise, we would have been unequally yoked together and would have been constantly pulling against the other person rather than pulling together and supporting each other.

Candy later said, "Before, whatever we did needed to be about me. I wanted to be in the spotlight. My unspoken attitude was, 'Kent may be a great preacher, but really, it is all about *me*.' Now, I can stand behind him and not feel that I am in his shadow. I am now able to be Kent's best cheerleader."

Although we could not have guessed what God had in mind for either of us, it is now clear that God was preparing Candy to be a servant not only to the church but to the lowest of the low in our community, and to identify with them.

Candy had a strong history of powerful prayer warriors in her extended family. Her grandfather, in particular, had an intimate relationship with God, maintained by prayer. He was the gold standard for her. He got up early each morning and spent at least an hour in prayer; throughout the day, he would spend several more hours in close communion with God in prayer and then another hour before he went to bed. By day's end, he usually spent at least four or five hours in intimate prayer, sometimes more. That was his pattern for decades.

Sometimes people came to him for counsel about a problem, and before they described the issue, he gave them the answer, because God had already revealed the situation to him during his time of prayer.

When Candy truly "sold out" to the Lord's will for her life, she felt a hunger for that kind of prayer life. She had always read the Bible and prayed, all the way through her depression, but now, since the Holy Spirit had taken over in her life, she had a renewed desire for deep prayer, for genuine communication with God, not merely throwing words toward the ceiling and praying louder in case God was hard of hearing. Now, she relished her time with the Lord because they had genuine fellowship together. She adopted as her own a statement attributed to David Wilkerson: "God always makes a way for those who pray."

She read books about deep prayer by authors such as Andrew Murray, Madame Guyon, and the Spanish Christian mystic Miguel de Molinos. She no longer yelled at God but rather entered His presence with a holy, reverential awe. And she found Him there, waiting for her.

In 2004, Candy went to a conference in St. Petersburg, and a man spoke a word of prophecy over her. He said, "Sister, God is going to do something different with you and your ministry, but it is going to take a lot of work."

He didn't explain what that meant, or perhaps he didn't know.

But we were soon to find out.

CHAPTER 22

The Most Unlikely

FEWER THAN SIX MONTHS after Candy's dramatic prayer closet experience, she met Brother Danny, a part-time minister who was laying tile in our relatives' home that was under construction. A kind, white-haired, grandfatherly fellow, probably close to seventy years of age, Brother Danny recognized Candy from seeing her on some Gaither videos, although he was shocked and concerned by her thin, frail appearance. On the videos, Candy's persona was that of a happy, vibrant woman, but now she wasn't, and Brother Danny noticed the difference. Over the course of several conversations, Danny told Candy about what he did in his spare time.

"I've been going to downtown Nashville below the underpass of Jefferson Street Bridge," he said, "where a lot of homeless people live. I grill some hamburgers or hot dogs for them and share the gospel with them."

Candy knew the area. Before she ever met Brother Danny, she had occasionally driven over Jefferson Street Bridge and prayed for the needy people who lived near or below it. She prayed, "God, where are the people? I know they aren't sitting in the nice, warm church with us, but I believe they are here."

She had even gone to one of the leading ministers in Nashville. "Maybe there is some way that you and your congregation might want to get involved in serving some of the homeless people who live under the bridge," she'd suggested.

The pastor dismissively placated Candy and almost condescendingly replied, "Oh, yes, we've been talking about that. I think we're going to do that."

But they never did.

A few months later, Candy met Brother Danny.

At that time, the area under Jefferson Street Bridge was known as an unsafe, dicey, tough part of town, so Candy was fascinated that Brother Danny was attempting to do spiritual evangelism and humanitarian work there single-handedly. "And will they listen to you when you talk to them about Jesus?" she asked. "Oh, sure," Danny said. "As long as I have food. Most of the folks under the bridge haven't eaten all day. Some haven't had a meal in much longer than that. So they are willing to listen to me. Are you really interested?"

"Yes, I am," Candy replied.

"Well, would you like to go downtown under the bridge and help me?" he asked.

"Yes!" Candy recalls answering without a moment of hesitation. She later said, "I didn't ask any of the logical questions such as, 'How many people are we going to feed? Is it safe for a woman to be there? Am I in danger of being robbed, raped, or worse? Is there any police presence or are there any strong men to protect us in case we have problems?' None of that even crossed my mind. I was fascinated by the opportunity to serve some homeless people in our own city.

"But Brother Danny wasn't convinced yet. He looked at me skeptically, standing there in my comfy, stylish clothes in my relatives' comfortable home, and asked, 'Can you cook?' By the tone of his voice and the twisted expression on his face, I was pretty sure he thought the answer was no."

"I surprised him," Candy remembers. "'Yes, I'm a Louisiana girl,' she said, 'and I can cook jambalaya in any size pot, for any size crowd.'

"He grinned in mock disbelief and said, 'Okay, how about next Tuesday evening?'"

"'I'll be there,'" I said.

The following Tuesday, Candy prepared a large pot of chicken and sausage jambalaya and drove to downtown Nashville by herself. It was January—dark, dirty, and cold under Jefferson Street Bridge. She met Danny there and they found an easily accessible spot where they could feed the homeless people out of the trunk of her car. Only a few homeless people came that night, quietly forming a line to receive the food that Candy had brought. Of those who showed up, all looked tired, sad, and disheveled; most were dirty, unshaven men, along with a few women. Many had no coats or gloves; few wore socks on their feet to help protect them from the frigid temperatures.

After the homeless people ate their food, Danny quickly shared the gospel with them in a short, concise form. He then asked if anyone wanted him to pray for them, and several did. Candy and Danny prayed for those who asked:

one or two for salvation, others for healing, and all for provision for themselves or for their children.

Almost immediately, Brother Danny said to Candy, "This is your ministry. Do whatever you want to do. Is there something you have in mind?"

"Well, I'd like to have someone come down and preach," she said.

"Okay," Brother Danny said.

When Candy came home that night, I could tell that something significant had transpired. She hadn't merely been helping to feed some homeless people; something had happened in her. Her entire demeanor seemed to have a radiance, and the spirit of depression that had hung over her for more than two years seemed to have been lifted off her. Her eyes sparkled again, and she seemed to nearly glow with a holy joy. She was so excited.

I noticed the change immediately.

"I'm going to the store tomorrow," Candy said. "I want to get some crackers and socks and peanut butter and gloves . . ." She was bubbling with enthusiasm. For the first time in a long time, Candy seemed to have purpose, and it wasn't about her. It was about helping some people who had no way to repay her.

Before long, Randy Barnett, a friend of ours, had loaded his pickup with groceries and other items Candy had secured from Goodwill and other places and helped us transport the goods for the homeless people. Eventually, Brother Danny moved on to other ministry opportunities, and Candy continued going downtown under the bridge every Tuesday evening. Whether on the coldest winter evenings or the steamiest, one-hundred-degree summer evenings,

Candy took food to the homeless people under the bridge. She recruited some preachers to share a brief message with the people who gathered. Eventually, some musicians joined her under the bridge on Tuesday nights as well. The ministry continued to grow, and as word got around, more needy people began showing up each week. Since that first night of taking jambalaya, Candy has been under the bridge herself or has made certain that somebody has been there to feed the homeless under the bridge every Tuesday night to this day.

It was hard work, but in many ways it was spiritually refreshing.

Candy and I had both been around church ministry and the gospel music world for most of our lives. We learned that every segment of these groups had their own silos of influence, their own hierarchies, their own "favorite flavors." To some people, we may be too Pentecostal; to others, not enough. Some thought we were too flamboyant; others thought we were too plain. Others in the music realm had their favorite styles of music.

When we went to the homeless people, they didn't care what our names were or how we looked or sounded. To them, only two things mattered: Do you have some food for me, and does this Jesus stuff really work?

It was so refreshing to us after being in the church for years. To Candy, especially, for the first time, there were no expectations about appearance or performance. It was all about sharing the love of God in tangible ways.

Perhaps that is why Candy's "spiritual death experience" was so important. God would not entrust the homeless to her when she was more worried about herself. Indeed, she could not enjoy His blessings or His power in her life until she came to the end of herself. Moreover, the persona of the "Perfectly Dressed and Coiffed Candy" that she had created and maintained for years could not show compassion to people who showed up with vomit streaked through their beards or smelling like urine.

Now, she could. Now, she wanted to love everyone she met. She got in the habit of shaking every person's hand and saying to every needy person she encountered under the bridge, "If no one has told you they love you today, let me be the first. I love you!" And she meant it.

I quickly realized that we had to guard against becoming disillusioned. Sometimes, I watched with a puzzled expression on my face as we passed out food to some people who appeared to be better off than we were. Some drove better vehicles than we did. Others were dressed better.

Did we get ripped off sometimes? Of course we did. But it was not for us to decide whether someone was telling us the truth about their need or not. We realized that our responsibility was simply to give to the homeless people and not to vet them to make sure they were truly needy.

Indeed, Candy and I felt it was necessary for us to sow into the ministry happening under the bridge, so we purchased the first truck to use in hauling chairs and food for the homeless. We weren't building a ministry; we were simply trying to help some people who could not possibly repay us—and we loved it!

There is a spiritual law of reaping and sowing: whatever you sow, you will also reap (see Galatians 6:7). For God to do what He wanted to do in and through us, to get us ready to go where He wanted us to go, we had to sow into the least of these. We didn't plan that or calculate that. We just did it.

We took our kids along with us to minister to the homeless. They were excited to be involved. We never worried about their safety, and the kids embraced the ministry wholeheartedly.

We made food, loaded a truck with chairs (and eventually a sound system), drove it all downtown and conducted services under the bridge, then went back home, where I washed the large pots and rinsed them using a hose outside in the yard till midnight. We were working harder than ever in our lives and enjoying it more than anything we had ever done.

We began receiving donations of food and clothing that we could distribute to needy people, so much that we didn't have enough space to store it between the weekly meetings under the bridge. We secured a warehouse locally where we could store the goods brought in for the homeless. Eventually, in 2004, we incorporated as a nonprofit organization and gave the ministry a name. Since we didn't want to limit the involvement to any one church (we welcomed people from all churches to join us in the work), we didn't want a "churchy-sounding" name. Instead, the obvious choice was simply The Bridge Ministry. Each week we provided a hot meal for the homeless, some clothing whenever we had it available, basic toiletries, and often a bag of groceries that folks could take with them at the end of the evening, after we held a short "church" service.

Occasionally, other ministries from far and wide joined us. Youth pastors sometimes brought their students to help serve under the bridge, and almost everyone left saying something like, "I came under the bridge to be a blessing to others, and I'm the one going away being blessed."

Ironically, I did not do well preaching under the bridge. As much as I could relate to the poverty and hopelessness, I felt no powerful unction of the Holy Ghost when I preached there. I was supportive of Candy's ministry, but I recognized it was not mine. This was something that God was doing in and through her.

Sometimes my association with The Bridge Ministry was actually awkward for me because I would go out in evangelistic services and preach my heart out, and the church would write a check for The Bridge Ministry! That was great for The Bridge Ministry, but the Christmas family paid our bills by the income that I brought in through Kent Christmas Ministries International.

Candy and I helped each other where we could, but we didn't place extra demands on each other. We understood that God gives people different kinds of ministries, and they may all be good and valid. It is easy to get upset when someone else doesn't buy into what God has given to you. It is also easy to get self-righteous and think, *Look at the good work I am doing. Why aren't you joining me? What's wrong with you?*

We were in a continual learning mode. Working each week with difficult cases under the bridge, we saw people who were bound by addictions. They'd pray and cry out to God, yet sometimes, they walked away just as addicted as before. Others were delivered and set free.

Our theology changed from "You just need to pray more" to "Okay, we are going to keep on praying for your healing." We knew the deliverance and healing were up to God, and we were responsible to do what He called us to do—which was love people, feed and clothe them, and present the gospel to them.

I wholeheartedly encouraged and supported Candy's ministry. I sometimes even thought, *This is it; the greater ministry will take place through my wife.*

Nevertheless, I couldn't shake the fact that Candy had received a word from God years earlier stating that my own ministry would thrive, that I would be a messenger to the nations.

Yet her ministry had taken off and had attracted the attention of such notables as Rev. Franklin Graham, First Lady Laura Bush, and the president of the United States. Hundreds of people showed up each Tuesday evening to help us feed more than four hundred homeless people and minister to their children. Businesses recognized the good work being done, and many contributed resources, including clothing and other basic needs. During the NFL draft held in Nashville in 2019, members of the Tennessee Titans football team worked right alongside us to feed homeless people under Jefferson Street Bridge. Eventually, The Bridge fed more than two thousand children each week, especially when school was not in session. Meanwhile, I was still speaking each week to fewer than a hundred folks at our church.

I watched as The Bridge drew in more than seven hundred people each week, while I had only a few people show up for prayer meeting at the church.[3] After a while, I concluded, *I will support and serve my wife's ministry in every way I can. If it means hauling equipment, or driving the food trucks, or washing pots and pans till midnight after the services on Tuesday night, I will do whatever is necessary. It isn't going to get any better than this.*

I could not have been more wrong.

CHAPTER 23

"Dad, I'm Gay"

"Dad, I'm gay," are words that rock any father's world. But if we allow love to rule and the Holy Spirit to guide us, those need not be the last words.

When my son Josh was about six or seven and my former wife, Patti, and I were still living in Washington, Josh became the victim of sexual abuse. An acquaintance of our family had a grown son who took advantage of Josh's innocence. I didn't know it at the time. I was working round-the-clock at the shipyard as well as pastoring a church, so I was oblivious to what was happening to our little boy.

Nor did I notice the shift in his personality, but his mother did. She later said that the happy little boy he had been prior to the abuse suddenly disappeared. Josh didn't say a word about the sexual abuse until nearly ten years later. Maybe that was God, in His mercy, shielding me from finding out about the abuser until I was living in

Tennessee. Otherwise, I may have lost control and done something that we all would have regretted. When we did find out about the abuse, in the midst of such emotional upheaval, we never thought about trying to find and prosecute the man who abused our son. Our main focus was to help Josh.

I had never told Josh why his mom and I had divorced. I did not want to say anything to besmirch the image of his mom in Josh's mind, so I simply kept quiet. But Josh may have suspected something was amiss, even though he was too young to process it all.

When Josh was eight, he saw his mom with a man in our home behaving in a manner indicating that they were more than friends. Josh did not tell me about what he saw, nor did he confront his mom. He simply buried that image in his mind and heart.

Carrying that intimate knowledge of his mom's infidelity, combined with the abuse he had experienced as a child and his parents' divorce, was a heavy load for a young boy. Years later, Josh acknowledged, "Those things didn't make me gay. But they did make me emotionally vulnerable."

After my divorce was finalized, I saw Josh for only a few weeks each year, when he came to Nashville to visit. During those years, I always told him, "If you ever want to come live with Candy and me, just let us know." He seemed content in Washington, living with his mom and her new husband, but then one day, when Josh was sixteen, he called me and asked, "Can I come live with you?" He had gone to a Christian school in Washington and had graduated early, so he was ready for a change.

"Sure," I said, "if that is okay with your mom."

Patti agreed and we began making plans for Josh to move across the country. Josh moved in with Candy, Jasmine, Nicholas, and me when he moved from Washington to Tennessee. He never said a negative word about his mom's new husband, and Josh was especially protective of his mom. It was as though he recognized that she was fragile and easily hurt.

Candy was only twenty-eight years old when Josh came to live with us, and she clicked with him immediately. Candy taught Josh about cooking, and he was a quick study. From the time he was sixteen, he had a natural proclivity for creating great-tasting food and gourmet-style meals.

Every Christmas season, Candy and I wanted to send gifts to the pastors who had engaged us throughout the year, but we really couldn't afford to purchase presents, so we made our own. Candy and Josh puttered, played, and worked in the kitchen for hours, coming up with special treats for our friends. Most of the pastors to whom we sent them expressed their delight at the delectable treats Josh and Candy had created. Josh loved being in the kitchen. Candy taught him how to make coconut bonbons, peanut butter balls, and all sorts of confectionery treats. They even made five-pound fudge, and everything they made tasted delicious.

We had a lot of fun together as a family, and Josh became a big brother to Jasmine and Nicholas. Being closer in age, he and Jasmine especially established a close camaraderie. Josh had an incredible memory and an amazing ability to process a large amount of detail. He had a propensity to recall theme songs from television shows or music from movies. He loved to sing worship music and knew every song, but he couldn't sing a note on key. He didn't care. And neither did we. During his early teen years, he worshipped so hard at church services or youth group functions. He wanted to enter in with all the other kids in their exuberant worship of the Lord. Josh was flat-footed and had no sense of rhythm, but he loved to get up and dance with all his might, working up a sweat as he worshipped.

Josh and I loved each other, but I sensed there was a barrier between us that I couldn't cross, no matter how hard I tried. From the time that he was eight years old—when Patti had left and then returned surreptitiously to Nashville and had taken him back to Washington with her—he felt that I had abandoned him, which I had not done. But throughout Josh's childhood, he believed that, and since he didn't know the real reason for his parents' divorce, he blamed me for anything that went wrong in his life.

Then, right before he left Washington to come live in Nashville, he ran into some girls at the mall whom he knew from church. They asked him, "Did your mom ever marry that guy she was seeing?" The knowledge that his own friends were aware of his mom's inappropriate behavior stunned Josh. Sadly, that's how he discovered the real reason why his mom and I had divorced.

When he moved to Nashville at sixteen, through his tears, he told Candy about the conversation at the mall. He wanted her to call his mom and tell her what those girls had said. "I don't belong anywhere," Josh said. "My parents will never be in the same room together again."

Candy reached out to Patti to let her know she was welcome in our home. Over the years, Candy had invited Patty to visit and to stay with her when I was away preaching.

Patti had visited for several days at a time, and the two women—my wife and my former wife—had developed a strong friendship.

Later, Patti sometimes visited us in Nashville on Mother's Day to see Josh. She had begged me to forgive her for what she had done to me, and I was glad to extend that forgiveness. In my heart, I had already forgiven Patti long before she asked. As awkward as it was, we all got along. Candy even taught Jasmine and Nicholas to refer to Patti as Aunt Patti, so they grew up with a special love in their hearts for her as well.

• • •

Josh did not "come out of the closet" suddenly. His experience with sexuality was more of an evolution of disclosure. As Josh was growing up, I noticed that he seemed more effeminate than other boys his age. The first time Josh and I talked about his sexuality was when he was a teenager. He had started crying. "Dad, I have these feelings," he said. Years later, he told our family, "At age eleven, my desire for male affirmation turned sexual."

"Son, are you struggling with homosexuality?" I asked straightforwardly.

"Yes," he said.

I knew that Josh had a hunger for the Lord, but that an evil spirit had gotten a strong hold on him somehow.

I talked with him, prayed with him, and arranged for him to spend time with some friends of ours who had a deliverance ministry in Louisiana, hoping he could receive spiritual help. When he returned home, Josh seemed to be doing better. His countenance had brightened, his eyes sparkled, and he was quicker to smile. He got a job at Gibson Guitar Company in Nashville, getting up before dawn and going to work, feeling a sense of purpose and accomplishment.

But it wasn't long before we heard that Josh was dabbling with homosexuality again, visiting gay bars and hanging out with people who did not have his best interests at heart. He moved out of our home and into his own apartment, and shortly after that he "came out" openly as a homosexual. He grew his hair longer and shaped his eyebrows into a conspicuous arch, which we later learned was a signal to his new friends that he was one of them.

For a while, he avoided our family members because he felt convicted, but we chose to love him no matter what, even though we did not condone his sin. That wasn't an easy balance to maintain. Once, when Josh had a problem with his car, he came to us for financial help, but I refused. I knew that he had been spending his money on things that were counterproductive to his spiritual life. We sat down in my office, and I said, "Son, there are consequences to your lifestyle. I want to help you, but I am not going to. I am not going to facilitate your sin."

I told him, "You're my son. I love you, and you are always welcome in our home. And I am not ashamed of you. I don't care if other people know that my son is gay."

I took a deep breath and continued, "But I do know that this thing will cost you your soul."

Josh had been sitting on the couch, and he slid down onto the floor. He lay on the floor and screamed and sobbed. "I know that this sin will send me to hell," he said, "but I've never seen anyone get free of it."

I knew that was a lie from the devil, but Josh was convinced that he had no choice regarding his sexuality. It turned me inside out to watch him suffering, but there was little else I could do but to love him unconditionally and pray for him. Like most families with prodigal children, we deeply grieved over the choices Josh continued to make. But we refused to say that Josh would remain imprisoned in the homosexual lifestyle forever; instead, we continued to pray and believe for his deliverance. We knew that Jesus had given us, as Spirit-filled believers, spiritual authority to break the power of that demon in Josh's life. We gave no place to hopelessness or despair. We never doubted that Josh would be set free. But for a long time, by external appearances, it didn't seem as though it would ever come to pass.

We prayed for Josh regularly for more than fourteen years. Then, in January 2006, Candy and I sensed that we needed to pray for Josh every day. By then, Josh was indulging in an openly gay lifestyle. He had his own parking spot at the gay bar and lived with a boyfriend.

Years ago, author and evangelist Oral Roberts, known for his emphasis on divine healing and deliverance, said the Lord had shown him that there are degrees of demonic spirits and that the demon associated with homosexuality is so vile and grotesque that other demons vomit when they come into its presence. This spirit is one of the most difficult to combat.

Candy and I could agree with that. We had battled that spirit alone for years, and we had grown weary. As far as we knew, none of our friends or fellow ministers had pointed fingers or wagged their heads in condemnation because our son was living a homosexual lifestyle. If anyone around us harbored such unbiblical attitudes, we were unaware of it. But in January 2006, we felt that we needed additional help to break through the spiritual strongholds in Josh's life. We approached five other ministers and their wives who knew how to pray, who understood the spiritual battle involved when ministering to homosexuals. We basically said, "We have been fighting this thing for fourteen years on our own. Would you help and join with us in praying for our son?" We knew that they were strong prayer warriors and had raised godly children. Those five couples committed to praying with us and for us, praying against the spirit that imprisoned Josh.

One of those friends, Pastor Val Treese, from Jackson, Tennessee, said, "I will help you pray, but we don't need to be praying buckshot prayers. We all need to be praying the same thing. I'll tell you how to pray. Pray that Josh comes to himself." We understood Pastor Treese's reference to the biblical account of the prodigal son, as told by Jesus (see Luke 15:11–24). It was only when the prodigal "came to himself" (v. 17) and realized that he had made a mess of his life and was willing to return with a repentant attitude that he was ready to change.

Pastor Treese continued, "And you need to get a plan in place, because when Josh comes to himself, you will need to have a plan ready that will lead him to full restoration and freedom. When he comes to himself, send him to me."

On June 6 of that year, Josh was at home with plans to go out when the Holy Ghost fell upon him.

That same day, Candy and I were returning home, coming back from California. We were in Fayetteville, Arkansas, at a Cracker Barrel restaurant, when my cell phone rang. I looked at my phone and saw that it was Josh calling. That, in itself, was unusual, because Josh rarely called me after he'd moved out of the house and into his own apartment.

I pressed the answer button on my phone. "Hey, Josh."

"Hey, Dad," Josh spoke emotionally. "I need you to pray."

"Okay, what's going on?"

"Dad, the Holy Ghost just came upon me in my apartment, and the Lord spoke to me, saying, 'Because of the prayers that have been prayed over you, because of the prayers of people who love you, I am setting you free from homosexuality.'"

I was so overwhelmed with joy, I could barely speak.

Josh continued, "Dad, I'm changed!"

He explained to Candy and me that he had planned to go out to a gay bar. He had just gotten out of the shower and was drying his hair when the Holy Ghost came upon him. He fell to his knees and began repenting, and right there, without being in church or receiving any instruction or encouragement, he started speaking in tongues.

Josh said that when he got up from his knees, he called every gay friend he knew and told them what had happened. The message was a strong one. (It must have been a clear line in the sand, as not one of them called him back ever again.)

He wanted to go to church but wasn't sure where to go in Nashville, since he was well-known there. But he'd heard that evangelist Reinhard Bonnke, known for astonishing healings and deliverances during his meetings, was speaking at Cornerstone Church, not far from our home.

Josh told his gay friends, "I can't go to the gay bar; I'm going to church."

The moment Josh put his foot over the threshold of Cornerstone Church, he started crying. "I cried the entire time I was there, all through the service," he later told us. "It was as though something was bubbling out of me."

The next morning, he went to his job at Yankee Candle in the Hickory Hollow Mall, in Antioch, about thirty miles away from where he had gone to church the previous night.

He was in the back stockroom when he heard a voice calling from the front of the store. "Hello! Hello?" the voice called. "Is anybody here?"

Josh went to the front and found an elderly gentleman standing at the counter, holding a cane. "Son, did you ever hear of Cornerstone Church?" the elderly man asked.

"Well, yeah," Josh said. "I was there last night."

"I was too," the old man said. "And the Lord sent me here today to tell you that everything is going to be all right." The man turned and walked out of the store.

Josh hurried out from behind the counter and tried to catch up with the elderly gentleman, but he could not find him. The man was gone; he had disappeared.

Josh was blown away. The experience left an indelible impression on him. Here was an old man in the candle store, nearly thirty miles away from where Josh had gone to church the night before. There are other malls closer to that church, and there was no reason why the old man should have come to the Hickory Hollow location. Yet he did.

And after he delivered his message, he disappeared.

Who was he? Why was he there? Could he have been an angel?

I believe he was. Angels are messengers from God, and that man delivered a vital message that Josh needed to hear.

Years later, Josh told his own story so others could hear how Jesus had delivered him from homosexuality. His testimony is easily accessible on YouTube, where he confidently declared, "There is nothing that my God cannot overcome!"[4]

Because of my experience with Josh, God has given me a sincere love for those who are caught up in the bondage of that spirit. So many churches condone the lifestyle of homosexuals, and others condemn them to hell. We don't compromise the truth of God's Word, which quite clearly labels homosexual activity as sin, just as the Bible condemns fornication (premarital sex) or adultery (sexual activity with a married person). But at the same time, we tell homosexuals, "God loves you, and there is hope." We encourage love, understanding, and compassion for the homosexual person. Many gay people who are engaging in homosexual acts do not want to live that lifestyle, and they struggle against their desires. They need encouragement rather than condemnation.

• • •

After Josh was touched by the Holy Spirit, we encouraged him to go spend some time with one of our pastor friends, Brother Val Treese. Josh drove over to Jackson, Tennessee, every week for several months for counseling and deliverance ministry. While there, he developed strong, healthy, and godly male relationships. The pastor's daughter and son-in-law invited Josh to move in with them so he would not have to make the long, weekly drive.

After he was there for a while, Josh was sitting in Brother Treese's office one day when a beautiful, dark-haired young woman walked in. She was Pastor Treese's niece, Carrie. She and Josh hit it off and the Holy Ghost said to Josh, "That's your wife."

Indeed, Carrie and Josh eventually became husband and wife. After they married, they lived in Jackson, often driving back to Nashville to spend the weekend with us.

It was a marvelous, ironic twist: God sent Josh to Jackson to help him remain free from sexual bondage, but He did not allow Josh to remain a sexual eunuch. Quite the contrary; in the same office where Josh confirmed his deliverance from homosexuality, God brought to him his beautiful wife, Carrie.

Josh continued counseling with Pastor Treese long after he was delivered, and it proved beneficial to him. He could now see through an adult's perspective some of those things that had happened in his childhood. Josh felt the extra effort was worth it and continued going to counseling.

Perhaps as a result of the counsel Josh had received, he felt compelled to call his mom and confront her about his childhood experience of discovering that she was bringing a man into their home to whom she was not married. He also told Candy, "You are the first person who tried to help me who ever asked, 'How are *you* feeling?' rather than giving me advice, whether right or wrong." Candy's newfound emphasis on the needs of others paid huge dividends in our own family.

Josh loved cooking, so he attended Middle Tennessee State University's culinary program to become a professional chef. He served as an intern at Chef's Market, a popular restaurant near our home.

Before long, Josh joined us under Jefferson Street Bridge every Tuesday night, helping to cook for the homeless people we fed there each week. He worked as a volunteer with The Bridge Ministry at first, then increasingly he got more involved. The Bridge Ministry didn't really have enough money to employ a full-time chef, but cooking for the homeless people gave Josh a sense of significance, and he soon worked himself into a job. He became the executive chef for The Bridge Ministry and threw himself into it with a passion, designing fabulous meals for hundreds of people each Tuesday evening, never really certain how many would show up, whether it was fifty hungry people or five hundred. It's difficult to plan a meal that way, but Josh did it. He loved serving the homeless. He felt a special connection with them and saw himself as one beggar helping another find the Bread of Life.

CHAPTER 24

A Solution to a Problem
That Doesn't Yet Exist

WHEN I WAS STILL WORKING IN EVANGELISM (about a year and half out from pastoring), the Lord challenged me to read through the entire New Testament every month. A friend of mine had done something similar and had profited immensely from it. "If you read nine chapters every day," he said, "you can read the entire New Testament every month." He had done that and had been blessed, so I felt sure I could do it too. And the Lord spoke to me, saying, "I want you to do that."

I started reading the New Testament through from Matthew to Revelation every month for a period of four years. Not only did I learn much more detail about Scripture, but I was able to see the whole of the message in ways I had never experienced previously. I was digging deeper.

Reading Scripture like that truly expanded my spiritual horizons. The practice also intensified my hunger for the Word of God. I saw things differently and more completely. My perspective toward life changed from a negative paradigm to a positive outlook. Charles Capps's twenty-seven-page booklet, *God's Creative Power*, was also valuable to me about that time. It taught me that my words could produce a power to impact my life. God showed me, "You are letting the devil curse you with your own mouth." I recognized that God wanted me to align my words with His Word. Most importantly, my faith increased. At the end of those four years, we started a church in Nashville known as Resting Place.

• • •

For some time prior to that, Candy had felt inclined to begin a church. I had adamantly declared that I would never pastor a church again, but I felt increasingly less comfortable continuing the evangelistic work in which I had been involved.

Jasmine had returned home from Lee University where she had been attending school, and she had met a man named JonMichael Brady, who was a drummer and drum technician who worked for a company that transported musical instruments for studio musicians in Nashville. JonMichael referred to Candy and me as "Mom" and "Dad" from day one. Within seven months, they were married. Jasmine and JonMichael quickly got involved with The Bridge Ministry, as did Nicholas. Josh and Carrie were with us for most weekends now, and they had plans to move to the Nashville area.

We were having some great services under the bridge each week, and hundreds of homeless people and their children were being fed, clothed, and ministered to regularly. We had no illusions about the homeless people attending our church but felt it would be a great rallying point for many of the people who were assisting us. We already had a warehouse building located in an industrial park that The Bridge Ministry used as its headquarters, so we began holding weekly services in a large room in the warehouse. Jasmine and JonMichael led the music, and Candy and I did the preaching. We called the church Resting Place, based on Scripture from 2 Chronicles 6 and referring to King Solomon's prayer at the dedication of the temple in Jerusalem. Solomon prayed, "Now, O my God, I pray, let Your eyes be open and Your ears attentive to the prayer offered in this place. Now therefore arise, O LORD God, to Your resting place, You and the ark of Your might; let Your priests, O LORD God, be clothed with salvation and let Your godly ones rejoice in what is good" (2 Chronicles 6:40–41 NASB 1995). It seemed like a perfect description of the sort of spiritual environment we hoped to foster—a place where God's presence could rest on us and His Spirit would be welcome. And for a while, it was.

The church chugged along, with fifty to seventy-five people attending. But God prompted me to declare that growth was part of our future. "There will come a day," I said with great unction and passion, "that you will have to get here early or you will not be able to find a seat." Most people in the warehouse looked at me as if I were naive or foolish. But I knew that the Lord had given me a word, so

I repeated it often: "One day there won't be an open seat in this place ... people will be lined up out the door, and the cars will be lined up down the road out front." Most people looked back at me condescendingly as if to say, "Poor Pastor Kent, he really has missed it this time." We carried on like that for several years.

One Sunday in February 2019 while I was preaching, right in the middle of my sermon, a woman got up out of her chair, walked to the front of the sanctuary, and laid some money on the altar area. I had not been speaking about money, so it seemed surprising. Nobody in our congregation had ever done anything like that previously. It was odd, but certainly not disruptive. I kept right on preaching as the woman returned to her seat. A few minutes later, another person followed the woman's example and brought an offering to the altar as well, then even more folks followed suit. At the close of the service, I said, "I feel there is a supernatural spirit of giving in the house. We are believing for and trying to save money for a church building other than the warehouse. If you want to give, please feel free to do so. I believe that God will bless you."

Many more people brought money to the church. Even Jasmine and JonMichael, still relatively newlyweds, made a large donation. So did my in-laws. Others did as well. Most people gave something; a few gave a lot.

"I believe God will double this amount of money in three months," I said. "If He doesn't, we will give all the money back."

During the next few months, several people in our congregation prospered at least twice as much as what they gave, and some prospered even more. Some, however, did not. At the end of three months, we had about one hundred thousand dollars but were still short of the amount needed to acquire a building.

Three of the leading couples in the church challenged me. "You said that God would double the money given within three months, or you would give it back. That has not happened, so you need to give people the money back."

After church one Sunday, we had an impromptu meeting of the church leaders. The atmosphere was tense but not explosive. "What would you like me to do?" I asked.

"We want you to give the money back," they said flatly.

I have always felt that if an offering is not enough for harvest and does not meet the need, then it should be used as a seed, hopefully to grow larger in time. Our church supported several missionaries, and I suggested that giving money to them may be a way to sow a seed of blessing if the people did not want their money returned. All the money given was still in a separate account. It had not been touched, not for payroll, repairs, or any other purpose. The three couples were adamant that the money should be returned to those who had given it.

The next day, I checked in with Mike Sircy, our church treasurer and chief financial officer, to get a list of the donors and to see how we should best handle matters. He pointed out to me that most people had already filed their income taxes for that year so it would not benefit them greatly to return the money and, indeed, could complicate their accounting.

I contacted each donor personally and explained the situation, asking what they would like to do regarding their financial gift. I told them, "We can cut you a check for the amount you gave, or we can give the money to missions."

Of the three couples who had initially challenged me about the matter, two wanted their money back; one had not given in the offering. Every other donor, with only one exception, essentially said, "Keep the money or give it to missions. We don't want the money back. We did not give it to you or even to the church; we gave it to God. Use it as you see fit."

The next Monday night, I called another meeting and informed the leaders, "I've done what you asked. I've contacted each donor and offered to give the money back to those who have requested it."

The three leaders who had raised the issue were virulent. "You did *not* do what we asked," they said. "You should have just cut checks to everyone who gave in the offering."

"I can't simply cut checks," I replied. "It is not quite that simple because of the tax situation and IRS regulations. Plus, most of the people do not want their money returned."

The leaders refused to accept my explanation. They stood and pointed their fingers at me, screaming accusations at me as though I were purposely trying to be deceptive or duplicitous. Their actions were offensive and vicious. The discussions grew increasingly heated. By the end of the evening, I simply sat down at the front of the warehouse church and cried. "Tell me how I can fix this," I said.

"You can't," one person said. "You need to just shut the church down and call it quits. It's over. We should shut the doors."

Another person later wrote to us, "You have dealt a mortal blow to the church. You will never recover."

I could hardly believe what these people were saying—people into whom we had poured our lives, people we loved and had ministered to for several years. Jasmine walked to the front of the church and stood beside me, her hand on my shoulder. Candy did the same, standing on my other side. Josh and Carrie were there as well.

The three offended couples left the church and encouraged others to do the same, causing a split in the congregation. Several of our key players in the ministry never showed up again.

It looked like it might be the end of Resting Place. For the next year or more, we struggled to keep the doors open.

When your enemy rejects you, that's no big deal. You expect that. But when your friends reject you, it hurts. And these had been close friends of ours who had provoked dissensions in the church. Once again, the Enemy tried to discourage me. "Why don't you just quit and do something else?" he tormented me. Admittedly, the thought crossed my mind.

Had I quit the ministry during that time, I'd have missed what God wanted to do in and through me. I had no clue that my best days were still ahead of me.

I now realize that God was preparing me for the work He wanted me to do later in my life. Preparation is essential for all of us. By getting so much Scripture into my heart and mind, God had helped me to be more biblically solid in my preaching and teaching as well as in my own life. And by forcing me to deal with overt opposition and unmerited accusations, He was also preparing me for a time when some people would misinterpret the message He wanted me to declare.

Moreover, it is not necessarily the case that *we* are not ready for God to use us. Sometimes the timing is not right; the conditions or the people are not yet ready for what God wants to do in and through us for them. Sometimes God prepares us as an arrow and then puts us back in the quiver because the target is not out there yet or not within sight.

In Isaiah 49:2, the prophet said, "He made me a polished arrow; in his quiver he hid me away" (ESV). As I studied, I discovered that arrows in Isaiah's time were made from acacia wood, which was a crooked but strong, durable hardwood. To straighten the arrow, its shaft was soaked in oil and then placed in a heavy press, which, over time, would hopefully straighten the arrow and prepare it for action. When the pressure was released, the shaft of the arrow was no longer crooked. Then the arrowhead and the feathers were attached so the arrow could fly straight and hit the target.

Sometimes God will put you under pressure to make your character straight and prepare you for action, but if the target is not there yet, He will put you back in the quiver until it is the right time for you and your work to be made public. In many ways, I felt that was what the Lord had done with me.

During that time of preparation, I often said to Candy, "We are the solution to a problem that doesn't exist yet."

She'd get upset with me and say, "Kent, stop saying that. It sounds like we are not relevant. There are plenty of problems in the world and lots of people who need the gospel message. We're not just going in circles, 'cold-trailing' like a hunting dog out on the tail of a prize that doesn't exist." Any time I mentioned us being on hold, Candy rebuffed me. "You said that again, and it makes us sound as though we are irrelevant. But we are relevant right now, not some day in the future."

"No, that's not what I'm implying," I replied, "but God has a season when He wants to do certain things in and through us, and in our world, so we can't jump ahead of that. We just have to remain faithful and obedient, doing what we know to do."

Some people struggle and claw, trying to fight their way to the top, whether in business or in ministry. But pride will come before a fall, and working "in the flesh" never glorifies God. It is always a recipe for failure. On the other hand, as we allow His Spirit to work through us, He can do far beyond what we can ask or even think!

I maintained that nine-chapter-per-day discipline for four years, but it was not easy to keep that pace, especially if I missed a day or two and tried to make up the number of chapters. Today, I still read the Bible all the way through, cover to cover, every year, but more methodically and not in as large of chunks.

Part of my learning process involved learning how to move in the prophetic vein, hearing the Spirit of God and honing the gift of prophecy that God had given to me.

As I was learning to trust the validity of what the Lord was saying through me, Candy and I accepted an invitation to minister at the church pastored by Lindell Cooley's parents' in Red Bay, Alabama. The Cooleys were friends in the ministry, and their son, Lindell, now a pastor in Tennessee, had been a key part of a prolonged revival in Pensacola, Florida.

During my sermon, I suddenly began to prophesy about their local church. "And this church will be on *fire!*" I proclaimed. "And you're going to move from the country to downtown," I stated.

Lindell's dad leaned over to his wife and said, "Well, I know Kent has missed it now." Their congregation was quite content where they were; moreover, they owned the property on which the church sat, and it was totally paid off.

Within three months, that country church caught on fire and burned to the ground.

Like most everyone else who had heard the word that day, Candy and I thought prophecy meant that the church was going to catch on fire spiritually, causing a great revival in the community. Instead, the building was consumed with physical fire. The congregation couldn't find a comparable place in which to meet, except for a property right downtown.

Candy facetiously quipped, "I have pictures of you out back of that church striking matches!"

Although we were saddened that our friends and their fellow believers had experienced that calamity, it was another confirmation to Candy and me that God was indeed speaking prophetically through me at times. I was learning to trust Him more and to be confident in the messages He presented through me.

I would need that confidence in the days ahead.

• • •

Admittedly, there were times when I felt like giving up. I thought, *Surely, we could do better if I simply got another blue-collar job. I'm not afraid of hard work.* Although I appreciated the kindness and generosity of Candy's family and our friends, it was demeaning always being the ones on the receiving end of their charity. "Hey, we're going on vacation. Why don't you guys come along with us?"

"Well, we can't really afford that."

"Don't worry about it; we'll pay your way."

That was kind and generous of them, but I was a grown man, more than fifty years of age, and I had nothing materially to show for a lifetime of service.

Every Wednesday night, I'd have about seventeen people show up for Bible study at the church. Not even the church leaders attended with any regularity. On most Sunday mornings, I preached to less than eighty people, sometimes as few as forty. It was rare when our attendance exceeded more than one hundred people. At times, I prayed, "God, why am I even doing this? What difference are we making? What good is this? What's the use?"

I did see the occasional miracle, and maybe God knew that I needed that to keep me going.

Candy had struggled with depression, so because we both loved dogs, we got a cute little poodle pup that we named Mozart. He was the coolest dog; if we simply looked at him, he seemed to know what we were thinking. He slept in our bed with us and often walked with me when I spent time in prayer. He stayed with Candy throughout her ordeal with depression, often accompanying her in her prayer closet. We took Mozart everywhere with us when we traveled. He was a special part of our family.

I sometimes laid hands on Mozart and prayed, "Lord, please protect him and give him a long life."

One day Candy and I were moving a piece of furniture out of the house, so we propped the front door open. Mozart saw an opportunity for some fun and shot out the door. He raced out into the road, chasing after a car, and a neighbor coming home in a large van hit him. The neighbor stopped and found him lying on the ground, his body stiff, bleeding out of his mouth; he was dead. The neighbor was distraught that he had hit and killed our dog. "I'm so sorry!" he cried. "I didn't see him." Another neighbor who had come out to assist looked on and said, "That's horrible."

I was angry, but not at our neighbor; I was frustrated with God. "Didn't I ask You not to let something like this happen?" I questioned the Lord. "I've laid hands on Mozart and I've asked You to protect him. You know how much I love this dog."

Candy went into the house and came back out with a towel. She tenderly wrapped Mozart's body in it. "What do you want to do?" she asked me.

"Well, the Bible says we can pray and God will raise the dead, so I'm going to pray and ask God to raise Mozart from the dead."

"Okay," she said slowly and quietly. Candy looked back at me respectfully but perhaps not totally convinced.

No matter. With our neighbors still standing there, I took Mozart into my lap and laid my hands on him, and I started to pray. "In the name of Jesus, I command the spirit of life to come back into Mozart."

Almost instantly, I felt that towel start to move. As I pulled off the towel, Mozart looked up and jumped out of my lap and down to the ground. He started running and did a couple of laps around the yard.

I took Mozart to the veterinarian to be checked out, and the vet examined him carefully and thoroughly. The vet looked at me and said, "There's not one thing wrong with him."

Our neighbor was freaked out by the dog that God had raised from the dead.

If seeing Mozart come back from the dead caused some friends to be astonished, that was nothing in comparison to what many of our friends grappled with when I spoke at the annual New Year's Eve service at the Rock Church in Virginia Beach.

CHAPTER 25

An Explosive Prophecy

WHEN THE PASTORS OF THE ROCK CHURCH invited me to preach, no other outside speakers were on the program that night.

I happily accepted their invitation, and as I prayed and prepared my heart and mind for what God wanted to say through me, I sensed that the message was a strong word of rebuke but also a positive word of hope. Still, there were several troubling issues that the Lord impressed on me.

Going into 2020, there was no indication that these things could happen, but I knew that I had heard from the Lord. I was so convinced that I carefully wrote down the prophecy word for word. I had never done such a thing before. I wasn't concerned about being embarrassed. As long as I was certain I had heard from the Lord, I was willing to say whatever He gave me, even if what I said was considered unpopular or made people feel uncomfortable. Still, I felt sure that the word God had given me to share that night was something out of the ordinary.

The pastors of the Rock Church greeted Candy and me warmly when we arrived for the service. The sanctuary was still decorated festively with dozens of potted poinsettias from the Christmas season placed in front of the Plexiglas podium. Hundreds of people showed up to welcome in the new year in the presence of the Lord and His people. The musicians led us in a marvelous time of praise and worship to the Lord, and then it was time for me to preach.

I put on my glasses and placed my notes on the podium so I could better present the prophecy I had received from the Lord. I started slowly, holding the microphone in my hand and emphasizing that this word was for the remnant of saints who had been faithful to the Lord. "In 2020, I am opening heaven for My saints who have been faithful, and I am opening it with the rain of favor," I began.

As I spoke, I felt empowered from on high, and although I tried to stay close to what I had written in my notes prior to the event, my mouth filled with words faster than my brain could comprehend them. Before I even had opportunity to process the message, I spoke rapidly and powerfully. I didn't pause to expound on each point; I simply delivered the word as it had come to me.

"As Elijah was on his knees till the cloud came, so has the remnant been in intercession. But no longer will intercession come out of your mouth, but the shout of victory and triumph. The favor that I am releasing on the remnant in the next four years is coming from the secular realm and not from inside the church.

This year I am lifting off the remnant the spirit of heaviness, and I am clothing you with the garments of praise," says the Lord.

"When I am done blessing My faithful people, the world will envy them for the blessing they walk under. I know how difficult it has been for the remnant to hold on to your faith the last few years, especially watching the lukewarm and the counterfeit prosper without paying the price of living by faith and sacrifice.

"But know this," says the Lord of Hosts: "What I am now releasing in the earth is going to be so glorious, both spiritually and in the natural realm, you will forget the pain and suffering that you have endured. When you leave this earth, you are going to leave in victory and not in defeat."

People in the audience began standing to their feet and lifting their hands in praise to God. I continued reading the word that the Lord had given to me:

"Two thousand nineteen was a year of shedding things in the Body of Christ—heaviness, discouragements, debts . . . all kinds of things," says the Lord. "It was a year of exchange. The first are now going to become last and the last are now going to become first. For all my children who have sowed in tears for many years, get ready, I am drying your eyes and now you shall reap in joy.

"This year, 2020, is the beginning of a last transfer of wealth in the earth. This final move of My presence and glory is not a revival for the Church, for revival is for the lukewarm. This final harvest is for the lost. This harvest is for a generation that did not reject Me, did not see what they wanted, but rejected the counterfeit church. The Church that is going to bring in the last harvest will not look like the church of past generations.

"Your pews are gonna have men and women on them with dyed hair and mohawks, and generational piercings, but they will be changed and washed by the blood of the Lamb and will give Me the glory that I have longed for in this hour.

"This harvest will primarily be a generation of younger men and women who have never felt the real presence of their Creator. They're going to be led by men and women who have a Joshua and Caleb spirit, who have had to live in the wilderness for years with the lukewarm and the unbelieving and the rebellious. But they did not become bitter waiting on Me to show up. I have preserved their call and purpose for this time.

"They are not famous people or well-known in the earth. But know this: They are famous and well-known in heaven and in hell. When they get on their knees to pray, the foundations of hell shake, and they are the ones," saith the Lord, "that the prophets have declared the people who know their God shall be strong and will do great exploits.

"The reason many of you have gone through trials and sufferings, I will now explain. When I got ready to release favor and blessings to Abraham, I tested him because I had to know that I could trust him, because what I was going to give him was greater than any man had ever had. What I am now releasing to the body of Christ is not a portion of Me, it is not a fragment of Me. But in 2020 it is the beginning of the fullness of who I am. Previous moves of God in the past were known for a portion of who I am. Some were known as healing moves. Some were known as moves of miracles. Some were known as a time of revelation; some were known as My presence.

"But not this time," saith the Lord. "This move will not be a portion. But the move of the Lord will be the fullness of the glory of God. I am now knowing this, that I have a remnant of people who have been broken and I can trust them. And because they will not promote themselves and say, 'Look at me,' they will not get off track and become drunk with their own blessings; I'm going to give you more," saith the Lord, "than you asked for."

• • •

One part of the 2019 New Year's Eve message was especially startling to some people. The Lord said through me, "Starting in 2020, I am going to begin to pull down strongholds that have ruled over this nation. The stronghold of abortion is going to be destroyed. The cry of the blood of innocent children has reached unto heaven. Because the devil took my seed in the womb, I'm going to take the children of this generation that Satan thought were his; I'm going to save them and make them a voice in the earth."

I went on, speaking a strong word about homosexuality, but probably not the word that everyone expected. The Lord led me to say,

"I am also going to send freedom and deliverance to the gay and to the lesbian men and women that the modern church has failed, because they had no power and no authority. These young men; these women who have been bound, that the church has ostracized, or else told them 'It was all right,' are men and women that I love dearly and that I died for.

"Out of the stronghold of homosexuality, I am going to raise up powerful worship leaders and musicians and songwriters who will not have the smell of sin on them," saith the Lord. "But there is a river of deliverance that is going to hit them in the name of the Lord.

"And to the families whom your young people have been taken captive, I make covenant with you," saith God, "that there is an authority and an anointing that is being released to the body of Christ that is going to break this foul demon, and your sons and daughters will be set free; they will bear you grandchildren," saith the Lord, "and they will stand on My platforms, set free by the power of God.

"They will lead as Judah did for Israel. All that My prophets have prophesied is now going to come to pass. For all of those who said that God's prophets have missed it, you will see it with your eyes, the prophecies fulfilled, but you will not be a part of it.

"I'm going to expose leadership in the church. [Those] who would not partake of the gospel of the Lord Jesus Christ, for all of the pastors and leaders who would not put any value on My presence, [who] watered down My message in their churches, who offered only a form of god without any power, so they can fill their pews and fill their pockets," saith the Lord, "I am going to take your congregations and give them to true shepherds who have labored in obscurity, who love sheep and smell like them."

I encouraged pastors to get among their people, to lay hands on them and to pray for them.

"In this move of God, I am going to uncover, and I am going to expose the devil, false prophets, wolves in sheep's clothing, both in the church and in the secular realm. I have placed an Elijah mantle and anointing in the earth now on chosen men to destroy the spirit of Jezebel, that witchcraft that has tried to destroy this nation, that foul spirit," saith the Lord, "that has permeated your government, permeated your colleges, and permeated your churches. The anointing of Elijah is going to destroy that foul demon," saith the Lord."

The words coming out of my mouth grew even more specific:

"I am going to put a muzzle on the mouth of the dishonest media that is going to be silenced for the righteous. And just as Haman built gallows to hang Mordecai, and died on them himself, so am I going to destroy evil politicians who have tried to impeach the man that I set in the White House. I am not setting men for a culture or a creed or a color.

"But I in heaven have decreed that he sit there. And I also have decreed that he will be elected, because that's who I have chosen.[5] I am God Almighty. I bow to no man. The earth is Mine and has always been.

"In 2020, I am starting recovery in the earth and in the church, and all that belongs to Me, that the devil has stolen," saith the Lord. "This is the beginning of a four-year harvest that is going to end at the end of 2024. There is going to be a reversal of profits for many in the next four years.

"Drug companies that have preyed on the weak are going to suffer. Not only because I will release physical healing. But I am also going to heal people's hearts, and I am coming after the demon of depression that has washed over this nation, and I am going to give men and women the joy of the Lord. As a lion roars over his prey, so you will hear the Lion of Judah roar over the wicked."

• • •

The audience was clearly stunned by the strong message, but the Lord had given me a further profound word to share with the people. I did not even pause as I continued pouring out a part of His message that surprised many in the audience and many more who would hear it later.

The Lord said, "Sports [are] going to see a huge decline in attendance because people are going to lose interest in them. This is My judgment on sports: Because they have dishonored Sundays and they have turned it into an idol, and they [have] stopped people from coming to worship on Sundays," God says, "This was My day and not theirs, and I'm taking it back."

Then, to make certain that people understood that these were not my words, I emphasized, "This is the Spirit of the Lord: 'I am also going to deal with Hollywood, who has bashed My name. I am going to judge them.'"

Although I did not notice at the time, Jasmine later told me that when she heard those words come from my mouth, she leaned over, grabbed JonMichael's arm, and whispered, "We are not even going to have a church after this!"

But the Lord was not done speaking:

"And the weapons of the secular world have been the ability to pass laws in Congress against righteousness. But know this, I am removing men who will not stand up for righteousness in government, and I am raising up a majority in government who will. As I did with Elijah, first there was the fire," saith the Lord, "and then there was the rain, so will I do now.

"Two thousand twenty will be remembered as a year of purifying both in the church and in the nation. I'm going to send fire," saith the Lord, "to this nation and to the church, and I'm going to purify her. And when the fire is done purifying," saith God, "I'm going to open the windows of heaven, and I'm going to cause it to rain on this nation, and on the remnant, and on the house of God.

"For all those who said that God is dead and we are out of touch, and that we are old in our methods, know this: Because you gave Me glory, and you put honor on My presence, the last shall be greater than the first." Hallelujah! "And I will release upon thee things that you did not ask. Even as Solomon asked of Me wisdom and not wealth, know this," saith God, "I am taking from the wicked that which they have said was 'ours,' and I am giving it to the righteous," saith the Lord.

"I am also going to be connecting men and women in the Spirit in the church that have never met each other. And I'm going to cause you to begin to form relationships with people that you've never met in the body of Christ. For the root system of the church is coming out of the ground, and I am raising up a church whose leaves shall be for the healing of the nations.

"I am also resurrecting ministries and gifts in people that have been dormant or that the church has refused to use. Men and women that sometimes, through failure, [have] disqualified themselves. But the gifts still burn in them. Know this," saith God, "because you have repented, and I've taken you through the process, My anointing on you is still strong."

And the Lord says, "I'm going to send men and women on platforms. Some are going to say, 'They are not worthy,' but My blood makes them worthy.

Because they have repented, the word of the Lord will come out of them."

God says the remnant church has been hidden in this nation. "Now," saith the Lord, "I am lifting the veil off the end-times church, as the bridegroom lifts the veil off his bride in that hour and beholds her glory."

I continued prophesying under a strong anointing from God. I then said something that astounded even me, something for which I had no advance knowledge or understanding. The words practically tumbled out of my mouth:

"In the next few months," saith God, "I am going to begin to cause the world to shake in her shoes. I am going to create situations where they will have no answers. Then I am going to release [the answers] in the house of God."

I didn't try to elaborate on what the Lord meant by this word; I simply delivered it as clearly and as accurately as I could. I had no scientific or political knowledge about what was about to happen on earth, but I knew what God had told me in advance that the best minds in the world would be baffled in trying to cope with what was coming.

The word continued through me:

"There have been many megachurches, and I am not against them," saith the Lord, "but I am demanding that every pastor and every congregation stand up and declare who you are and whose side you are on.

For the years that you have paid the price, for the years that you would not break ranks, I saw it," says God. "And tonight I make covenant with thee that the greatest days are upon thee.

"The days of weeping are over. The days of testing are over. The womb is being pulsated with a birth of faith," saith God, "that is getting ready to come out. I say to thee that the end-times church is going to cast out demons. They're going to raise the dead; they're going to walk in hospitals and lay hands on the sick, and by the scores they will get up and walk out.

"To your children that education told them that God did not live. I am invading your colleges; I am going to deal with the professors that have challenged me and said that I am not real and that I do not exist. I am going to show up in their classrooms, and I am going to release the baptism of the Holy Ghost upon men and women across this nation because the earth is Mine," saith the Lord.

"It is My hour that I am going to lift up the church. So be encouraged," saith the Lord. "The best is yet to come. Hold on. Weeping may endure for a night, but joy cometh in the morning."

• • •

Altogether, I prophesied for less than twenty minutes, and when I was done, I was totally spent, so I simply said to the audience, "Stand to your feet!" We entered a time of praise and thanks to the Lord as we brought in the new year.

The look on Candy's face as I concluded this word told me that I had scared even her, but I knew the message was from God, and I appreciated Candy's trust in me. She knew that the word had not originated from my own ideas and that I would not prophesy anything that I was not convinced came from the Lord.

My job was simply to be the messenger. Still, it was interesting to see what connected with the audience there in the church. Undoubtedly, the message about abortion in America being dismantled resonated with the crowd, but two other aspects of the message seemed to surprise people even more—that sports and Hollywood were going to shut down.

Some of my friends fretted aloud, "Oh, my! That is crazy. Sports shut down? No way. Nobody going to the movie theaters? Impossible. Kent must have really missed it this time."

I had several people actually tell me, "I enjoy listening to you, but you really missed it here."

I didn't blame them.

After all, at that time, the sports world was gearing up for the annual, end-of-season collegiate bowl games, not to mention the NFL's playoff games and Super Bowl, and the professional hockey and basketball leagues were just hitting their seasonal stride. Within six weeks, Major League Baseball would open spring training camps. So, for me to say that people were going to suddenly lose interest in sports and that the venues would be closed was a totally outlandish statement—unless it came true.

Similarly, the motion picture industry was prepping for the Academy Awards and the numerous other self-congratulating ceremonies usually held early in each new year. Why would theaters close or have fewer customers when movies were about to be lauded all over the world? There would be even more people in the theaters, not less—unless the word of the Lord came true.

Word soon circulated that I had predicted that sports stadiums would be empty and that theaters would be vacant as well. That was not precisely the word that God had given to me or that I delivered (the full message can be found online), but that's what people heard.[6]

Then, in late February and early March of 2020, COVID-19 overran the world. Like most nonmedical people, I was relatively unfamiliar with coronaviruses and had not even heard of COVID-19 prior to that. Nor did I have any knowledge of its potential medical implications or what the world might do to combat the virus. Who could possibly have imagined the impact of a worldwide pandemic? Nobody in my lifetime had experienced anything similar. The closest we had ever come to such a nightmare in America was the Spanish Flu epidemic caused by the H1N1 influenza virus that killed more than 650,000 people in the United States around the end of World War I. Before it was contained, an estimated 500 million people worldwide were infected.

But less than three months after God prompted me to prophesy that word, the stadiums and theaters around the world were empty. So were most of our highways, schools, restaurants, churches, factories, and other workplaces.

And the best minds in the world were baffled in trying to combat a virus that touched not merely one or two nations, but the entire earth.

God's Word had been fulfilled.

Rock Church put the video of the 2019 New Year's Eve prophecy on YouTube, and the message received more than two million hits. Thousands of people watched it in its entirety and sent it on to friends and family members. The responses varied, but by the spring of 2020, few people doubted that our world was being rocked.

Certainly, some people were offended by the word I had given. I couldn't help that, and I made no attempt to explain to them or to placate their concerns.

Because of my prayer life over the years, I'd grown accustomed to talking conversationally with God. I don't feel the need to use fancy or flowery phrases; I simply talk with God as a Friend, always mindful and respectful that He is the Lord, yet confident that He has invited me into His presence and given me access through Jesus. Although He does not speak to me in an audible voice, Jesus said His sheep would know His voice, so I've learned to discern His voice, and I can hear God's Spirit talking to my spirit.

Many of the prophesies that the Lord has given to me over the years have been clearly delineated, either black or white; there were no gray areas. Sometimes I'd think, *Oh, Lord, You are taking me way out on a limb here*, but I learned that obedience was not optional. Still, there have been times when I have protested, saying to God or to myself, "I ain't sayin' that!" God and I would then have conversations, and although He never rebuked me, I knew better than to stretch the boundaries of His patience or His grace.

In most prophetic words that I have received, I merely repeat what God has spoken to me. Although it is not a perfect analogy, the process is similar to an interpreter in a foreign country who is translating a message from one language to another, hearing what the speaker says, then translating it into a language the audience can understand. I hear the word from the Lord and then speak it forth in my own words, attempting to accurately reflect the message as best I can. As I understand Scripture, that is how the Old Testament prophets functioned. The Lord did not *possess* them, as some want to imply nowadays, pretending that the human personality disappears when someone is prophesying. No, God filled them with Himself and His Word. It was still Isaiah's voice, or Daniel's, or Jeremiah's, or Ezekiel's that the people heard speak in their own languages and idioms, but in a real way, the message was directly from God.

Is it possible to make mistakes in this process or misunderstand what the Lord is saying? Of course. Perhaps even in genuine prophetic words, there is a small measure of "flesh" that unintentionally gets included in the message the Spirit is speaking through a human being. But to the best of my ability, I attempt to discern what the Holy Ghost is saying, and I repeat it unvarnished and unabridged.

Often, what I hear from the Holy Ghost is not a message I have previously thought about. The words do not originate with me. I don't worry about being embarrassed, and maybe that's one of the reasons why God gives me these strong messages: He knows I will say them. My first responsibility is to be loyal and obedient to God, not to people's opinions of me.

• • •

The Rock Church invited me back to speak at their New Year's Eve service in 2020. Again, I presented a firm word to the church, but then I also felt strongly led to repeat similar statements regarding sports and Hollywood not only being abandoned and the facilities empty but never fully rebounding or ever being the same again.

When it comes to prophesying, I'm really careful. I never speak my own ideas, even if they are correct. Nor do I ever tell someone who is sick that they are going to live unless it is the Lord saying it. I've never told someone he is going to live and then that person has died.

I had a woman come and ask me to speak life over her, but I couldn't. The Lord did not give me that word for her. On another occasion, a well-known Christian musician asked me to pray for him and share with him what the Lord showed me. I did, but it was not necessarily a positive affirmation. I could not help that. I am merely the messenger, the conveyor, the wire over which the word is carried, not the initiator of the message.

I understand the potential damage a prophetic word can have if it is wrong. Most of my prophetic ministry has usually been more corporate correction to the church rather than direction for a specific individual's life. I've never been one to sit around for an hour or two, giving personal prophecies to people. While I don't normally denigrate that sort of ministry in others, that has not been the sort of ministry that God has given to me. My prophetic role has been more corrective and encouraging, more forthtelling than foretelling, especially in presenting messages to His church.

Maybe that is one reason why God opened the door for me to speak to a much larger audience. But the way it happened was so outlandish, I knew it had to be God!

CHAPTER 26

Dots Connected by God

PRIOR TO THE SUMMER OF 2020, I had never met Kevin Jessip, the founder of The Return, but although I was unaware of his ministry, he evidently knew of me. In August 2020, Kevin was in Nashville for advance meetings, raising support and awareness for a massive prayer and praise event he planned to undertake in Washington, DC, in September 2020. He had already been working on the project for nearly two years. In what seemed like a serendipitous meeting, our friend Danny Gokey bumped into Kevin in Nashville. "We're having a little get-together and prayer meeting at our house tonight," Danny told Kevin, "so why don't you come by?" Kevin agreed to attend.

Candy and I had also received an invitation from Danny and his wife, Leyicet, to attend the prayer meeting. When Candy mentioned it to me, my initial response was, "I ain't goin' to that." We had been to Danny and Leyicet's home previously, along with our daughter, Jasmine, and her husband, JonMichael, so my reluctance wasn't because of the hosts. We loved Danny and Leyicet. But I also knew there would be numerous "prophetic types" at the gathering, and I felt no compulsion to join that party.

Certainly, there is a valid spiritual gift of prophecy, in which God communicates a message directly through a person who speaks on His behalf. The prophetic gift may involve forth-telling, speaking God's truth into a situation, or foretelling, which may be more predictive of future events. Sometimes, it involves both. But nowadays, the prophetic ministry has been used and abused so much that it sometimes verges on cartoonish or worse. Many of today's so-called prophets speak in spiritual gibberish or in such ambiguous terms that nobody can understand what they are conveying—not even the other prophets, which, incidentally, violates a Scriptural requirement for valid prophetic ministry.

Other prophetic ministers seem to think it is incumbent on them to present a word of prophecy, even if it is not God speaking directly through them. Because they may have spoken a valid prophetic word previously at some point, they seem to feel that other people in the room *expect* them to "speak for God" any time an opportunity arises. They don't want to disappoint people. But that is not the way the genuine gift of prophecy works, and it is all too easy to get into trouble when someone portends that he or she is speaking for God when, in fact, they are merely expressing their own thoughts and beliefs or, worse yet, opinions.

In some cases, it seems the more outlandish the prophecy sounds, the more spiritually esteemed it is regarded by some people. That's hogwash!

One "prophetess" told me about some of the revelations God had given her during one of the thirty or more times that Jesus transported her to heaven and back.

"Okay . . ." I said, staring back at her dumbfounded, having nothing further to say. What's a person to do with that? I didn't really believe her, but I didn't want to call her a liar either.

More problematic, many "conspiracy theory" folks—sincere but misguided people of every ilk and across political lines—tend to follow prophetic ministries and often reinterpret spiritual messages as clarion calls that did not emanate from God. They regard a "word from the Lord" almost like fortune-telling. Rather than taking the time to seek God on their own, they'd rather roll the Urim and Thummim,[7] or have a prophet hear from God on their behalf. That can be dangerous, divisive, and possibly even play right into the hands of the devil's destructive efforts.

Moreover, I get nervous when someone introduces himself or herself ostentatiously. "Hello, I'm Prophet Joe" or "I'm Prophetess Mary." True ministers of God do not have to promote themselves. God can put them before kings and presidents. He can open doors others say are impossible to enter. On the other hand, the old saying still rings true: "Self-promotion stinks." And it doesn't always take a spiritual gift of discernment to smell it.

So, for a number of reasons, I wasn't excited about attending the event at our friends' home.

"We must go," Candy said. "We're going. Danny and Leyicet are dear friends and have been so supportive of our work in feeding the homeless people under the bridge. The least we can do is to attend the prayer meeting at their house."

I groused a bit more and eventually agreed that we would go, but my expectations were minimal.

About twenty or thirty people had gathered at the Gokeys' home for the prayer time. I recognized a few renowned "prophets," but many were simply God-loving folks who wanted to see Him move in and transform our city and our nation. Prior to the prayer time, most people engaged in casual conversation and some light refreshments before Leyicet called the group into a large living room area. After a brief introduction, Danny and Leyicet began calling out prayer requests, and it didn't take long for various people in the room to begin jockeying for position, chomping at the bit, it seemed, to offer their two cents.

A fellow well-known in prophetic circles set the tone for the evening. "Well, you all know me," he said whimsically. "I'm over here percolating."

Say what? *Percolating? What does that mean?* I wondered.

Early in the prayer time, Danny looked in my direction. "We want Brother Kent to pray over our nation and concerning the pedophilia that is going on in Washington."

What? He wanted me to pray about *what?* I was not to ask God's wisdom and favor on the Christian members of Congress and the Supreme Court? Not even to pray against the evil perpetrated legally through legislation that flew in the face of Almighty God? No, Danny wanted me to pray about the pedophilia in our nation's capital—a matter I knew nothing about.

I was aware of a few headlines in the news, but I had no more insight than anyone else about the situation. I looked across the room and caught the eye of my son Josh, who was cracking up in laughter at the unusual request. Jasmine and

JonMichael were chuckling as well. They could tell that I was bumfuzzled by the strange request, and they loved it! In fact, the more miserable I was, the more our kids were tickled.

But Danny knew that occasionally I spoke prophetically, and I had previously prayed specifically for Danny and his ministry. I assumed that was why he had asked me to pray, so I was willing to do that. Still, I'm not good at "prayers on demand"; God is not a slot machine into which you toss some coins and hope for the best. But I could sincerely pray for the protection of our children and the conviction of sin on the perpetrators. My request was heartfelt, but it wasn't anything "prophetic," and that was okay by me. When it came to prophetic words, I had learned long ago that it is impossible to make God talk to you or through you. If God isn't speaking, forget it. So, I prayed, "Lord, please protect our children and expose the perversion and break the demonic holds," and then resumed my usual role of quietly listening to others.

The meeting moved on, and one person after another sought the ears of the other participants. Some had good, solid words and provided encouragement to the group. Others were simply nauseating with their bombastic grasping for approval.

One man didn't offer a word all evening long. Indeed, he seemed quite reserved.

I hadn't met Kevin Jessip previously, but I noticed him at the Gokeys' home. With slightly graying hair and stodgy, traditional glasses, he looked more like a banker than a huge event promoter. Still, he was hard to miss since most of the others in the group seemed to be either casually dressed, hip-looking musical artists or "prophet types," attired mostly in black. Kevin was one of the few people there wearing a dress shirt, suit, and tie. I watched Kevin throughout the evening, and while others in the room seemed to be jockeying for position and anxious to speak out what they felt God was saying to them, I noticed that Kevin did not speak out a word during the prayer time. He was quiet and unassuming, even though he was probably the most powerful promoter in the house.

Before the evening concluded and we all departed, Candy and I walked over to Kevin and greeted him.

"Hello, Kevin. I'm Kent Christmas."

"I know who you are, brother," Kevin said. "I've watched some of your prophetic messages online."

We struck up a conversation, and Kevin told me that he was in town to raise awareness about an event that he was planning to hold in Washington in September. He told me some of the speakers and musicians who had agreed to participate. "We would really like for you to come and join us," he said. We talked further, and he gave me more details about the event. I enjoyed talking with Kevin, and he struck me as the real deal—a pure spirit.

As much as I felt a strong spiritual connection with Kevin, as soon as I got in the car, I turned to Candy and said, "I ain't doin' that."

We hadn't even driven off the Gokeys' property yet.

"It will be symbolism with no substance," I said.

Candy looked back at me and said, "Babe, I believe that God wants to release a word. God wants to speak to the nation. You have to go." She was convinced that Kevin's invitation was a divine appointment. Candy also knew how much I despised symbolism without substance—going through a bunch of spiritual motions that have no lasting benefit. She understood that I needed some extra prompting to attend the event in Washington.

About a week later, Kevin sent me an email outlining the particulars of his invitation. The Return would cover my hotel costs for the night before and after my presentation, but my travel expenses and other costs would be my responsibility. Nor would there be any honorarium offered.

Looking back on it, I'm sure God was smiling, because everything about my being at The Return was so divinely orchestrated. Details and connections that appeared at first glance to be nothing more than chance, we later realized, were dots connected by God.

CHAPTER 27

The Lion of Judah
Will Roar Again!

CANDY AND I HAD NO IDEA WHAT TO EXPECT regarding The Return. We saw it simply as a window of opportunity.

Steve Huffman, one of my best friends, came into the church office one day. Steve is not known to speak out prophetically, but he felt that he had something important to tell me. "The Lord spoke to me about this thing, The Return. This is going to bring you world renown," he said matter-of-factly. We talked briefly about what that might mean, and then Steve said, "But it will also bring out the haters."

I tried to process the implications of Steve's words. "Well, okay. Nothing has ever been easy for me, Steve." I said with a laugh. "You know that!"

Steve knew my story well. He knew that for years in ministry, I had enjoyed little success as a pastor or as an evangelist. I wasn't lazy, and I worked hard, but I never seemed to get ahead.

At times I felt as though there were demons on an assignment from hell, tempting me to give up the ministry. Occasionally, I wondered aloud, "What if? What if I had not gone into the ministry? I could have done well in business or at some other sort of job." It was as if the Enemy recognized the potential influence I could have for the kingdom of God, so he attempted to head me off at the pass by enticing me toward other occupations.

Yet, ironically, every so often, I felt a wave of God's anointing flow over me, speaking through me and touching other people's lives. I knew that individuals were being healed not merely physically but spiritually. I wondered, *Is there more that God wants to do in and through my life?*

I was not scheduled to speak at The Return until Saturday night. Burton Gaar, my good friend and trusted coworker at the church and The Bridge Ministry, accompanied me on the trip from Nashville. We arrived in Washington on Friday and decided to visit the National Mall that evening to attend a portion of The Return and get a feel for the event. I didn't plan to meet with Kevin Jessip prior to the event, but when Burton and I got out of the hotel van that had transported us to the Mall, Kevin was arriving in a car with Rabbi Jonathan Cahn, one of the main speakers at The Return.

I attempted to enter the perimeter of the greenroom tent near the backstage area, but security would not grant us access since I did not have the proper credentials. Kevin saw me and waved off the guard. "Oh, he's fine. Let him in."

Kevin came over and hugged me and introduced me to Rabbi Cahn, who was dressed in his traditional black rabbinical suit. A Jewish rabbi who trusted Jesus, Rabbi Cahn was friendly and easygoing but also passionate about his faith. I was impressed by his genuine spirit.

Since we were on the precipice of the US presidential election in November 2020, both secular and Christian television networks had reporters and cameras covering the event—everyone from the Trinity Broadcasting Network and Daystar to Fox News and CNN clamored for scoops and details.

I noticed numerous protesters gathered on the outskirts of the Mall. Some were upset at the Christians in attendance who held strong, biblical views about marriage designed by God as between one man and one woman. Most all of the true believers gathered on the Mall were also opposed to abortion—the murder of nearly sixty million babies in our nation since *Roe v. Wade* passed in the 1970s. Many in the gathering were fervent supporters of Israel as God's chosen people.

Consequently, although the organizers tried to avoid anything political, that was nearly impossible since it was only a matter of weeks until the election. Some protesters simply seemed mad at President Trump. Some people thought that he might greet the crowd or send some sort of message. At one point, he flew over the Mall in Marine One, but he did not appear as part of the event.

I arrived at The Return having not studied or prepared for the event. I wasn't being lazy or cocky or arrogantly dismissive of the need to prepare to speak to the tens of thousands of people at the event—and potentially millions more who might see it online. I simply didn't know how to prepare for it. Kevin had provided the schedule with some loose guidelines and time limits, but other than that, each speaker was on his or her own.

I went to Washington thinking that The Return was going to be similar to America for Jesus, another event I had participated in a number of years earlier. That gathering was intended to be a giant, two-day-long prayer meeting held on Independence Mall in Philadelphia, with a multitude of Christian leaders directing the crowd in prayer—a great idea in theory. The City of Brotherly Love was, after all, the first capital of the United States. It was also the site of the signing of the Declaration of Independence and the ratifying of the US Constitution. Moreover, it was a focal point of the Great Awakening, a time of spiritual revival and renewal in colonial America in the 1730s. As such, this rich symbolism offered hope to millions of Christians that the gathering could spur our corrupt nation to a time of national revival. This event was also not intended to be in any way political; it was meant to be a catalyst for confession of sin, repentance, and renewal. I traveled to Philadelphia with high hopes that God was going to move in our country.

But once there, I felt disappointed. As I arrived at Independence Mall, I recognized many of the speakers and other participants. Most were immaculately dressed, with not a hair out of place, as though they were ready for their next televised appearance. Fake smiles and meaningless banter held sway. It seemed like a convention of Christian celebrities with a bunch of egos on display. I also noted the presence of several so-called Christian leaders who were openly gay. I didn't fit in, and I wasn't sure I wanted to. I thought to myself, *This isn't me.*

When the event began, it was as though all the speakers were on parade, a showcase of top Christian personalities strutting their stuff. Most prayed bland, innocuous, politically correct prayers, perhaps sincerely, but the prayers seemed to get stuck on the ceiling of the staging platform. I didn't feel any sense of anointing at all. As I had been instructed, I prayed a relatively brief prayer and left the platform, with neither the audience nor myself transformed in any significant manner.

It seemed the spiritual atmosphere did not lend itself to the Spirit of God having His way or doing anything supernatural. To me, it really was symbolism without substance. I left America for Jesus feeling that it had been an ineffective waste of time.

So, when I was invited to participate in The Return in September 2020, I hoped for better but did not greatly anticipate any lasting results. I thought, *This is going to be another America for Jesus, a glad-handing weekend, little more.*

The Return had scheduled ninety speakers and worship leaders over several days. Most were well-known preachers or ministry leaders as well as a few Christian political leaders. A few of those on the program I recognized were from Nashville, including Pastor Steve Berger, who, at the time, led a congregation of more than eight thousand members. Grammy Award–winning artist Michael W. Smith, whom Candy knew but I did not, sang during the event, as did Ricky Skaggs, an award-winning member of the Country Music Hall of Fame. Ricky and I knew each other casually but not well. Consequently, I didn't draw any great nerve-soothing solace by having some Tennesseans on the program. Although the Nashville group served well, their efforts produced few rumbles among the massive crowd on the Mall.

During the weekend, it seemed we repented of our actions and attitudes, and we apologized to every minority group anyone could drum up. But it struck me how little genuine repentance there was to God. I attended Friday's spectacle and left perplexed.

I was scheduled to speak on Saturday evening, near the close of the event. Saturday morning, Burton Gaar and I went back to the Mall and stayed till afternoon and left before I'd had enough. I had been asking God what He wanted me to speak about, but I had received no word. Nothing. I had zero leading about what I was to share and no unction from His Spirit. "Let's go back to the hotel for a while," I said to Burton. We walked out of The Return and headed to our hotel.

Later that afternoon, I went outside and walked along the bank of the Potomac River and up and down some of the streets in our nation's capital. I sought the Lord's guidance as I walked, but I still didn't sense His leading. I had nothing, and it was nearing the time for us to go back for the evening session. I changed my clothes and put on a black shirt and a pair of black jeans. Burton dressed as decked out as Burton normally gets—a casual pair of gray jeans, a T-shirt, and sneakers.

I caught a glimpse of the National Mall as we rode back to the event. The crowd had greatly diminished from a few hours earlier when the renowned Rabbi Cahn had stirred the audience with his challenging message. Now, the Mall was practically empty compared to what it had been Friday evening and Saturday morning.

People must have already gone home, I thought. *The people stayed for the better-known speakers who addressed a big crowd, and now I will be looking at an empty lawn!* I figured that I'd be speaking to a few faithful and to the tourists at the Washington Monument.

We exited the sponsors' van and went inside the green-room tent to await my time to speak. I didn't know anyone there, although I later discovered that several people in the tent were known to millions of other people. No doubt, I was unknown to them as well. After all, just a few weeks earlier, a grand total of eighty-three people had shown up at our Sunday morning church service in Nashville. Clearly, I was not a household name to most of America or even to most Christians. I understood that, so I simply kept to myself in the speakers' tent. I wasn't nervous but I wasn't totally calm either, since I had no clue what I was going to speak about. As my time approached, one of the leaders came and found me. He said, "We're going to bring you up to the side of the stage. Then, when it's your time to speak, we'll move you to the other side."

"Okay, fine. Thank you," I replied. Burton and I followed him to the location he indicated. I sat down and watched, trying to get a sense of what God was doing. A man was exhorting the crowd, but it was difficult to hear what he was saying because of the backstage commotion. The audience seemed quiet and unresponsive. The evening skies were already dark, and the crowd had been on the Mall for more than nine hours that day. Earlier, the audience had heard messages from world-renown speakers and familiar personalities, people such as Pat Boone, Kathie Lee Gifford, and

Rick Scarborough, president of Recover America. Everyone seemed tired and sluggish, ready to go home.

A pastor whom I did not know prayed right before me. As he did, the stage manager came and ushered me to the other side of the stage, where I sat on a stool by myself. "You're up next," a female stagehand said. "In two minutes, you'll go on. Watch that red light. When it comes on, that means it is time for you to conclude. Don't go over that, or we'll turn your microphone off."

"Okay," I said. I still had no leading from the Holy Spirit. I figured, *I'll just pray and sit down.*

It was about that time that I received a text message from Phil Cappuccio wishing me well and promising to pray for me. I quickly responded, "I've got nothing. It's going to be really good or really bad."

From somewhere offstage, I heard the stage manager say to me, "You're on. Remember to keep an eye on the red light." I stepped briskly to the podium in front of the enormous crowd that now numbered about 130,000 people on the National Mall, with millions more watching online. I still had nothing prepared to say, but as I leaned into the podium and opened my mouth, completely uncertain of what—if anything—might come out, the Holy Spirit hit me, and I boldly spoke, releasing the word of the Lord, saying what came to my heart and mind.

I kept my head down as I began to speak:

"By the authority of the Holy Ghost, we take dominion today over the powers of darkness that have ruled over our nation, and we command that they be broken in the name of Jesus. For this is the hour of the church," says the Lord, "and not the hour of man. And by the end of this year," says God, "the greatest outpouring that you have ever seen is going to hit the United States of America."

I heard a stirring among the crowd in front of me as people cheered in agreement. I continued:

Starting January 20 in this year, hallelujah, God is going to begin to declare that there is a release of an unprecedented move of the Holy Ghost like we've never seen in our lifetime. Thus sayeth God, "I'm coming after the strongholds that have ruled over this nation for decades, and I am pulling them down by the power of the Spirit of God."

I heard the crowd cheering, but I kept speaking the word that seemed to almost bubble out of me with an increasing intensity.

"For the violence that you see in the land and the roaring that you hear over our nation is demon spirits that are crying out because the angels of the Lord have come to silence them for this hour. And just as the world has put a mask on the church and just as the world has put a muzzle on the people of God— the spirit of intimidation that has risen against the church—I, the Lord thy God, now am going to take that spirit, and I am going to put it on the world, and the heavens that have been brass," says the Lord, "I am breaking by the power of the Holy Ghost. For four years," saith God, "from 2021 to 2024, this is the last final harvest," saith God, "that is going to hit this church."

I felt the power of God surging through me, and my voice raised in intensity and tone as I declared,

"No demon will be able to stop the glory of the Lord that is coming. Get ready," says the Lord, "for the holiness of God is coming up in this hour. And I, the Lord thy God, will take no back seat to a man. For what I'm getting ready to do," says the Lord, "will not be known by personality or name, but it will be known by the power of the Holy Ghost."

I felt almost as though I was in a trance as I spoke in a more rapid-fire manner, louder and faster, with more urgency.

"I'm going to pull down strongholds over this nation! Sports will not recover, though they say they will; theaters are going to remain empty," saith God. "And the church is going to begin to fill up. And the glitter of sin that has drawn the sinner to the world is now going to be tarnished. And I'm going to cause the church," saith the Lord, "to rise to her feet. There is a *roar* of the Lion of Judah," saith God.

I heard the crowd in front of me roaring as well; I kept my eyes straight ahead and continued delivering God's message.

"I am going to release divine healing upon the nation. I am also coming after a generation of young people that have never been in church, never known God. I'm going to invade the homosexual community, and I am going to set them free by the power of the Holy Ghost. There is anointing," saith the Lord, "that I am releasing over this nation. Just as the laws have come out of this city in the natural," saith God, "so now is there a law being released out of heaven that says My church will not be silent, for I am raising up, hallelujah, mighty men."

I raised my head a bit and heard the crowd thundering all over the National Mall. My head had been tilted slightly downward as I spoke, my eyes focused intently. Suddenly, I heard a loud roar from the crowd, and when I lifted my gaze, I saw that thousands of people on the Mall were standing with their hands raised heavenward, shouting to God and praising Him. I wasn't preaching hard as I prophesied, yet I had a calm authority and firmness about my voice. I continued speaking under the anointing of the Holy Spirit. I sensed His presence and knew that this was not me merely speaking off the cuff. Anyone who ever has spoken with the anointing of God can tell the difference when something beyond ordinary human effort is involved. That was definitely the case here. I continued:

"For the spirit of Jezebel has ruled over this nation for a century, but I have raised up an Elijah anointing," saith God, "that's going to break the spirit of Jezebel, and there's going to be peace in the land; there's going to be silence among the liberals," saith the Lord, "and I'm going to put a roar in the mouth of My people. Even to the age of young five- and six-year-olds, the glory of God is getting ready to come down upon this nation. Give a shout," saith the Lord!

I could feel the words pouring out of me with supernatural power and intensity. The crowd was on its feet and was roaring.

"For I have not forgotten thee. I will never leave thee. I will never forsake thee. In 1906, holiness preacher William Seymour said this: 'There is another revival coming in about one hundred years. And the Blood line is going to cross the color line.'"

Hear God today: This is not about color. This is not about culture. This is about the church. And God said, "The church is My body. So today I release healing into you. I release a spirit of boldness upon you. Rise up," saith God.

"Whatever you bind, I will bind! Whatever you loose, I will loose. For greater is He who is in you than he that is in the world. There is a liberty," saith the Lord. "I am releasing over this land, and it is a harvest of souls. Your churches are going to fill up. Your children are going to praise the Lord. Your bodies are going to be healed, because I declare it," says God.

"And it shall be done," saith God."

• • •

I finished speaking even before the red light came on. Someone later told me that I had spoken for only four minutes and twenty seconds. A mighty roar continued to rise from the crowd on the Mall—not in praise of me but in humble awe in the presence of our God. It was a sound I will never forget.

I felt exhausted but exhilarated, as though Someone had turned me upside down, drained out everything that was within me, and then refilled me with the peace of God. It did not even occur to me that some of the things I had prophesied that night were precisely what God had revealed to me in a dream more than thirty years earlier. Now, I was the old man in the vision, proclaiming, "The Lion of Judah will roar again!"

When I was done, I simply turned and walked offstage in the direction from which I had come. A stagehand who had been working as a sound engineer for the event all weekend ran over to me. "Oh, my!" he gushed. "That was really powerful!" He vigorously shook my hand as he spoke.

I thanked him and went around to the other side of the stage, where I reunited with Burton. Together we descended the steps from the elevated stage. Burton later told me, "Before you started, few people onstage were paying attention; everyone was busy talking among themselves. But when you started, everyone shut up. And several people asked, 'Who is that speaking?'"

God had chosen that moment to speak through me, and apparently it had moved those people. They recognized that something different was happening.

Burton and I went back through the staging area to the greenroom to pick up my bag. Ricky Skaggs was still there, and he walked over and hugged me. "Brother, that reminds me of old-time Pentecost," he said.

I thanked him as several other people expressed their gratitude for the message. Nobody asked, "What does this mean?" or "How will this word be fulfilled?" The message, apparently, was obvious enough for all to understand. Afterward, Burton and I made a hasty exit and headed toward the street, hoping to get a taxi back to our hotel. I was scheduled to preach in Nashville the following morning, and we were already confirmed on a predawn flight, so we did not remain for the end of the event. A number of people made kind comments or tried to talk with me as we walked by, so I nodded in appreciation, but I kept moving.

I had no idea at the time that the word the Lord had given me would reach at least 110 countries. Millions of people viewed it online in the months following the event. Some estimates say that more than a billion people have now heard the word that I delivered that evening at The Return.

As leader of the Church of God (Cleveland, Tennessee), Tim Hill put the message out on the Internet. His social media received more than two million hits gushing about The Return, particularly about the message God had me share.

Burton and I arrived back in Nashville by 8:00 a.m. on Sunday, and we went straight to the church, where we arrived in time for the service. Meanwhile, my phone was blowing up with messages about the word I had delivered.

I knew something significant had happened, but I had no idea how enormous the ongoing impact might be.

Not all the response I received was positive. One disturbing call came from a Christian leader for whom I had always had great respect. I don't know how he got my number (we had never had any previous phone conversations), but a few days after The Return, this minister called me directly on my cell phone. I was surprised but pleased to hear from him.

"I saw what you did at The Return," he began. Although we had met previously, we really didn't know each other well, and had no formal relationship, but almost immediately, he began to correct me—and continued to do so for nearly forty-five minutes. "You inferred that for there to be an end-time revival, Donald Trump had to be president. You don't need to make the church feel that for there to be a revival, the nation needs to put Donald Trump back in office," he said.

I had no clue what the man was talking about. Although The Return took place in September 2020 and the upcoming presidential election had loomed over the event like a gathering storm cloud, I had not remotely mentioned President Trump or addressed him in any way. Yes, I had called the church to get clean, and declared that the Lion of Judah was ready to roar again, but I had not referred to President Trump in any specific way during my time behind the microphone.

This man continued talking to me in a rebuking sort of tone, and during that entire time, I spoke for less than two minutes. I was never so sorely disappointed in a person I had admired so greatly.

There was nothing I could do to placate him. I could not have changed the message God had given me to speak, even if I had wanted to do so. I had learned that lesson years earlier. My priority was not to please people, or even other preachers or prophets, but to be a vessel through which the Lord could speak. Still, I was thankful that this preacher's opinions did not reflect those of the majority of people, who were positively impacted by the message I had delivered.

CHAPTER 28

Something Must Be Going On

THE SOUND THAT ERUPTED FROM THE PEOPLE on the National Mall at The Return will remain in my heart and mind forever.

Perhaps more importantly, though, the responses we received in emails and letters from people from all over the United States and from many locations around the world were truly astounding. Most of those letters said something like, "Thank you for giving me hope."

Following The Return, I went back to work in Nashville as usual, preaching and praying at our warehouse church just as I always did. Like many other churches, we had conducted mostly online services during the shutdowns and quarantines of the first few months of the COVID-19 pandemic. During that time, we had rebranded our church name and now called ourselves Regeneration Nashville. Occasionally, someone might mention to me something about my message at The Return, but for the most part, we carried on in the normal fashion. We celebrated Thanksgiving and Christmas with our eighty or so parishioners and planned to continue our routine into the coming new year of 2021.

But on Sunday morning, December 27, as Candy and I arrived at the church around 9:30 for a 10:30 worship service, we both noticed the long line of automobiles on the road leading to the business park where the warehouse was located. Cars snaked down the road for nearly half a mile. "What are all these cars doing here on a Sunday?" Candy asked. "Something must be going on at the business park."

It was nearly an hour before the service was scheduled to begin, and the building was already packed with people. Candy's face wrinkled in pleasant surprise and her eyes opened wide as she walked into my office. "What is going on?" she asked.

"Carmel, I don't know," I replied. "I'm as shocked as you are."

It was a mere two days after Christmas, normally one of the most sparsely attended church services of the year, so I couldn't fathom the fact that the building was jammed full.

When we opened the service that morning, I quipped to the congregation, "Where did all of you people come from?"

Not only had they shown up, but they were enthusiastic, standing on their feet and worshipping the Lord, their hands raised, their voices shouting His praises.

I wasn't used to that at our little warehouse church.

We had a marvelous service that morning doing what we normally would any Sunday, starting by taking time for our musicians and singers to lead us in praise and worship. After about forty-five minutes, I stood to preach in my normal fashion.

I realized that all these people were a ripple effect of The Return. Apparently, during the Christmas vacation, many of them had discovered me online and responded by coming to Nashville in droves.

In many ways, I was more surprised by what happened on December 27 than I was by what had happened at The Return. When I walked in to see our building packed with people, I was overwhelmed.

I had prophesied several years prior to that morning that one day such a thing would happen—although I had no idea how or when—and now it had come to pass. For three years, with fewer than one hundred people sitting in the room, I had given several prophetic words such as, "The Lord says that there will come a day, unless you show up early, you won't get a seat because the building will be jammed and the cars will be lined up down the road."

It seemed impossible at the time, but I believed what God had said. No doubt, some people in our congregation may have said amongst themselves, "Oh my. Kent has really lost it now. Look, the room is half empty. You can show up a half hour late and still find a seat. But Kent is saying a day is coming when the place will be packed. Surely, he is either naive or misguided."

But I wasn't.

I spoke what I believed God wanted me to say even though it seemed to defy all logic.

And now it had happened.

The following Sunday, we didn't do anything differently, yet more than 350 people showed up. I wondered when the crowds might diminish or even disappear.

That didn't happen. Instead, the people kept coming. Our attendance increased by about a hundred people each week.

A month after the first explosion of new people attending, we had 526 people at the warehouse. It was packed to capacity, and we set up rows of chairs and a large screen to accommodate the people crowded into the lobby. Week after week, I wondered whether I would walk out from behind the curtain and find only a tiny group of people again. That didn't happen. Candy also confessed, "For the first few months after The Return, while driving to church each week, I was literally terrified, wondering if or when we might go back to the 'usual.'"

We never did.

I didn't feel it was incumbent on me to prepare more diligently or to seek some new sort of truth that might keep the people coming. Quite the opposite. I often wondered if what was happening was simply a flash in the pan, that one day we'd come to church and the warehouse would be largely empty. It took me several months before I realized that these folks weren't going anywhere.

Indeed, they kept coming, at first an hour before service time, then even earlier. Often, if a married couple didn't arrive early enough, there were not two adjacent chairs where the husband and wife could sit together. People came from miles around; many came from various states. The big difference was that they came expecting that God was going to meet their needs, that He could and would perform a miracle if necessary. They felt strongly that they needed to be there, in His presence. They came with a wide variety of needs and kept on coming.

The warehouse could seat more than 250 people comfortably. Prior to my appearance at The Return, the room we used as a sanctuary had plenty of leftover seating available. But on December 27, we continued putting out chairs; from then on, we lined the walls with folding chairs, squeezing in seats everywhere, in any space we could find. Our good friend Sonya Isaacs said, "We have about seventy chairs in our basement. They aren't the same color as the ones you have, but you are welcome to them." We took Sonya's offer, and there were still not enough chairs or space to accommodate the crowds. The lobby was always crammed full of people, and they didn't mind sitting in the overflow section. They simply wanted to be there.

At the close of the service, while I prayed for people in the sanctuary, Candy and our son Josh went out to the lobby and prayed for people there. They recruited elders and deacons and several other people from our congregation who knew how to address the deep spiritual needs people brought with them— everything from a desperate need for physical healing to deliverance from demonic oppression or possession. We prayed for everyone who asked, and the ministry continued to thrive, growing more numerous almost each week.

I was keenly aware that apart from God's divine plans, I should never have been a speaker at The Return. Even afterward, multitudes of people commented on social media, asking, "Who in the world is Kent Christmas? Where did he come from? Why haven't we heard of him before?"

I was still me, still doing what I had always done. But suddenly, the audience had expanded exponentially.

It was an odd transition for us. Candy and I had lived rather quietly and frugally for years, and we were content and happy, even though we constantly scratched to eke out a living. Now, almost overnight, we went from receiving meager offerings to having an abundance. We had never asked for money, and still haven't, but it was as though the floodgates of heaven had opened and God poured out financial blessings such as we had never before seen.

In 1994, Candy and I had filed our income taxes based on a yearly income of around $8,000—filing jointly! Now, suddenly, from that last Sunday in December 2020, our coffers filled continually. It was as though God were saying, "These blessings are rewards for all the years of sacrifice."

In a similar way, we felt released to focus more on God and what He was saying in and through us, rather than simply trying to persuade people to attend church services. For years, Candy and I had felt as though we were oxen pulling a cart, begging and dragging people to church. "Please come join us," we'd implore. "Please come to pray." When we had only eighty people, we needed everyone to faithfully attend. Some members of our congregation yawned and responded, "Well, maybe. We'll come if we feel like it, as long as we don't get company, or there's nothing to watch on television, or something else doesn't come up." Now, suddenly, people needed to get to the church early or they would not be able to find a seat— and even then, few empty seats were available.

Despite COVID-19, as Easter 2021 approached, the sanctuary was full, and we packed 126 people into our warehouse *lobby*. We believed that we had to take special steps to accommodate the crowds of people we anticipated might come to celebrate the resurrection of our Lord. We struck an agreement with the leaders of a large sister church in our area that could seat nearly three thousand people. Cornerstone Church—only a few miles from where Candy and I had lived for years—was willing to rent their facilities to us at three o'clock on Easter Sunday afternoon.

People came from miles around, and a number of people came from neighboring states. "We found you on the Internet after we saw you on The Return," more than a few visitors told us. Some came to visit; many came to stay. In the weeks and months following, some people were so hungry to hear from God, they literally moved their families from out of state to the Nashville area so they could be a more active part of Regeneration Nashville. People came to Tennessee from Idaho, Minnesota, Virginia, Texas, and New York. One woman sold her home in Alaska and moved to Nashville to join our church.

These days, we have nearly one thousand people in the church sanctuary. Burton Gaar, our director of broadcasting, told me recently that we now have three thousand eight hundred people who have joined our church, and more than twelve thousand people gave financially to our ministry in 2021. Our services now go into one hundred countries or more every week. It is God's sovereignty doing this phenomenal work. I know better than to think it is about me!

I continue to do the same thing, preaching the same way on the same biblical truths. We don't hawk "spiritual" items such as medallions, oil, prayer cloths, or any other spiritual accoutrements (although we do have a line of products such as shirts, music, and books). We don't beg for money, but people give generously.

Two years earlier, in February 2019, we experienced an uprising by three leaders in our church that broke our hearts and nearly killed us. It devastated me almost as much as going through a divorce. At the time, we had about seventy-eight people regularly worshipping with us on a Sunday morning. I didn't know if we would survive, so I considered retiring from the church.

Now, both the church and my ministry known as Kent Christmas Ministries International were bursting at the seams, and there seemed to be no end in sight. Every week, people showed up, and beyond merely attending, they gave of themselves, generously offering their time, talents, and treasures. We received donations, not simply from residents in our city but from people across the country. It was exciting, and we had to make rapid adjustments. Our newfound prosperity allowed us to hire dedicated, competent staff members who possessed attitudes of excellence and used their talents and gifts to take portions of our ministry to levels we had never before considered. Besides enjoying the results of their giftings, these new coworkers set Candy and me free to focus on the Lord and what He wanted us to do next. We felt less encumbered overall.

The most astounding aspect of this new phenomenon was that I wasn't doing anything different from what I had been doing for years. I was exactly the same. I preached no new content or themes in my messages; I presented no new, recently discovered truths; nor did I speak in a new style, tone of voice, or in a prophetic form. Yet the Holy Spirit showed up and continued to work in and through us, and miracles took place.

Occasionally, in the midst of my prepared message, God would speak through me prophetically, mostly to the church rather than to individuals, and usually in a forthtelling mode, not necessarily in a predictive sense of prophecy. But we didn't center our services on that, and we made no attempt to build our church on the prophetic. The church was built on Jesus and His Word. And the overflow continued.

Suddenly, I was no longer invisible. In fact, people now recognized me any time Candy and I went outside of our home. After The Return, we were at a mall in Nashville one day, and Candy had gone upstairs to a store she wanted to visit, while I remained on the first floor by myself. Before long, some people noticed me.

"Excuse me, are you Kent Christmas?" one woman asked.

"Yes, I am," I replied.

"Can we get a picture with you?"

"With me?" I could not imagine why they would want a photograph with me, but I was glad to comply.

"Yes, I've watched you online."

I looked up and saw Candy looking down over the railing. She was chuckling. She knew how awkward and uncomfortable I felt with people recognizing me.

Candy and I had gone from nearly losing our home to suddenly having enough to purchase a new home with spacious property. For twenty-five years, we had driven around the Nashville area, declaring and believing that one day we were going to have a large, beautiful home with enough land that our children could build homes nearby if they chose to do so. All the while, for most of those years, we were broke. We couldn't afford the electric bill at one of those huge houses.

The Lord confirmed our faith, and now we saw His promises fulfilled, almost overnight.

CHAPTER 29

Blessing Others

SINCE GOD HAD BLESSED US SO ABUNDANTLY at Regeneration Nashville, we wanted to be a blessing to other churches, so we decided to hold a pastors' conference and invite spiritual leaders from all across the country to gather in Nashville for a time of spiritual encouragement. We called the event Elijah Co, a conference founded in the prophetic ministry demonstrated most powerfully in the Bible by the prophet Elijah.

For the first Elijah Co, we invited popular prophetic speaker Dutch Sheets to minister to the group of pastors and evangelists and their spouses that assembled at a local hotel ballroom. Since we had no precedent, we wondered how many people would show up. More than five hundred did, most of them hungrily seeking a fresh touch from God. I wanted to pour into them and encourage them. "You just need to be consistent and faithful in what you are doing," I told them. "I lived where you do—for decades. And I want to tell you that this stuff we believe really works."

I spoke to the ministers from three passages of Scripture, beginning with Luke 10:2, where it says the harvest is plentiful but the laborers are few, so pray for the laborers. I then turned to John 4:35, which reveals an important truth: Don't keep saying that the harvest is coming; it is already here! The harvest is prepared; millions of people around the world are ready to receive the gospel. I also looked at Matthew 13, a profound passage that is so relevant for our time. Jesus told His disciples that the "field" is the world. Certainly, it is important to find the sphere of influence in which we are to work. You will not be successful if you attempt to work in an area over which God has given you no authority. Prophecy can be released only by the unction of the Holy Ghost. But there is a place in the field for each of us.

> Yes, there is a harvest at the end of the age in which the reapers are the angels, but there is also a harvest in which you and I are involved. We are now in an age where everything that has been planted is about to come up.
>
> Certainly, there will be wolves in the midst of the harvest time. An angelic army will deal with the wolves, so I believe there will be deaths of people who have stood in the way of God's harvest and the final, huge ingathering of souls. But I also believe we are going to come into the greatest season of joy because of this harvest.
>
> As the harvest unfolds, God will release three things: wealth, fame (in the sense that He will

uncover people previously unknown), and power to His designated laborers. We need to rid ourselves of a poverty mentality. If God calls us to do something, He will provide what we need to accomplish His plans.

Sadly, most people, even sincere Christians, can't handle wealth or fame, and they abuse power because they have never been tested by suffering. The only way you are ready for wealth is to live in lack until you learn how to be content even without money, or attention, or supernatural manifestations, and to have victory even in the midst of poverty—when you learn to have victory without abundance and you can still praise God.

I noticed a number of the pastors nodding their heads, but others were gazing at me quizzically, as though saying, "Come on, Kent. You are pastoring a large church now and people all over the world know your name. It's easy for you to say these things now." So I wanted to assure them that I understood their struggles.

I told them about attending a pastors' conference and not having enough money to stay at a beautiful hotel such as the one in which we were meeting. I couldn't afford to dine in the hotel restaurant with the other ministers, so I slipped out to my van and ate lunch meat sandwiches from the cooler I had brought along. Again, I could see several of the pastors nodding their heads as I told the story. A few gazed at me in astonishment.

"God brought me to a place where money no longer controlled my joy," I told them, "and I learned to walk in victory without money. I have money now, but it is not the source of my joy. It won't stop me from praying, nor will it cause me to forsake God. I learned how to have joy when I didn't have it, so when prosperity came, it didn't change me."

I then reminded the ministers of Philippians 4:12, where Paul said, "I know how to be abased, and I know how to abound" (NKJV). To be abased means to be ranked below others who are being promoted or elevated. It means to have a modest opinion of oneself.

"Everybody that God is going to use in the final harvest will have learned how to live triumphantly and to trust God when they were abased."

I told the pastors that I knew what it was like to preach hard, to study for hours, and to have only seventeen people show up for the midweek service. I could see in the faces of some of the ministers that they could identify with what I was saying.

My wife and I came to the place where if we were in the will of God, it was enough. When life and ministry don't give you what you expect, it will either make you bitter or drive you into the arms of the Father. And you never know when God is going to flip the switch; He doesn't tell you.

The reason I'm telling you this is because a lot of you are pastoring churches that are small. But you have to reach a place where "smallness" does not drive you from your calling. If that is what the Father has called you to do, when you function in your gift, you can do it with all your heart and strength.

God rewards faithfulness, but you will never be successful if you give in to weariness and accusations against God.

Our attitude needs to be, "If this is what you have called me to do, Lord, I'll do it."

If you can't learn to have victory in anonymity, if God gives you sudden exposure, it will kill you. As you go to the cross and die to yourself, fame doesn't matter anymore.

My prayer these days is, "I'll be as famous as You need me to be, Lord." But to be truthful, I enjoy being alone. If you've never gone through the process of suffering, if being famous is your driving force, it will make you compromise your principles. Promotion without God's favor will cause you to take shortcuts. Jesus wasn't looking to be famous; He wanted to be in the presence of His Father. Everyone has a season in their lives. I didn't understand that for a long time. I thought that if I lived a holy life, God would promote me. For most of my life, He didn't. That was frustrating to me, but when God says it is time, you will find that things work.

I once heard the popular author T. D. Jakes offer a key insight when he said, "You see our success now, but you are seeing the end of the movie. You didn't see the beginning of the story."

Now, I understood.

"Ten years ago, nobody wanted to hear my kind of preaching," I admitted to the ministers. "Now, I turn down invitations every week because I can't handle so many requests. What am I doing differently? Nothing. But now it is the time."

Many of the laborers that God is raising up have never been known previously, even within the Christian community. An older generation of leaders is basically done, and God is using a new group. It is their time. In an emotional moment, I confided to the pastors,

> Maybe you don't know my story, but I preached for fifty years before I ever saw God give me success. So I learned to find my fulfillment in my relationship with the Lord and not in my ministry. Whenever your joy comes more from your gifting and being used than your relationship with Christ, you will have a frustrated life.
>
> The most outstanding aspect of the ministry of Jesus was His compassion. He was not ministering to people because He wanted something from them. He was ministering so He could give something good to them.
>
> Compassion is not merely a gift. It is something that is experienced, and it only comes through suffering. Some Christians believe that if you are properly serving the Lord, you will never suffer. Everything in life is going to be easy. But that is not biblical.
>
> If you are going to shake hell, and if you are going to bring in the harvest, you must learn to live where you are going to lead. You will never be able to lead where you have never been.

If you are called of God, then God will come through for you. If God's hand is on your life and has called you to pastor, and you have only forty people, then you do it with joy and do it with His power. When God hears you preach in the midst of pain, He responds by saying, "I'm going to use that person for My glory."

We must accept the sovereignty of God. Would I have liked to have pastored a church of a thousand people when I was thirty? Absolutely, but I didn't have the maturity; I hadn't died enough. I wasn't ready.

It can happen overnight. Don't think that you and I are in different leagues. We are not. I've been *you*. I can tell where you are, because I was your neighbor for most of my life.

The harvest we are to bring in must be done by human laborers, not angels. And Jesus said, "I'm going to allow you to go into fields that you didn't plant." The harvest has already been planted over the previous decades by men and women faithfully sharing the gospel. Now, it is time to bring in the harvest from the seed that others have planted. The seeds planted by others have come to maturation. The harvest is here, and we are in the middle of it.

Many of us thought we were failures because we couldn't see the harvest coming in. And God has shown us, "It wasn't about you. I was preparing laborers for the harvest."

I desperately wanted the pastors and their families to understand that their efforts mattered, that they were not laboring in vain, even if they did not see large numbers of people in their churches.

> You've lived in frustration, anonymity, and without money, and you've asked God, "Lord, what are You doing?" and He says, "I've been preparing you to be a laborer who has compassion."
>
> How do you get compassion? You have to experience the pain of the people you are getting ready to see get saved. God comforts us in our troubles so we can comfort others with the same sort of comfort He has given to us [see 2 Corinthians 1:4].
>
> I have been able to minister to people who have gone through divorce, because I've been there. I can identify with their pain. I can tell you about the electricity being shut off in your house because you couldn't afford to pay the bill. I know how despondent that can make you feel. I've experienced it.
>
> The key is not to allow the person in need to pull you down, but for you to lift that person up. If you have fought cancer and God has healed you, it is easy for you to look at someone who has been diagnosed with cancer and say, "Honey, God is going to heal you." And when the person looks back at you and asks, "How do you know?" you can say, "Because He has healed me."

I shared one of my frustrations with the group.

God doesn't always explain Himself; He doesn't tell us in advance what He has planned for us. The just must walk by faith, not by sight. But God can put such love in you that you can say, "Nothing will separate me from the love of God."

We've had people tell us at Regeneration, "What you are experiencing is only a flash. It is temporary success. Sooner or later, it will all go away." If it does, okay, but I'm going to keep doing what I'm doing, because my relationship with God is not based on my ministry—my ministry flows out of my relationship with God.

When I went through divorce after fifteen years in the ministry, although I was anointed of God to preach, I was still a hard man. I had little mercy and little compassion. I was just noise without love.

When God broke me, I discovered an important truth: the more resistant you are to the will of God and the harder your spirit is, the stronger the blow God will use to break you. I was hard, and it took a heavy blow from God to bring me to the place of brokenness.

But when I found that place of brokenness with God that I had never known before, God put a prophetic mantle on me. That's important because the two go together. Prophets who have no mercy will wound or possibly even kill the body of Christ, God's people.

Now, I weep all the time. I understand the suffering that people go through ... I'm grateful for God's blessings, but I'm even more thankful that God made me *nice*. He took away my heart of stone; He used the "oil of His Holy Spirit" to soften my heart, and He gave me a heart more like His, a heart of love and compassion.

That was a big deal to me. I firmly believe that we will be unable to make a difference in the lives of people who are hurting if we cannot relate to what they are going through.

You will never be a laborer in God's final harvest without compassion. And you will not have compassion without first being broken by God. You can gauge your maturity with the Lord by how rapidly you say yes when He tells you to do something. Now, when the Lord gives me instructions, I say yes as quickly as possible. Why? Because I know I am going to do it eventually anyhow. I might as well agree with Him quickly.

Understand, not everyone is meant to lead a thousand or five thousand people. Some people are meant to influence fifty people. You will always walk in more joy working with fifty people than you will with five hundred if that is not where God put you. It is important to be content wherever God has placed you and to serve Him there with all your heart.

I went for a lot of years trying to make things happen. The early disciples rejoiced that they were counted worthy to suffer for His name. It has only been in the past few years that I realized it was an honor that God allowed me to suffer for Him on behalf of Christ.

God gives the most difficult ministry assignments to the people He trusts the most. He knows they will complete the task; they won't run from it. If God takes you through great suffering, it is because He values you and trusts you. It doesn't mean that you love pain; it means that you love the Lord.

God has prepared you as His laborer to be thrust into the harvest that He has been getting ready, the harvest that is here. People who do not pray are not laborers; people who merely have gifts are not laborers. People who have money without concern for the lost are not laborers. The laborers that God will use are those who have concern and compassion. Keep in mind: God does not judge on the outward appearance; He judges the heart.

In closing my session, I reminded the pastors of Stephen, one of the deacons who waited on tables and took care of the widows in the early church, the first martyr mentioned in the New Testament. He was a good man, full of faith and filled with the Holy Spirit of Jesus, who boldly spoke up when he had opportunity. But the crowd did not respond positively. In fact, the opposition picked up rocks and began hurling them at Stephen. As he was being pummeled by rocks, being stoned to death, Scripture calls attention to the fact that in heaven, Jesus was not seated at the right hand of God, but He was standing up and Stephen saw Him (see Acts 7:55)!

Stephen died an ignominious death, but that was not the end of the story. Watching nearby was a brilliant young man who knew the Old Testament. He was guarding the coats of the men who were stoning Stephen. His name was Paul, and his life would never be the same after witnessing the real thing in a man willing to give his life for Christ. Paul would not only be converted shortly after that, and become the greatest missionary in the early church, but would go on to write much of the New Testament.

"When the rewards are passed out in heaven, I believe much of Paul's reward will be shared with the fellow the world never knew—Stephen. But Jesus knew him, and Jesus gave him a 'standing ovation' in heaven," I said.

I encouraged the pastors to work with that attitude, to please Jesus.

Later that year at our Fresh Fire Conference, the event moved along beautifully, with every speaker presenting relevant messages, until, on Saturday, our friend Pastor Val Treese suddenly appeared to have a heart attack. We called for an ambulance and the paramedics rushed in and tried to resuscitate Brother Treese. Meanwhile, the conference attendees prayed for him. His face was pale, his body was cold, his eyes were fixed in one position, and the EMTs said, "He's gone. He is dead." I knew that we had a great deal of faith in the crowd, so I went back to where Val was lying, laid hands on him, and slid my body over his, praying and asking God to raise him from the dead. Val stirred and I felt him move. Before long, he was back on his feet.

He preached from his own pulpit the following Sunday. As I write these words, Brother Val is still alive and well.

Jesus said that all things are possible to those who believe.

CHAPTER 30

Healing Happens

THE CHRISTMAS FAMILY HAS LIVED from one miraculous event to another, and Candy and I taught our kids to seek God first, not simply as our "last resort." We were thankful for doctors and nurses and medicines and had no qualms about making use of hospitals and the medical resources available to us, but whenever anyone in our family had some physical ailment, our first response was to ask God for healing.

When Jasmine was nine and Nick about five, Jasmine was playing in the garage with a red aluminum softball bat, hitting golf balls with the bat and sending them soaring. She didn't notice that Nick had moved right behind her and was walking directly toward her when she took a full swing with the bat, smacking him right in the face, crunching his nose, and knocking him instantly to the concrete. His face immediately began swelling and he was bleeding profusely. He lay on his back on the ground silently.

Jasmine ran into the house, screaming, "I didn't mean to do it!"

I could not imagine what had happened, but I hustled out to the garage and found Nick dazed, bleeding, and lying on the garage floor, just as Candy drove up in her car. I said to Candy, "Carmel, we're going to walk this thing out. Either we're going to believe this thing or not. We're going to pray right now."

I scooped him up and we both began to pray for him, declaring healing. I laid my hands on Nicholas and prayed, "Lord, we declare that he will have no broken bones. We declare that he is perfectly fine and that he is healed right now. I declare by faith that he will not have a broken bone."

We rushed him to the hospital, praying all the way. By the time we arrived there, his face was blue and swollen and he looked like a character from a science fiction B-movie.

The doctor took one look at Nick and said, "We don't know what sort of damage is done. His nose is obviously broken. But we need to do an X-ray to make sure there are no shards of bone that could move to his brain and that his skull is not fractured."

We sat and prayed in the waiting area as the doctors took Nick for tests.

The doctor came out after a while, shaking his head. "I don't understand it," he said. "He does not have one broken bone." He promised that Nick would be fine and instructed us to take him home and put some ice on his bruises. Nick came through the ordeal with two black eyes but no broken bones or negative residual effects.

Our kids grew up expecting God to heal and were surprised when He did not. Because of our own experiences, we expected God to heal other people when we prayed for them, according to the instructions in His Word. In a similar manner, whenever Candy or I had a physical problem, we took it first to the Lord, asking Him to touch our bodies with His healing power.

For instance, in 2015 I was scheduled to speak at a church near Atlanta, Georgia, on a Sunday morning, so I planned to make the four-hour drive from Nashville the night before. I had been lifting weights earlier on Saturday as part of my regular workout regimen, when suddenly I felt pain sear through my shoulder. I knew instantly that I had torn a muscle. The pain was excruciating. I felt as if I had been stabbed, and it hurt to breathe. I could barely move my arm and couldn't raise it high enough to wash my hair in the shower.

What could I do? I knew that I had to drive 250 miles and preach the next day.

I recalled a friend who had suffered a similar torn muscle injury, and he had told me that he'd prayed for healing and the Lord had healed him instantly.

I prayed, "Lord, I know You are not a respecter of persons, so I declare in the name of the Lord that my shoulder is healed."

Immediately, I felt a warmth hit me. I lifted my arm, was able to take a shower, and drove to Atlanta to preach pain-free. It was one of the few times in my life when the Lord healed me instantly.

Sometimes God heals instantly; at other times, He uses therapy and doctors, medicine, and other means. The logic is sometimes difficult to understand; His ways are not our ways. Oddly enough, the same fellow whose shoulder had been healed still wore a hearing aid. "I don't know why God has not healed me of my hearing problems," he admitted.

Oral Roberts was frustrated over the people for whom he prayed and were not healed, but the Lord revealed to him, "What about the people who *do* get healed?"

We discovered a principle about healing: do what you are to do—pray and believe—and leave the results up to God.

• • •

A woman named Patti Reavis drove a great distance to bring her husband, Dennis, to attend our fall 2021 conference in hopes that he might be healed. Dennis suffered from severe Parkinson's disease and could barely stand to his feet, much less walk by himself.

I had already completed a time of praying for the sick when Patti struggled to get Dennis to the front of the room, where she told Nicholas of the situation. Nicholas passed the word on to Candy, who asked me, "Can you pray for one more person?" She knew I was already exhausted and had been praying for people for roughly half an hour.

When I looked over to the side of the platform and saw Dennis, I felt overwhelming compassion for him.

"Yes," I said to Candy. "I can pray for one more person."

His family had secured him in a chair, but he slouched backward, all slumped down. Looking at the man, I knew that only God could make him well, and I believed He could. I wrapped my arms around him and tears welled in my eyes. I didn't ask his name; I simply laid my hands on him, prayed for him, and commanded the spirit of Parkinson's disease to leave him. I spoke directly to the disease, not to the man.

The man stiffened and started to shake on the chair, almost causing it to scoot backward.

After I prayed for him, I walked across the platform in the opposite direction from where the man was sitting, with my back turned partially away from him. Just then, I heard a huge roar from the crowd. I turned around and saw that the man had jumped up from the chair and was running back and forth across the platform. He grabbed his wife and they embraced on the stage. They danced all the way across the platform.

He was healed!

The entire episode was captured on video.[8] I'm glad that it was, because skeptics often want to diminish the reality of divine healing, but in this case, the evidence is on video for all to see. I hadn't done anything unusual; I had simply prayed for him in the name of Jesus, and God had done the rest. Still, before Dennis left the platform, he ran back across the stage and hugged me. A sense of joy and wonder pervaded the church, and I was elated as well.

On the other hand, I've prayed with just as much faith and fervor for other people with Parkinson's disease, and they were not healed instantly. I've learned that the healing doesn't depend on me. My responsibility is to pray, believe, and trust God with the results.

During our services at Regeneration, we have witnessed numerous people healed of stage IV cancer. Others whom we have prayed for with equal amounts of faith have not been healed. What makes the difference? We don't know, but we are certain that God honors faith, so we continue to pray for everyone who asks.

People often come to our ministry as a last resort, after they've tried the best that the medical profession can offer and have found no relief. Sometimes I know that they are looking at us as their last hope. That places some pressure on me. Of course, I want all who come to us with a need to be healed. But I also know that nothing about me can heal them. Still, I take a great responsibility for being a clean channel, a pure vessel that the Lord can work through. I don't want anything in my life that might block the flow of God's Spirit using me as a blessing to someone else.

How can you tell if something is blocking the flow of His Spirit in your life? Simple. Just ask Him, "Lord, is there anything in me that displeases You? Are there any sinful actions, attitudes, or thought patterns in me that might disrupt or disqualify me as a vessel of honor that You can use? If there are, please cleanse me of those things right now. I want to be completely Yours, completely clean, and available to You." Otherwise, I can pray the same sort of prayers, but no Holy Ghost power is released, and it all becomes futile and discouraging. When you pray for miracles all the time and none ever happen, that can shake your faith. Perhaps that's why some "faith healers" and evangelists attempt to conjure up their own miracles. Not smart. (Remember Simon the Sorcerer in Acts 8.)

Candy and I have been to meetings where someone claims to operate in the miraculous, but so much of that is chicanery and possibly even spiritual manipulation. We try to get out of there as quickly as we can. We don't want anything to do with such shenanigans.

Either God does the healing or not, but we don't go for nonsense. We don't engage in nonbiblical gamesmanship simply to attract attention or to give people false hope. Our job is to believe, to pray, and to leave the work up to God.

Some people want to "prove" God, or test Him, similar to what Gideon did by laying out a fleece in the Old Testament. Okay, but if we are going to test God, we need to be prepared for Him to test us as well. Be careful what you ask for; if you read Scripture carefully, you'll notice that God's testings usually involve severe emotional or physical pain.

In February 2022, a wheelchair-bound woman named Betty wrote me a sweet letter in which she posed a question: "I want to know if you are going to be at your church on February 27, because if you are, my daughter will bring me from Ohio to Tennessee. I want you to pray for me."

She didn't mention that she was confined to a wheelchair and unable to walk, but her letter touched my heart, so I called her. "I can't believe it's you!" she gushed when I identified myself on the phone. She further expressed her surprise that I would call her personally.

"I received your letter, Betty, asking if we will be at the service on February 27 of this year. The answer is 'Yes, the Lord willing, we will be there.'" I told her, "Betty, you come on. I'm going to be at the church on that Sunday, and when you get here, tell one of the ushers that Pastor Kent said to bring you up to the platform so we can pray for you."

She was elated, and her faith exuded all the way from Ohio to Tennessee.

In late February 2022, her daughter drove Betty from Ohio to Tennessee simply so we could pray for her. Could she have had someone pray for her at her own church? Of course. But something connected her faith with ours, and they felt it was worth the extra effort to make the trip.

When the ushers brought Betty up to the platform, I was surprised. I didn't know that she was confined to the wheelchair. Nevertheless, I was honored to pray for her.

I prayed a simple prayer for Betty, and she stood up in front of her wheelchair. Then she started to walk! She kicked up her leg and walked all the way across the platform.

Betty began crying and laughing at the same time, and the audience erupted in praise to the Lord. Afterward, somebody pushed the wheelchair over toward Betty so she could sit down.

"I don't need that!" Betty exclaimed. "I'm healed!"

God did it. Not me.

I've prayed that same sort of prayer for other people who did *not* get out of their wheelchairs. But I've seen God do so many marvelous things. I know He loves people, so when I pray for someone in need, I expect to see God work.

Truth is, I don't fully understand divine healing—especially why some people are healed and others are not. I know that God can do anything, and as I've studied the New Testament, I've noticed that Jesus healed everyone who came to Him with a need. Everywhere He went, people were healed, except in His hometown of Nazareth, where He did only a few miracles because they did not believe Him or honor Him.

Although I know that Jesus is the Healer, not me, many people believe that if I lay hands on them and pray for them, they will be healed. Some people have driven up to a thousand miles just so I can pray for them in person. I appreciate their faith, and I examine myself and search my soul any time I pray for someone and that person does not get healed. "Lord, is there something in me preventing You from working?" I'll ask. "Am I doing something wrong?"

Most often, that is not the case, and I have to relax and know that He is God and I am not. He is the Sovereign Lord, not me. His ways are not our ways, and His plans are much higher than ours.

Certainly, faith is the crux of the matter—Jesus often told someone, "Your faith has made you whole." So, we know faith is crucial, and yes, it helps to have someone with the gift of healing and people who have faith that God can and wants to heal us. But Jesus promised that wherever two or three of us agree on something in His name, it will be done. So, could God use *you* to pray for someone who needs to be healed of cancer or heart disease or leukemia or AIDS? Absolutely. God will use anybody who doesn't attempt to steal the glory from Him or take the credit for what He does.

For most of our ministry, we had about eighty people attending our church. We haven't started doing anything differently, nor have I been presenting any new biblical truths, yet large numbers of people have started coming, and we have seen miraculous results.

What made the difference?

The only answer I can come up with is that the people who are coming to us with such deep needs also have great faith. They come expectantly, and they go away satisfied, because, as Scripture promises, "Whoever believes in Him will not be disappointed" (Romans 10:11 NASB 1995).

CHAPTER 31

Expecting Life

WE NEVER THOUGHT WE'D HAVE ANOTHER GREAT LOSS in our life. The church was thriving, and our family was prospering. People were being saved; others were being delivered; serious, life-threatening physical ailments were being healed. We were going from blessing to blessing, and life was good. I felt like Abraham after he encountered Jehovah Jireh, "The Lord Provides," on the mountaintop. I certainly didn't think we'd have to go through more heartrending experiences.

But we weren't in heaven yet, and our family was about to walk through one of the darkest, most hellish experiences we could ever imagine.

The horror started late afternoon on January 12, 2022, when our son Josh was picking up his kids. Earlier that day, he had planned to join me in walking a piece of property that Candy and I were considering as a possible purchase. About a half hour drive out of Nashville, the property had a home and a barn already on it. The accompanying land that was available could easily support additional homes for Josh and Carrie, Jasmine and JonMichael, and Nicholas.

The property had piqued our interest when Candy and I had viewed it previously. The woman who owned it had allowed us to walk through the home. Our kids had not seen it, though, so I made arrangements with the real estate agent for all of us to visit when the owner was not at home. I drove out to the property accompanied by Candy and Carrie. Josh planned to join us to look around the property for a possible homesite.

I had called him earlier and said, "We're going out to view the property and see the house. Would you like to come along?" Josh said that he would.

About midday, Josh called me and said, "Dad, I'm sorry. I'm not going to make it out there today. I'm just not feeling up to it, and I have a cough. I'll go out with you next time."

Candy asked Josh, "Are you feeling all right?"

"Yeah, I just feel sleepy," he said. "I don't really feel well today. I'll come out another time."

"Okay," I replied. "I'm excited about you seeing it."

"I love you, Dad," he said.

"I love you, too, son."

In January 2022, our church was engaged in three days of prayer and fasting, voluntarily sacrificing meals to focus our attention on the Lord for a period of time. It was a practice we did at the beginning of each quarter of the year, so it was not unusual. It was the first day of the fast, but Candy and I had already fasted three days during the previous week in addition to three more days prior to the church's fast.

Because we had finished our fast, I planned to grab something to eat before joining Candy, along with members of our congregation, for a time of focused prayer later that evening. Our daughter-in-law, Carrie, planned to meet us at the church, but Josh and Carrie's son Charlie had a guitar lesson that afternoon at Guitar Center, a large music store. Carrie took Charlie for his lesson and Josh kept their younger son, Cash, with him, waiting in the car for Carrie to bring Charlie out, after which Josh planned to take the boys home while Carrie went on to the prayer meeting at church.

Josh pulled the car into the parking lot and kept the engine running to keep warm on that bitterly cold January day. After a while, he fell asleep and started snoring loudly and gurgling.

When Carrie came outside after Charlie's guitar lesson, she found Josh asleep behind the wheel, and Cash was in a huff.

"Mom!" Cash said with frustration in his voice. "Dad is asleep and he won't wake up." In his innocence, he thought his dad was playing a game with him.

But this was no game. Carrie recognized that something was wrong. She tried to awaken Josh, but he was unresponsive. She sent Charlie back into the store to get help, and she then performed CPR until the ambulance came. At 5:00 that evening, Josh was rushed to the emergency room.

Meanwhile, unknown yet to me, Carrie had called Candy, as she was in the front row praying. Candy recalls Carrie speaking rapidly and emotionally: "Mom, the ambulance has just taken Josh to Skyline Hospital. I came out of Guitar Center and he was not responsive. I sent Charlie back into Guitar Center to get a couple of guys to help, and they came and dragged him out of the car. I did CPR on him until the ambulance got here."

"Tell me where you are," Candy said, trying to remain calm.

"I'm at Guitar Center."

"Okay, I'm coming now," Candy replied.

"No, they've already loaded him into the ambulance," Carrie said, "and they are taking him to Skyline. Meet me at Skyline."

I was at Chef's Market around 5:00 p.m. when Candy called and informed me about what had happened. I misunderstood her message and thought that she, Carrie, and Josh were still at Guitar Center, so I raced over to the parking lot, only to discover that none of my family members were there. I called Candy, and she told me that she and Carrie were already at the hospital. I jumped back in the car and rushed to Skyline.

Strict COVID-19 protocols were still in place for medical facilities throughout much of the country in early 2022, so when I arrived at the hospital, a security guard stopped me and would not permit me to enter the building.

Almost immediately, family and friends began showing up and congregating outside the hospital: Nick, JonMichael (Jasmine was in quarantine because she had come down with COVID), Steve and Terri Huffman, Josh and Amy Rodgers, Mike Sircy, Pastor Linda Hilliard, and others. It was freezing cold outside, but the hospital would not allow us into the foyer or main waiting room.

Since this had happened during the restrictive isolations forced on our society by COVID-19, the hospital staff was extremely concerned about protocols and refused to let us in to see Josh. They allowed only one person inside the hospital.

Security permitted Carrie inside only as far as a reception desk so she could provide Josh's insurance information and sign some papers, and then she, too, had to return outside with us in the cold. It was frustrating.

Our distress and confusion were exacerbated by the hospital's adamant refusal to let us inside. For us to even stand outside the hospital in the cold, the guard required that we go through a metal detector, put on masks, sign a document acknowledging that we were in danger, and then go back outdoors.

We stood outside the hospital in the cold and dark for more than two hours. A few of the people in our group were not even wearing winter coats.

As the evening wore on, Candy approached the front desk and said, "I want to know what is going on with Josh Christmas."

"May I ask who you are?" asked the woman at the desk.

"I'm his mom," Candy answered.

"Well, I can't let you in, and I can't tell you anything, but I can tell you that he has vitals. They are not yet stable, but he does have vitals."

Vitals? Of course he has vitals.

We had no idea how serious Josh's condition really was.

The woman said, "They are working on him right now, and when his vitals are stable, I will come find you. But you cannot stay inside the hospital."

Carrie was overwhelmed with emotion concerning Josh and their children. "My boys," she said. "I have to get my boys." The boys had been with Josh when the incident had occurred. After Josh had been transported to the hospital, Carrie's mom, Lilly, had met her, picked up the boys, and taken them to Chick-fil-A to get something to eat and to distract them from worrying about their dad.

"Don't worry about the boys," Candy told Carrie. "I'll go get them and bring them back to you." Candy went to get the boys, and they anxiously told her what had happened. They didn't understand the seriousness of the situation and were frustrated that Josh had been unable to play with them.

"Gigi, my dad was snoring and I couldn't wake him up," Cash told Candy.

"I know, Cash. It's okay. Let's just pray for Daddy."

• • •

After our group had remained outside in the freezing cold for more than two hours, the hospital finally permitted us to enter the building and gather in a small room that had a few seats in it. Some people sat on the chairs, but most of us clustered together on the floor.

After a while, a doctor came in and spoke to us. He did not provide any more information than was necessary. "Josh has suffered a brain aneurism," he said. "A blood vessel burst, and it has occurred at the most critical part of the brain, where the nerves from the spinal cord go up to the brain stem. Because of where it is located at the base of the brain, we cannot do surgery, so we are going to send him to ICU." The doctor did not explain any further.

"We have him stable," he said. "He's going to ICU. You can see him in the morning." He casually raised his hand as if to say, "No questions." Then he repeated, "We'll see you tomorrow."

Living in Nashville, we had several other fine hospitals nearby, so I wanted Josh transferred to Vanderbilt University Medical Center, one of the top hospitals in the country. Skyline was not cooperative, so I called a friend, Dr. Cole Barfield. He talked me down off the ledge and called the hospital, then called me back. "Skyline is really good at dealing with Level V trauma, and I've talked with the neurosurgeon," he said, "and here's what you are dealing with." Dr. Barfield explained a bit about Josh's condition and then continued, "They are not going to be able to do any more at Vanderbilt than what they are doing right there. Probably the best thing is not to move Josh and let them continue to do the treatment that they are doing there."

I thanked him and gathered everyone together to pray for Josh. We asked God to give us calm and peace, and of course we prayed for Josh's healing. Our friends hugged us and each other, and we all planned to return in the morning, believing that everything would be all right.

Candy and I headed for our car when a nurse chased us down, calling out our names. "His COVID test just came back, and he is not going to ICU," the nurse told us, "but he is going to the COVID unit in the hospital, so you will not be able to see him tomorrow."

That put a new wrinkle in the situation.

I asked to speak to the neurologist at the hospital. "Are you sure he has COVID?" I asked.

"We didn't do a rapid test," the neurologist responded. "We did a more thorough test."

"Really? How did you get the results back within sixty minutes?"

He didn't answer. I later heard that the hospital received an additional $3,800 for every positive COVID case they dealt with. I didn't want to think the hospital was being duplicitous, especially with Josh in dire need of assistance, but the thought crossed my mind.

I didn't think that Josh had COVID, but we had no idea what we were dealing with and no way to be certain during the strange, secretive days of COVID-19. Regardless, we felt that Josh may have to remain in the hospital for a few days at the most, and then all would be well.

Our church was already in fasting mode, so we continued praying fervently for Josh's recovery as well as for other needs within our congregation.

I called Josh's mom and informed her of the situation. Ironically, Patti had been scheduled to visit with Josh and our family during Christmastime, but she had contracted COVID and had been unable to come. After her recovery, she rebooked her flight from the West Coast to Nashville and was able to be with us soon after Josh suffered the aneurism.

• • •

When word got out that Josh had suffered a cerebral aneurism, multiple people contacted us or sent notes of encouragement, saying, "I went through something similar. I had a debilitating aneurism, and I went through thirty days of physical therapy, and I'm now back at work, feeling great." Other letters said, "My mom [or son or daughter] experienced something similar, and she woke up after a few days and has done fine ever since."

We appreciated these notes, and they bolstered our faith. Indeed, our faith never wavered. Throughout Josh's hospitalization, we had no doubt that God was going to heal him. We figured that if God had done it for all these other people, of course He would heal Josh.

As we went along, however, the doctors repeatedly gave us mixed opinions. Some said there was no hope for Josh, that he was brain-dead; others said they were going to send him to long-term care—basically, to a nursing home. Still others hinted that they wanted to unplug Josh from life support machines. The mixed communications baffled and concerned us, but we continued praying, believing, expecting Josh to walk out of the hospital.

We were shocked when he didn't. Instead, Josh remained in the hospital for twenty-five days.

During most of that time, Josh was in the COVID unit, so the family members were not permitted in to see him. "You will never see your son again," one of the hospital representatives coldly reported to Candy.

Exasperated, Candy sought help from everyone who had any clout, including people in the office of Tennessee's governor. Governor Bill Lee is an outspoken believer in Jesus, so we hoped that if we could get a message to him, he might understand our plight. The governor had signed a bill stating that a family member of a COVID patient could get in to see his or her loved one. At last, we were allowed in the hospital room to see our son.

The doctor met with us and spoke bluntly. "The only reason Josh is still living is because he is on life support." It was clear that the doctor favored turning off the machines.

As Josh's wife, Carrie bore the burden of dealing with those difficult end-of-life decisions. Candy and I emphasized to Carrie that we would support her decisions, whether it meant keeping Josh on life support machines or turning them off. We did not want to add to Carrie's pain by heaping guilt on her if she decided one way or another.

After more than three weeks with no improvement, Carrie consented to turn off the life support machines. It was a difficult decision, but Candy and I supported her. The doctor came into Josh's room, turned off the machine, and then stood there, waiting for Josh to die.

Prominent healing evangelist and author Andrew Wommack called me precisely at that juncture, just as the machines fell silent. Years earlier, Andrew's own son had been raised from the dead. He had been in a morgue for five hours with a tag on his toe. His body was already turning black. Andrew drove five hours to get there to pray for his son, who miraculously came back to life. I knew that if anyone understood what I was feeling, both the pain and the faith, Andrew did.

"Andrew, I need to know how you prayed, so I can pray over my son."

Andrew understood. "Kent, the moment I laid hands on my son, the color began to return to his skin."

"How long did you pray before you began to see a change?" I asked.

"As soon as I prayed, he immediately began to get his color back," he replied. "It was an almost immediate thing. But you need to know that Josh's will is involved in this."

His will? I thought. *What does his will have to do with anything? He's incapacitated.* I thought I understood what Andrew was saying, but I did not want to even entertain those thoughts, so I rejected his words. I hung up with Andrew, and an hour later, the life support machines remained off, and Josh was still breathing.

The medical personnel seemed almost disappointed that he was still alive. A nurse came in to give Josh a large dose of morphine, which would slow down his organs.

"No," I said. "You can give him morphine, but not that much. If you want to give him morphine every few hours to ease his discomfort, okay, but not that much at one time."

"Well, he's in a lot of pain," the doctor said.

"How do you know he is in pain?" I asked. Josh couldn't speak; he barely moved. His breathing seemed regular, and the monitors showed no disturbances.

A nurse disconnected the feeding tube as well as the saline fluids.

"We're going to move him to comfort care," she said, "and then the whole family can be in there as much as you want." We made the move and Josh's condition remained the same. After a day or two, I said to the head nurse, "You need to hook him up the machines again."

"We can't do that," she replied.

"Why not?" I asked. "You people said he was going to die when you disconnected him from life support and from the feeding tube and saline. But he is still living, so you need to hook him back up to the feeding tube. You can't just starve him to death."

The nurse looked irked. "If we do that, we will need to move him back to ICU or to the COVID unit," she said. "Then you and your family cannot come in to see him."

"You have already told us that you think he is going to die," I repeated. "Why do you care if we have him hooked up to a feeding tube?"

The nurse glared at me, making little effort to hide the exasperated expression on her face. "I'll give you guys a few more hours then," she said. "But since you want him on a feeding tube, I'm going to have to move him back upstairs and you won't be able to see him."

She walked out the door, and that's how she left it.

As the ordeal dragged on, I got to the place where I didn't really want to go to the hospital, sitting there all day long, hour after hour, day after day, with Josh remaining unresponsive. Despite the COVID threats, Carrie, Candy, and I and a few other family members had been going into his hospital room. We played Christian worship music, laid hands on Josh, and prayed for him in the Spirit.

But his condition remained horrendous.

One day, Carrie said, "Pop, I just can't go to the hospital today. Can you go and sit with Josh?"

"Certainly," I said, knowing that it would be heart-wrenching to fulfill her request, but even more so to beg off.

When I walked into Josh's room, the sight sickened me. Even though Josh was forty-three years of age, he was still my boy. My mind repeatedly went back to holding his hand as a little boy, playing ball with him, and relishing other experiences in Josh's childhood. The emotional aspect of twenty-five days of watching our boy die ripped my heart to shreds. Again and again, I silently wailed, *My boy! My son, my firstborn son.*

From his first day in the hospital, the doctors had placed a tracheotomy tube in Josh's throat, but in recent days, they had taken him off life support and the hospital had removed the trach.

Seeing him in that condition was gut-wrenching. The wound was still open where the doctors had removed the trach. All the pungent, grotesque smells emanating from his dying body seemed to ooze from that wound. It was horrific. I was in the room by myself with Josh and I noticed he was gurgling. I moved closer to him. Suddenly, he coughed and blew blood out the tracheotomy slot, splattering blood all over me, including my face, nose, and mouth.

I gazed at my helpless son in the hospital bed. The doctors were giving him no hope of survival, but I still believed that God could heal him regardless.

At one point, Josh was bleeding from every orifice in his body. His tongue hung out of his mouth, and it was black and swollen from where the tongue depressor had been clamped onto it to keep him from biting or swallowing his tongue. The sight was more than we could bear.

Nevertheless, we did not share these details with anyone but family members. The Old Testament prophet Isaiah said that the Messiah, Jesus, would be acquainted with sorrow and grief (Isaiah 53). My life was acquainted with grief, but I did not want to pass that on to others in a negative context.

It is easy for grief to infect a congregation and spread from person to person, resulting in a spirit of gloom. It is difficult to overcome such a pervasive attitude once it has invaded so many hearts. I determined in my heart and mind that I didn't want that to happen to our congregation, so I attempted to maintain "faith" and an upbeat perspective even in the face of overwhelming medical odds. I set my face like a flint to restrain my emotions in front of our fellow believers, and I decided early on that I would not speak publicly about Josh's condition unless I could engender faith. I did not want our family to be discouraged, and I certainly didn't want that spirit of negativity in our congregation.

I recalled in Scripture when David wept after his son Absalom died. Absalom had rebelled against his father, the king, and had gone so far as to have sex out in public with one of David's concubines. He was killed by troops loyal to King David, but when David received the news, he was so stricken with grief, he refused to celebrate his return to the kingdom. Consequently, when the nation could have been celebrating the victory, they wept in shame because they took on what their king expressed.

I refused to let that sort of spirit get loose in our church through our family or me. I knew our grief had to be kept more private for the time being.

Even at home, Candy and I fought to keep our faith strong. One day, Candy was struggling so hard. Standing in our kitchen, right next to the refrigerator, she could not stop crying. I saw her, so I went to her and laid my hands on her shoulders. I commanded that spirit of grief to leave her. That very day, her uncontrollable sobbing stopped, and a peaceful calm came over her. She was still sad, but her faith was resolute.

Since December 27, 2021, we had experienced a sovereign move of God in our church congregation. Josh was an integral part of the fabric of our church. He had always loved my preaching, even when he was a little boy. He was our Pentecostal "holy roller," and later in his life he still enjoyed watching Pentecostal choirs worshipping through music more than almost anything in life.

He participated in all the inner workings of our church. He was involved in everything, especially the communion services, when he often preached mini sermons to bolster people's faith. Perhaps not surprisingly, Josh had been one of the leading proponents of praying for the sick, leading us into an emphasis on divine healing at our church. He often told our congregation, "If you can't have faith for your healing, I will have the faith *for* you." Josh ate, drank, and slept divine healing. The license plate on his car read, "HEAL SICK." People who saw it often asked him if he was a doctor. One of his favorite sayings was a quote from Kathryn Kuhlman: "I don't believe what I see; I see what I believe."

Josh had earned the respect and love of our congregation. Our church family members cared deeply for him and looked to us for how they should respond to his hospitalization.

We could barely believe that this had happened, much less process it in some way that made sense, and we refused to believe that Josh would die. We did not even know a mortician or a funeral home director. We weren't prepared for death. Despite the overwhelming odds, we expected life.

CHAPTER 32

Believing for the Best

CANDY SPENT THE NIGHT IN JOSH'S HOSPITAL ROOM on Saturday, February 5, 2022. Meanwhile, his temperature was soaring. She called me and said, "His fever is 104 and his oxygen level has gone down. I think you better come over here."

With Josh's condition continuing to decline, on Sunday, February 6, I got up early in the morning and went to the hospital to see him. I prayed for him again, then around noon, Candy and I went back home. I was getting dressed to go to the church to preach at our service beginning at 3:00 p.m. About that time, Carrie called Candy. "Mom, Josh's temperature has spiked to 107 degrees," she said. "His oxygen level has dropped down to barely 20 percent. You better come quickly."

I called Dee Jay Shoulders, a local minister, whose Sunday service was held earlier than ours. "Can you come and preach for me this afternoon?" I asked him. "We have a family emergency."

"I'm at lunch," Dee Jay said, "but I will head right over to the church."

Interestingly, our friend Ricky Skaggs had called and asked if he could come to the church to sing that day. Ricky is an internationally known music artist with a full schedule of personal appearances. He did not need another performance. But he and his wife Sharon had been praying for us. Without us even asking, Ricky said he felt compelled to come to the church and participate in the service. We were deeply grateful and welcomed Ricky's help.

Our daughter Jasmine, out of quarantine and feeling strong and healthy, handled the entire service that day. As much as she wanted to be with Josh, the Holy Spirit empowered her to conduct Candy's part of the service, introduce Ricky, then introduce Pastor Dee Jay. She also handled the invitation for people with spiritual needs to respond at the close of the service. Afterward, she and JonMichael headed to the hospital.

Candy and I had planned to return to the hospital later that day after the church service, but when we got the call about Josh's rapidly declining condition, we rushed back to the hospital immediately. By the time we got there, his temperature had risen to 108 degrees. Carrie was already there, as was Patty. Josh's face was bright red; his hands were swollen, as was his entire body. I still believed that, at any moment, he was going to open his eyes and snap out of it, and we'd celebrate what God had done. I walked to my son's bedside and laid my hand on Josh. My hands were still on him when I felt him take his last breath. It was 3:02 in the afternoon. I knew at that moment that he had died.

"He just passed," I said quietly. None of us cried because we all believed that God could raise Josh from the dead. I had faith that God was going to do it. A supernatural wave of peace permeated that room. It was truly a peace that passed understanding. No one shed a tear. We did not believe that it was over.

I crawled up onto Josh's body, as the prophet Elisha had done when he had prayed for the Shunammite woman's son who had died (2 Kings 4:34). I pressed my face to Josh's face, my eyes to his eyes, my lips to his, with his blackened tongue rubbing against mine, and I prayed just as Elisha had done. I felt Josh's bodily fluids squirting out of the tracheotomy onto me, but I didn't care. A grotesque smell filled the room. I continued praying with unabashed faith that God would raise my son from the dead. I spoke to him calmly, "Son, wake up. In the name of Jesus, wake up." After a while, I slid off Josh and walked around the room praying, then I climbed back on top of him again. My family members and I stayed right there and prayed for several hours. We played praise and worship music, including songs such as "His Goodness Is Running after Me" and "Ain't No Grave (Gonna Hold Me Down)," and we prayed and worshipped. We played a video of some of Josh's communion messages that he had preached at our church, with Josh himself declaring divine healing for others. It was comforting to hear his voice, and we sat calmly in the room, waiting for God to raise Josh to life.

I could feel urine on me from Josh's bladder that had burst. Although time was passing and the color had drained from Josh's face, and the swelling had diminished, revealing his emaciated features, I still believed and declared that God would raise him from the dead. Jasmine and JonMichael arrived, as did Nicholas, and they joined us in praying and believing that God would raise Josh from the dead.

But He didn't. Our son did not move; he didn't take another breath. He did not rise—yet.

After a few hours, we realized that this was not God's way, so we had no intention of keeping Josh's body in the morgue or doing anything else weird. No doubt, the hospital personnel thought we were nuts already, but we weren't concerned about their opinions.

What I didn't know was that my son had been experiencing stroke-level blood pressure issues for some time prior to the brain aneurism. He had taken prescription medications to reduce his high blood pressure from the time he was in his late thirties. But over the last three years or so of his life, Josh had embraced some messages about divine healing that he heard—recorded messages from Kathryn Kuhlman, A. A. Allen, Andrew Wommack, and other ministers with an emphasis on healing.

Instead of taking his blood pressure medicine, Josh took communion every day—the bread and wine (or grape juice) symbolic of the body and blood of Jesus Christ. No doubt, Josh believed that God would take care of him physically because of his faith. None of his family members, including Carrie, Candy, or me, knew about the blood pressure concerns. We all noticed that Josh's face was often flushed red, but we didn't give that a second thought. We knew he had been taking blood pressure medications for years, but none of us realized that he had recently stopped taking them.

We later learned that months before Josh died, he had gone to an eye doctor, where a friend from another congregation worked. When they did a glaucoma test, they discovered that he was at stroke level.

The eye doctor told Josh, "You need to go to the hospital; your blood pressure is dangerously high."

Josh shrugged his shoulders, smiled, thanked them for the information, and walked out of the office. He did nothing to stave off the effects of the high blood pressure.

Apparently, he felt that since he was walking by faith and taking communion every day, he didn't need to seek the help of the medical community. But he was wrong.

Candy and I believe in divine healing, but we also believe that God has given us common sense, along with wisdom to use the resources we have available to us. We are thankful for doctors and the great health-care expertise we enjoy in America. Certainly, when we get sick or have an accident, our first response is to pray, but we also believe that God often uses the medical knowledge He has given to others to help His children. A hospital in the middle of the jungle in Kenya has a large, hand-painted sign outside its property bearing the slogan "We treat; Jesus heals." That is our attitude as well.

Josh was forty-three years old, an adult man making his own decisions, but had I known about his blood pressure issues, I would have strongly encouraged him to seek medical attention.

• • •

A popular Nashville songwriter had passed away six weeks or so prior to Josh's death. Tara, the funeral director's assistant at Spring Hill funeral home, had called and asked if I would be willing to lead the songwriter's funeral service, but I did not feel comfortable about it. I didn't know the songwriter or his family. Nor had they ever attended our church. I referred the funeral director to our friend, Pastor Dee Jay Shoulders, who was not only a local pastor but also a chaplain for the Nashville police force. He was accustomed to conducting funeral services for people he didn't know and for those who had not attended his church. Pastor Shoulders was willing to help.

When Josh passed, we did not even have a funeral home in mind, because we were convinced that he would live. Nor did Carrie, and we wanted to respect her wishes as Josh's wife. She looked to us concerning how we should handle Josh's death.

Carrie was distraught and asked us to guide her as to what to do, so Candy called Tara from the hospital and apprised her of our circumstances. "What do we do, Tara? We don't even know where to begin," Candy told her.

"You don't need to do anything," Tara said. "We will take care of everything. Stay as long as you wish, say your good-byes to Josh, and then just leave when you are ready."

We stayed for a while longer, and I gathered everyone around Josh and prayed again, committing Josh's soul to the Lord and asking for His peace in our hearts and minds. We all hugged each other and then we simply left.

It was a hard time but a precious time.

I grappled with what we had experienced: I had believed that God was going to heal Josh; I had declared by faith publicly that God would heal Josh; and when he died, I had still expected God would raise him from the dead.

He didn't.

Josh died.

What does a preacher who believes in a God who heals do with that?

All of that was hard enough. Telling Charlie, Josh's eleven-year-old son, that his daddy had died was even more difficult. Carrie was grieving hard, and I knew it would be stressful for her to explain to the children, so I volunteered to do it. The days ahead would not be easy for her, I knew, as she poured herself into raising two young boys.

I hugged Charlie and held on to him tightly. I said, "You know that your daddy has been sick for a long time. You know that, right?"

"Yeah..."

"Well, he went on to be with Jesus."

Charlie sobbed in my arms.

After a while, he asked, "Can my daddy see me?"

Candy said, "Yes, he can. And he loves you." It was a heart-wrenching moment, but we wanted Charlie to know that the story wasn't over. "And we will see your daddy again when we get to heaven."

When Candy's mom had died, we grieved, but she was ready to go to heaven, and we didn't want her to suffer anymore. "Lay hands on me, and pray that I will die," she said. Of course we didn't. But she was ready to leave.

The untimely aspect of Josh's death, however, threw us.

CHAPTER 33

Someday We Will Understand—but Not Yet

THE NEXT DAY, I GOT ALONE TO PRAY, and I leveled with God. "I will never pray for another sick person," I said. "Why should I? It doesn't work. You said if we ask anything in Your name, believing that we will receive, it will be done. You said if we lay hands on the sick and pray for them, they will recover. I did everything Your Word says to do, and Josh still died. How can You expect me to get back on the platform and pray for others when I no longer believe it works?"

A few weeks after Josh had suffered the aneurism and was still lying motionless in the hospital, I had preached hard on faith and God's power to heal our bodies. "Either this stuff works or it doesn't," I said publicly at our church. "When God raises up Josh, when He heals Josh, we're going to roll a coffin in here and I'm going to stand on that coffin and preach."

The day after Josh died, that statement came back to haunt me, and the devil used it to taunt me. I had made public statements of faith. Now the Enemy tried to use my own words against me.

As I was lamenting to God in prayer, the Lord spoke to me: "Call Brother Bowen."

I rarely ever interrupt my prayer time for anything or anyone, but I sensed that this was a specific instruction from the Lord. I called Rev. Rich Bowen.

"I need to know what the Lord showed you," I said.

Reverend Rich Bowen had called me a few days before Josh had died, but I was in the hospital and had not answered my phone. Rich had left a message: "Call me back when you get time." In the blur of activities surrounding Josh's final hours, I had forgotten to call Rich.

Now Reverend Bowen said, "I wanted to share with you that Josh was not coming back. I wanted to tell you before Josh died, but I couldn't get a release for it." Brother Bowen told me that he had seen a vision two weeks before Josh passed. The Lord showed him a conversation between Josh and the Lord in which Josh expressed to God that he did not want to return to earth. In the Lord's conversation with Josh, He said, "I'm going to send you back."

But Josh said, "I don't want to go back." So, the Lord allowed Josh to stay there in heaven.

Clearly, with all the prayers going up for Josh, the possibility of him returning existed, but Josh's will was involved, and he chose to remain in heaven, knowing that we would soon join him there.

I think God knew I would not pray for sick people anymore unless I received an answer, because, in believing for Josh's healing, I had done everything that I knew from the Bible to do. So, in His wisdom and kindness, God gave Rich Bowen the message I needed to hear. Perhaps had God not given Brother Rich Bowen that word, that Josh did not want to leave heaven and return to earth, I may not have been able to carry on in ministry in the same way. Most of us don't consider that the sick or dying person has a part in the healing process. But they do, and I believe that although God is sovereign, He often honors the will of the person for whom we are praying.

We shared Brother Bowen's message at Josh's funeral, and afterward, we received letters and emails from people in various parts of the world saying that those words helped them as well.

Jasmine had experienced something similar, almost as though the Lord were preparing her in advance. On Sunday night, one week before Josh died, she had a dream. In her dream, she walked into what she thought was a hotel, but she later realized it was a hospital.

"Your brother has died," a hospital staff member informed her.

"Where is he?" Jasmine asked.

"He's in the morgue."

"Please take me to him." They led Jasmine to the basement and there sat Josh, awake and alive.

"I need you to get up," Jasmine said in her dream, "and I need you to live."

"No," Josh said. "I'm not going to . . ."

"Josh, I need you to get up," Jasmine repeated. "And I need you to live."

"No, I am not going to."

The dream was so real to Jasmine that she sobbed for hours that night. She kept the dream to herself. She still believed and functioned in faith, but one week before Josh died, Jasmine knew.

I now understand that when the Lord asked Josh about returning, Josh had made a good choice. I also believe that God could have healed him of his high blood pressure. I do know that God took him, and his future is forever sealed in heaven, so I rest in the sovereignty of God and trust that our separation is only temporary. Josh is already living where the rest of our family wants to go. The pain of separation and the temporary loss is real, but it is dulled by the knowledge that this is not forever. We will see Josh again, alive and well in heaven.

• • •

Although I had attended and conducted many funerals over my ministerial career, I didn't know where to start in planning a celebration of Josh's life. Nor did we have a cemetery plot in which to bury Josh. Carrie and Candy and I went out to a cemetery with the funeral director and found a perfect location. We bought a plot in the cemetery and later learned that the section in which we had purchased the gravesite was known as the Garden of the Prophets, with a large statue of Elijah looking over the graves.

During the days before the service celebrating Josh's life, the Lord asked Candy, "Do you want to bury him, or do you want to plant him?" That seemed like such an odd question until we realized that we had a choice between merely burying Josh or sowing him as a seed.

In the days after Josh died, Candy could not pray. She could only cry with intense grief. One day, she told the Lord, "You have to lift this off me. I can't function with this kind of grief." "If you can't feel it, I can't work My purpose in you," she sensed God saying. The Bible says we do not have a High Priest who has not been touched with the infirmities of others. "You have a choice," the Lord told Candy. "You can bury Josh in sorrow and grief and unbelief, or you can plant Josh in faith and reap a harvest."

We chose to "plant" Josh in faith. We believe we are going to reap a harvest of miracles. What's the difference? If you bury something, it is over, but if you plant it, there is growth. A few days before He died, Jesus said, "Truly, truly, I say to you, unless a grain of wheat falls into the earth and dies, it remains alone; but if it dies, it bears much fruit" (John 12:24 NASB 1995). What the Enemy tried to destroy through Josh's death, I believe God is going to use to birth something new, something supernatural and miraculous, and raise up a new emphasis on healing. We have already seen people healed during our church services, but I believe there is a much greater harvest coming.

We know what it is like to hurt. That's why the superficial stuff in some Christian circles is difficult for me to tolerate. The shallowness is almost offensive. Now, I realize that the reason I am on the earth is to advance the kingdom of God, regardless of the cost.

But let's be honest: if you are going to change the world, you have to go through a lot of pain. When Josh suffered a brain aneurism, although my heart was broken, I refused to allow my faith in God to be shaken. I knew God was good despite the circumstances. When Josh went to heaven, even after we had prayed and fervently believed that the Lord would raise him up from his hospital bed, I remained unshaken, steady as a rock. Nothing could shake me from my faith and trust in Jesus. But that doesn't mean we were not crushed.

Candy was terribly distraught following Josh's death, as was our daughter-in-law, who was shaken to her core. But somehow, the experiences that God had used to shape me earlier in life helped me to be strong for my family in the aftermath of Josh's passing.

With the women traumatized and the family crumbling emotionally, I needed to be a rock. Candy and Carrie mourned grievously, and I felt it was my responsibility to help pull them through the despair. I wanted to be strong for my family and friends.

Candy later said, "I knew that Jesus dealt with my sin on the cross. And I knew that His blood also paid the price for our healing. But I didn't know or realize what it meant to experience the truth that 'surely He has borne our sorrows and carried our grief.' Now, I did, and to me that was monumental. Because that is what He did for me. If that had not become a reality in our lives, we could not function. Not merely from the stress but from the pain and grief. My heart ached, literally. I felt as though I had a physical pain and a hole in my heart."

Candy noted, "There is a confusion that accompanies grief. It is hard to think straight or to concentrate. Everything went back to Josh. We saw him everywhere and the things he loved. The power of Christ had to set us free from the grief. Had it not been for our relationship with the Lord, our grief would have been incapacitating."

It was still walking on eggshells for all of us, including me. Weeks after Josh died, I'd hear something interesting about some missionary, and I'd pick up the phone to call Josh. "Oh," I'd suddenly realize. "Josh is not here."

A person can get used to pain, and I had felt that sort of pain before, following the death of my father. I don't normally cry. But I cried at Josh's funeral during the first few minutes, and I cried at the gravesite.

Letting go is difficult.

• • •

You cannot change what has happened to you, or everything that strikes your life, but you can choose how it will affect your future. Your own experiences become the platform for your message to be presented. Chinese Christian leader Watchmen Nee, martyred for his faith in 1972, often said, "It is not enough to know the message; you have to *become* the message." That's when you are powerfully effective—when you *are* what you are preaching. Indeed, that's what many of the Old Testament prophets illustrated, whether Ezekiel or Hosea, Jeremiah or Jonah, they all illustrated the messages God gave to them through their own lives, and along with their spoken messages came perpetual troubles and often personal humiliation. Our family could identify with that and understood the sacrifices.

Jesus said, "In the world you have tribulation, but . . . I have overcome the world" (John 16:33 NASB 1995). Part of my great joy is that Josh left this world full of faith, full of the Holy Ghost—there is no greater joy than that.

Do I still have questions about Josh's death? Absolutely. But I choose to trust God. I know the goodness of God is working for us, not against us. I'm so grateful for His kindness and goodness. Whenever we need to know, to have His assurance, God will facilitate that. We don't have to have all the answers right now. We can trust the Lord to see us through. As Jasmine said at Josh's funeral, "If I had all the answers, then I wouldn't need God, and who would I run to? So, I would rather not know and have the Lord than know and not have God."

Josh and Carrie had not purchased life insurance. At the funeral, Candy mentioned that we had T-shirts with an imprint of one of Josh's favorite quotes, "I don't believe what I see; I see what I believe." Many people wanted those T-shirts after the funeral, so we made them available. People generously contributed a large amount of money to help Carrie cover her expenses and pay off her home mortgage.

Our family decided early on that we couldn't make this about us. Our loss was about using our suffering as a comfort to others. Many people were going through pain much worse than ours. Scripture says in 2 Corinthians 1:4 that we should comfort others with the same comfort we have received, so that's what we attempted to do.

Numerous people deal with the same questions we did. "God, why have things turned out as they have? We prayed, we believed, we did all that Your Word instructed us to do, but we did not get the results we were hoping for."

There is always a reason why the Word doesn't work the way we expected, even if God doesn't tell us the reason right now. We live by faith, and there are times when God chooses not to explain Himself—at least not yet. Even though we do not yet know the answer, that does not mean the answer does not exist. One day, we will know all that we need to know.

• • •

Questions abounded as the weekend approached. Could we control our emotions during our Sunday service at Regeneration Nashville? Should we get someone else to handle the music and the preaching while our family took a day of rest and sat in the audience? Should we attend at all or remain home and heal? What would it be like the first time someone asked me to pray for their healing? Would there be a reticence to pray for someone else in the aftermath of our many prayers for Josh?

Our entire family determined that we were not going to do things differently on Sunday, February 13, the first gathering of our congregation after Josh's funeral. Some people may have been surprised that I did not take that Sunday off, but I knew where my proper place was and where God wanted me to be—with His people, preaching His Word, and praying for those who needed healing.

Our son Nicholas, now a powerful man of God, set the tone for the service that day when he declared in his opening prayer that "healing is in the house." Jasmine led the congregation in worship, singing, "You are the Alpha and Omega, the beginning and the end." Anyone attending for the first time would not have imagined the ordeal our church family had just come through. The presence of the Lord was so real, and after several more worship songs, Jasmine brought that portion of the service to a conclusion and led the audience in singing, "Hallelujah! Praise the Lord! My heart sings His praise *again*."

Candy rose to assure the crowd that we had not abandoned our post. "There is healing flowing through this room right now," she said. "Do you still believe Jesus answers prayer?" she asked, without stating the obvious: *Do you believe, despite the fact that we prayed for Josh to be healed in this life, but he went on to heaven?*

The audience cheered and applauded.

"Do you still believe that we serve a miracle-working God?" Candy pressed.

Again, the crowd responded enthusiastically.

"Do you still believe in the power of prayer?" Candy asked as the congregation applauded and affirmed.

"So, we must move forward," Candy declared. Then, as she led the congregation in prayer, she declared, "The atmosphere is seeded for miracles."

As if to put an exclamation point on Candy's prayer, Ricky Skaggs, the Isaacs, Rebecca Lynn Howard, and Burton Gaar sang the triumphant song "Ain't No Grave (Gonna Hold My Body Down)."

I walked to the platform, and the crowd stood and applauded before I said a word. It was an emotionally overwhelming experience, and I knew they were not merely supporting me but lifting up my arms as Aaron and Hur had lifted the arms of Moses so the work of the Lord could continue (see Exodus 17:8–12).

I raised my arms in the air and said, "There is a spirit of victory in the atmosphere!" I sensed a strong anointing of the Lord and felt an incredible freedom in preaching His Word. Although I don't consider myself a great singer, especially in the company of the professional musicians in the room, at one point in the message, I broke into song, singing, "I'm undone by the mercy of Jesus . . . I've got Jesus; how could I want more?"

About thirty minutes into my message, I gave a prophetic word that I did not fully understand at the time. I declared that a move of the Lord was coming that would not be defined by time or location but by the abiding presence of the Spirit of God. I said, "There will be times at three and four in the morning when there will be buildings full of crowds beholding the majesty of the Lord Jesus Christ." Interestingly, what became known as the Asbury University Revival broke out one year later, on February 8, 2023, when crowds thronged into auditoriums on the campus in worship, repentance, and calling out to God all day long and all night long for more than two straight weeks. Tens of thousands of people traveled to the campus, simply to be in the presence of God. From there, the revival spilled over to various universities and churches around our country.

Near the end of my sermon, I spoke about the authority believers have because of the resurrection of Jesus Christ and the power of the Holy Ghost. "I can preach like this today," I said, "less than a week after my son was lying here . . ." I glanced down to where Josh's casket had been a few days earlier, and my words caught a bit in my throat. "Do you know why I can?" I asked. "Because there is resurrection in the atmosphere. Death has no authority over believers."

At the close of the service, I invited people to come to the front of the platform for prayer, and many responded. Without hesitation, I knelt down on the floor and wrapped my arms around the shoulders of a young man who had stepped to the front of the stage for prayer. I didn't flinch in asking God to do what He had promised to do in His Word. Our prayer team continued praying for the numerous people who had gathered at the front. Several people walked up onto the platform, asking for specific needs to be met, and with as much confidence as I'd had before Josh's passing, I prayed that God would heal them.

Candy and I prayed for Nancy Alcorn, the founder of Mercy Multiplied, a ministry that has affected thousands of young women for more than four decades. Then, as Jasmine led the audience in singing, "Through it all, I've learned to trust in Jesus ... I've learned to depend upon His Word," in a special moment, Candy and our good friend Terri Huffman prayed for Josh's mom, Patti, who had joined us in the service that day. Candy closed the service by leading a prayer for those wanting to know Jesus. A marvelous spirit of love and healing pervaded the atmosphere.

Yes, the Enemy had hit us with a hard shot, trying to rob, kill, and destroy, but God turned it around and used it for good. I knew that He would continue to do so.

These days, the pain is less piercing, but it is still there. But God is still there too; He is right there with us, even when it hurts. Several months after Josh went to heaven, his son Cash graduated from kindergarten. Our family members went along with Carrie to the celebration. Candy was visibly upset and was having difficulty holding back her tears as we sat there without Josh, knowing how much he loved his boys and how proud he would be— even at Cash's kindergarten graduation. Josh was always so proud of his boys and so active in their lives. A few months earlier, none of us could have imagined Josh not being with us at Cash's milestone, and now he was gone and we could not see him . . . for a while.

While Josh went home to Jesus, Carrie went home alone with five-year-old and eleven-year-old sons. She grieved hard. Now, although she had our help and encouragement, as well as that of our church congregation, she was a single mom raising two young children, and she missed her loving husband terribly.

One Sunday during our church service, I felt led to call her out of the congregation and come to the front of the sanctuary. We placed our hands on her shoulders, and the entire congregation prayed for her.

Carrie later said, "I felt that heaviness lift from me, and I have not grieved the same way since."

• • •

Josh had never been bashful about sharing his testimony of God's goodness with others. My heart overflowed with joy when I heard him say many times, "Don't tell me that a gay person can't be anything but gay, that a gay person can't change." He'd raise his hands in the air and declare, "Fourteen years—free!" We were so proud of Josh, how he had overcome homosexuality, how he had served the homeless people in Nashville, and how he had led our congregation in believing God for healing. We had worked together and had gone on vacations together, and we loved being a family. Jasmine especially had grown close to her big brother.

That didn't mean that everything came easily for him. Josh never really got over the rejection he had experienced as a child. He had made great strides, but it was still there as late as three years prior to his passing. He had, however, conquered much of the residual bitterness he had carried since childhood. Years later, a counselor helped Josh to see the truth more clearly and to be more open and loving with me. In 2021, Josh called his mom and found reconciliation about their past. His mom had repented years earlier and had lived as a godly woman, but it was important for Josh to speak truth into their relationship. It took great courage on his part to do that, and it was a milestone for him.

In the midst of our own grieving process, as well as moving forward, Candy and I felt that we needed to be there for Carrie and to let her talk about Josh. Some people are afraid to be around someone who is grieving, but it is not necessary to have all the answers. Just be there. We talked about the fun times we'd enjoyed together and the funny things Josh often said. And, of course, everyone acknowledged what an amazing chef Josh had become.

Even after he and Carrie married, Josh still made bonbons and other candy treats to earn extra money for the Christmas season. One year, he came up with a delicious cinnamon roll mixture and made a thousand cinnamon rolls at the warehouse.

For Thanksgiving and Christmas every year, he deep-fried at least thirty-five to forty turkeys and sold them to other people who wanted to enjoy his great cooking expertise.

Despite the popularity of his recipes, we recalled with great joy that in 2021, it was the first time in years that Josh didn't work through the holidays making fried turkey for others. Instead, he and Carrie and the boys went with us to Destin, Florida, along with our other family members, and we had the best Thanksgiving we'd had in years. Looking back, we can now see that God gave us that special time together before Josh died.

Somewhere around the 2021 holiday season, Josh began praying about his life having a larger impact. He talked to us about going into full-time ministry with the church rather than merely being the chef for The Bridge Ministry. We could not have imagined the greater ministry that Josh's life would have.

CHAPTER 34

What's Next?

MY WHOLE LIFE HAS BEEN PREPARATION for this season—everything I have experienced, both good and bad, has pointed me toward and prepared me for now. Moreover, I believe that all that I have experienced in life has been preparatory for what God wants me to do for the rest of my life. Perhaps that is why I did not enjoy success early on in life. Success that comes too easily can often breed pride, arrogance, an inordinate love of comfort, or complacency. God had to build a large reservoir of faith in me so I would be ready to help others. He did not break me to hurt me; He broke me to soften my heart and bring me to the place where I would trust and obey Him, where I would believe that He would guide my steps and bring good out of what the Enemy intended for evil.

I would not be the person I am had I not married Candy. She was the woman God picked for me. When the Lord brought us together, for the first time in my adult life, I had someone who truly believed in me and encouraged me to be the man God wants me to be. It's not been easy for her. I know that I am different, and not every woman would put up with my sort of quirks. But God knew I needed her. We work well together, and we believe together.

Although I appreciate the gift of prophecy that propelled me to a prominence I had never known previously, I believe one of the important gifts that God has for me is to pray for people who are sick. I feel a fresh anointing presence of the Lord, and He has given me a new sense of compassion for people in need. For years, I could not cry. Today, I cry easily with the people I pastor; tears sometimes well in my eyes during conversations when an emotional or spiritual subject arises. I often cry when I am praying over someone in need; whatever pain they are suffering is mine as well.

I sense that God is going to do miraculous healings in the days ahead. I believe we will experience in a fresh way the manifested presence of the Lord, where the glory of God and His Spirit settle over us and people are delivered, set free, and healed.

Since The Return, most evenings Candy and I and members of our church can be found praying for people who have contacted us from all over the country, and some from other countries, asking us to pray for them. We are seeing amazing results from these concentrated times of prayer for healing. Healings at our church are expected by the people and often take place. Several people with stage IV cancer have been healed. We prayed for another young man who had been totally paralyzed since birth. He was not healed instantly, but his mom emailed us and wrote, "Something is happening to him. The therapist is fascinated. He is moving in ways he hasn't moved in years."

I can't preach something I don't believe, but when I preach about God's power to heal our bodies, I believe He will do something supernatural. I pray for anyone who comes asking in faith. Not everyone I have prayed for has received divine healing—yet. For instance, a fellow named Jezreel has come to our services several times in a wheelchair, asking me to pray for him so he can walk. When Jezreel is wheeled up onto our platform, I pray for him specifically. So far, he is still wheelchair-bound, but we continue to believe that God will heal him. I have zero reticence about that, because I trust wholeheartedly in God's ability to heal. That's why I believe we will see paralyzed people and blind people healed. We have not yet seen the fullness of what God has in mind to do, and we believe our best days are ahead of us.

I'm convinced people everywhere need a fresh visitation of the presence of the Lord. Throughout Scripture, we can see that God will do what He has said He will do. When His people obey Him, He shows up in power and glory. That is the kind of supernatural presence we long for today. People who experienced Kathryn Kuhlman's ministry in the 1950s and 1960s said that at times they could see a haze in the room, and researcher Roberts Liardon revealed that people in attendance could feel a vibration of the Lord in that place.[9] In such a powerful spiritual environment, doubters and even atheists may find God, because they come into contact with something they cannot explain—the power and presence of the Lord—and they are convinced God is real.

If we build on what human beings can do, we will build in vain, and our works won't stand. But if we base everything we do on the presence of the Lord, we will have an influence that will last not merely for a few years, but throughout eternity.

I believe that in the days ahead, our heavenly Father will transform many of our local churches into healing centers and places where people can find a genuine relationship with Jesus Christ. I believe God is shifting us from the prophetic ministry to the apostolic, so we need to prepare and make room for that change.

In recent years, I've been associated with prophetic ministries, and I know that God has spoken prophetic words through me, for which I am humbly grateful. But we didn't build our church on prophecy. In fact, 95 percent of my ministry is in preaching the Word, helping people to understand the Bible and how it applies to our daily lives in practical ways. Certainly, there have been times when I've been preaching a sermon, and suddenly, the Spirit of Prophecy will come upon me, and I know it is the Lord speaking directly through me. But for the most part, I preach the messages He has helped me prepare in advance.

In studying the Old Testament, I noticed that in the holy of holies, in the temple of God in Jerusalem, there was a gold-covered table, three feet long and eighteen inches wide. On this table of showbread were twelve loaves of a special, holy bread, also known as the bread of His presence. Stacked in two pillars of six trays, one on each side of the table, this bread could be eaten only by the priests. The bread on that table was replaced every Sabbath. Think of that: the leaders of God's people in the Old Testament received fresh bread in their sanctuary every week.

In our nation today, we have "bread" that has been on the same table for thirty to fifty years. Much of that bread has been stale for a long time. Sadly, some churches have no bread at all. Consequently, the congregation is spiritually starving.

Many people nowadays—even people who believe in God—have allowed their hearts to grow calloused, hard, and cold. When people refuse to obey God or believe His Word, the Holy Spirit is quenched in their lives. They are no longer convicted of sin, righteousness, or the judgment of God. Their lifestyles are essentially the same as people who don't know God. Others may believe in the Father and the Son, the Lord Jesus, but they do not have the power of the Holy Ghost. Consequently, they fall back on what they think might keep them in touch with God. They slide into a heady intellectualism, assuming mere knowledge of the world or even the Word will draw them closer to God. Or they slip into legalism. "I need to keep all the rules. I'll give some money to the church or help feed some homeless folks. I won't do this or that, go here, or there." They think that by their good works they can scratch, claw, and climb their way into the supernatural presence of God. That won't happen. We desperately need the softening that comes by the oil of the Holy Spirit.

At Regeneration Nashville, we continually seek to be renewed and refreshed by God's presence. Maybe that is why our ministry looks to many people as though it happened overnight. In fact, we spent years getting ready. We were similar to a bamboo shoot that remains small for a long time and then suddenly shoots up and grows stronger and more numerous as it covers the ground in the area.

God was bringing me to a place where I would depend on Him. And to see what God has done reminds us how much He loves His people. To understand what He yet wants to do in and through us is exciting.

What is it that God wants to do through His Church in the days ahead? Scripture tells us that Jesus came to heal the brokenhearted, so that's what we're about.

We are not trying to attract attention to ourselves. Some ministry people become so ambitious, driven to succeed, driven to be up in front of others, to have a large congregation, to be on television, or to write the best-selling book. Those things aren't necessarily wrong, but they can distract a person from truly serving God where he or she is right now. We want to be a place of healing, where people can find freedom from guilt, cleansing of sin, the fullness of God's Spirit, and the healing of their physical bodies in *this* life, not simply in heaven, one of these days.

God allowed me to serve in obscurity for so long that it burned the unholy ambitions out of me. Similar to the apostle Paul, I learned to love God and live contentedly whether in poverty or abundance.

Before The Return, I had long since stopped dreaming of any significant or widespread ministry. Over the years, I had experienced the bursting of so many of my idealistic spiritual balloons, I no longer expected any of them to float higher than where I could see. I still longed to do more for God, but I was okay to serve wherever and however He chose. If He wanted me to wash pots and pans after Candy fed hundreds of people under Nashville's Jefferson Street Bridge each week, I would be the best dishwasher I could be. I had grown content and was willing to minister in obscurity if that is where God could best use my life to glorify Jesus and point some people to Him.

My guest appearance at The Return was sort of an uncovering. After living more than sixty-five years, I was brought to a place of public prominence I had never previously known or imagined.

I could easily relate to the biblical character John the Baptist, who lived his first thirty years in obscurity and then ministered in the wilderness for a mere six months before he was beheaded at the vicious demand of King Herod's wife. Yet it was John the Baptist who first pointed the public's attention to Jesus: "Behold, the Lamb of God who takes away the sin of the world!" (John 1:29 NASB 1995). John never claimed to be a big deal; he was simply a voice preparing the way for Jesus. Maybe that's what I am to be as well—a voice preparing the way for someone more prominent or more spiritually powerful than I am who will come to the forefront. Certainly, I've sensed that I am a voice preparing people for the last days before the Lord's return, the final outpouring of God's healing grace, and the great harvest of people coming to know Jesus.

For years before now, I felt that I had been born out of season, that my time had not yet come. My sort of ministry did not do well during the "prosperity season" of the church, in the late 1970s through the mid-2000s. At a time when megachurches were growing and the Church was thriving and prosperous, I was preaching holiness and sacrifice and dedication. That message was not popular.

On occasion, I felt a strong anointing from God, aware that He wanted to do something special in and through me. But for some reason, it was not the right time. I'd take two steps forward and three steps backward. Nevertheless, every major loss I experienced in the past has had something to do with my ministry now and in the future. I didn't understand that earlier in my life, but I do now. Looking back, I can see that God has been shaping me, getting me ready for what He wants to do in the days ahead. The Lord told me, "I took you through the fires and developed your anointing on the inside so it will support the anointing I want to put on the outside."

In the meantime, Candy and I and our church congregation did everything we knew to do, even some "outside of the box" attempts at evangelism in the Nashville area. For instance, we rented a billboard in downtown Nashville above the Hustler shop, a venue known for purveying pornographic materials. We posted a picture of Candy and me, along with an invitation to attend our church. As far as we know, nobody decided to attend our services because of that billboard, but it did attract some attention.

But since the 2020s, things have changed in America, and people are looking for hope and truth. Many are asking, "Can God supernaturally change these circumstances?" Suddenly, the message has become relevant. The only difference is that people have sensed they cannot solve the problems that face us; they are desperate for God's supernatural intervention.

When the bright lights are shining and the electricity is on, there's no need for a flashlight. But now that the lights in America have grown dim, people are looking for a light. We were the flashlight while the electricity was still on. Few people even noticed us.

We weren't needed as much, until the lights went out in the world. Suddenly, we became necessary.

I've been hidden in a drawer for a long time, and now that the lights are out, people have discovered me. That gives me more understanding of my purpose, even though it has been lonely and painful at times. On the other hand, it is hard to dissuade me of the truth; I'm not going to change the message. It was real then, and it is real now. Because I have experienced so many jarring jolts in life, I have found what matters, and it is hard to shake me from my positions. I know where I am going. My interior spiritual compass has a strong "due North," and I will not be swayed by success, failure, or people's fickle opinions.

Nowadays, our services at Regeneration Nashville are seen in more than one hundred countries. More than two hundred thousand people tune in online every week, and multitudes more view our services later. We continue to see people healed. Several people have reported that they were healed of cancer. During one service, we prayed for a woman who had been diagnosed with terminal cancer. Almost immediately after I prayed for her, she vomited a black bile-like substance and had to leave the service. But a few months later, she came back. She stood in front of the entire congregation and witnessed that she had been healed of the cancer!

In July 2022, fewer than five months after Josh went to heaven, a man named Chuck Twelves drove from Choctaw, Oklahoma, to Nashville so he could receive prayer during our service. Chuck had suffered for years with aortic stenosis, and his condition continued to worsen as he aged.

I did not know Chuck and knew nothing about what ailed him as he stepped onto the platform. But as I prayed for him, I felt moved to ask the Lord specifically for healing of Chuck's back and his heart.

When Chuck returned home, he was examined by his doctor. Afterward, he received the report from the cardiac stenographer, saying, "There is no aortic stenosis." It was gone!

Chuck later wrote to us, "My back pain has changed and I'm no longer crippled by this anymore!"

We heard of another account in which a little boy was healed of autism. We take no credit for these things; only God can do these sorts of wonders. But because our church is becoming known as a house of healing, people seem drawn to us, and we pray for as many as we can. During most of our evenings, people from our congregation are praying on the phones with needy people from all over the United States. Candy's team of prayer warriors gathers at the church almost every day to pray for the many needs of people who are coming our way. We prayed for a person with stage IV brain cancer, and when the individual went back to the doctor, the doctor said, "I don't know what has happened or how to explain it, but I can't find the cancer. It is gone."[10]

One of our prayers, of course, is that multitudes of believers will pick up this mantle of prayer. We believe there will be a reversal in the spirit world when God's people pick up the weapons of spiritual warfare and put the Enemy's troops to flight.

The growth of our congregation has freed Candy and me in many ways. Our success has allowed us to hire people who are wise, skilled, and able to do the work of the ministry. It has freed us to be more intentional about what we do rather than neglecting our top priorities.

Moreover, God has freed us to seek Him more whole-heartedly. Our focus has changed. Our time is used more wisely and more efficiently. I can spend most of my time during the day praying. Candy and I lead a simple life, dominated these days by praying for people in need and adoring our grandkids.

Additionally, one of the great delights of my life has been seeing Candy regain the joy of singing after more than twenty years of rarely ever singing a solo in public. The depression that led to the formation of The Bridge Ministry is gone, and in 2022, I watched and listened in amazement when Candy conducted a funeral for our friends Steve and Terri's son-in-law. During the service, Candy sang "Master of the Wind," and as she began singing, I thought, *Oh, my! I hear the Candy I knew who could sing like an angel. She's back!*

These days, we simply want to do what God wants us to do. My prayer is, "God, let us see Your glory. Expand our horizons, that the eyes of our understanding may be enlightened."

I often pray in these tumultuous times, "Lord, You said that You would reveal Yourself to Your prophets, but right now nobody knows what You are doing." There are things we need to know.

God often uses types and shadows to show us previews of things yet to come. For instance, when God took the Hebrew people out of Egypt and into their inheritance in the Promised Land, the trip should have taken only eleven days. Instead, because of their lack of faith, it took forty years. Meanwhile, as God's people made their way toward new life and freedom, a death angel was released in Egypt.

A death of similar sorts will come upon the earth, especially the United States. Years ago, the Lord said to me, "There will come a day when there will be so many dead bodies, there will be no space in the funeral homes." It was an ominous word, but I delivered it, knowing that the word was *through* me but not *from* me. I was simply the messenger. That prophecy has not yet come to pass, but we learned through COVID how quickly life on planet Earth can change.

Nowadays, we get too caught up in looking to our political leaders for answers. President Trump wasn't our savior, nor was President Biden, nor any other world leader, and neither the Democrats nor the Republicans are our enemy. Satan is our Enemy, and we need to learn how to overcome him by the blood of the Lamb, the word of our testimony, and by being willing to lay down our lives for the cause of Christ if necessary (see Revelation 12:11).

We need to keep our hearts and minds open in the days ahead to hear and discern prophetic statements. Keep in mind, not every prophet who claims to speak for God is authentic, so we must discern the spirits and weigh the prophecies that are spoken. Still, prophetic words will remain important in the end times. It seems that prophecy is often opposite of what is happening at the moment, or else it wouldn't be needed, so we need to listen and observe carefully.

Nevertheless, as tenuous as the times are, I believe our best days are still ahead of us. Your best days are ahead of you! Yes, the times are serious. The hour in which we live is not an easy one; corruption and perversion seem pervasive, but we should never despair or walk around with a gloom-and-doom attitude; we have good years ahead. This is not the first time that corruption and perversion have run rampant throughout society. Throughout Scripture we see it. We also see it in the history of ancient Greece and Rome.

We see disturbing similarities in our present society. Just because the US Supreme Court says something is legal or illegal does not change the standards of God. Base your actions and attitudes on His Word. Stand on His Word and you will be secure.

When you feel you have done all God has told you to do, and circumstances have not changed for the better, and indeed, you suffer for doing what is right, that is where you must trust that God will turn things around for His glory and for your good. In the days ahead, you will see His blessing if you don't give up.

As I mentioned earlier, I'm convinced that I am only on the earth for one reason, and that is to help God build His kingdom. There is no price too high or pain too difficult. As missionary pioneer C. T. Studd said, "If Jesus Christ be God and died for me, no sacrifice I make for Him is too great."[11]

Some people who know me well have told me, "You seem to be two different people—one sort when you preach and another person in private when you are not preaching." They did not mean that my character or personality traits changed, only my demeanor. In some ways, they spoke correctly. Outside of the pulpit, I am rather quiet and reserved, but when speaking for God, I speak forcefully, sometimes loudly, and always passionately.

But my manner of speaking is largely irrelevant. I've learned that it is not my words or insights that can touch and change anyone's life. It is only the presence of God and the power of the Holy Spirit that can transform a person. To me, that's all that matters. But that does put me out of sync with many contemporary pastors and preachers who are more glad-handing, people-oriented movers and shakers.

That's simply not me.

I love people and care passionately about their spiritual welfare, but I don't want to talk on the telephone or sit on a couch for several hours and talk about things that don't matter. Nor do I wish to enter into useless debates online. I've never been impressed by people, parties, or political influence. I'm not worried about being part of the in-crowd. I'm not obsessed with promoting myself. In truth, even writing this book has been a stretch for me. But I know it is not about me; it is ultimately about Him.

Candy grew up in gospel music circles, where self-promotion was considered a necessary given and an expected form of publicizing. In our desert years, she sometimes subtly encouraged me, "Maybe if you'd just put yourself out there a little more, doors might open easier." She often tried to gently pull me out of my comfort zone—which I appreciated—and sometimes suggested that I meet certain influential individuals who might be able to enhance our ministry.

"I ain't doing that," I said. "If God doesn't open the doors, I'm not going to try to break them down." For me to minister in the way I do, I know there is a price tag. Some people don't understand and don't appreciate that I am disconnected from many ordinary, mundane matters. I want to focus on things that are eternal. Everything else takes a lower priority to me.

I'm not a motivational speaker touting six steps to the Holy Spirit or five secrets to your personal healing or four keys to spiritual bliss and blessing. The flippant spirituality and fad Christianity that is in vogue today isn't real and will be eviscerated when times get tough. If God isn't in the message, I want nothing to do with it.

I want what is eternal. We need to be about things that will make a difference forever. On judgment day, how many saints will be standing? How much of what we have poured our lives into will have any lasting value? Certainly, we have to function in this present world—living as though Jesus could come tomorrow, because He might. He has not instructed us to quit our jobs, leave our families, and go hide on a mountaintop somewhere until He returns, as some misguided groups have done in the past. No, He has called us to live in the world and by the power of His Spirit, to point people to Him and to bring in the harvest.

Yes, the dynamic of ministry matters and social interaction with people is meaningful; relationships and fellowship with others are vital. I understand that, but that is not most important to me. My goal is to make God's vision come true. I'm here only for one reason, to promote the vision of Christ. I often ask God, "What do You want to see happen today? What is *Your* dream?"

As true Christian believers who seek to walk in God's will, we are already secure. I'm not worried about that. We're going to be fine in eternity. If I am in the will of God, I am always safe. No matter what circumstances we go through, we will come out of them better than we were before. But I do want to be led and empowered by His Holy Spirit.

We don't have to be profound, but we do need to be anointed. At our church, we have people from a broad spectrum of life, women and men, rich and poor, educated and uneducated, and people from various ethnic backgrounds. They are all looking for Jesus. He is the only One who can satisfy the deep longings of our souls. So, I am continually grateful for our pasts and all that God has brought our family through. God had to bring me to the point where I had nothing but Him, and I learned that Jesus is enough. God always stayed near to me. At my worst moments, I never felt that He had left me. Having Him near during those difficult times kept me balanced. I never thought He was mad at me. I felt that I had failed Him in some ways, but He never left me.

The Lord allows us to hold on to the memories even of things that hurt us, but He takes the pain out of them. We all have scars, but we no longer have wounds. Paul said, "I bear on my body the marks" (Galatians 6:17 ESV), but his wounds, like yours and mine, have been healed.

I now realize that until you have walked through the fires of failure, you will not be ready to handle the blessings of God.

There is also the unmentionable factor that few people today are willing to discuss. A prayer that I have rarely shared (until now) opened my eyes and helped me understand what God was doing in me all that time. I had been discouraged and a bit envious of what God was doing in some prosperous businesspeople and high-profile ministries led by some individuals who I felt sure were either misguided or not sold out to Him. So, in my usual straightforward way, I complained to God, "Lord, I don't understand why these people, who are less dedicated with less anointing, are so wildly successful. Why can't I seem to break into this circle and have some success in my ministry?"

God answered me just as straightforwardly. "Because one day I am going to destroy this system, and when I do, I don't want to have to destroy this system in you." This system included any ministry that could function successfully without the presence of the Lord. I understood that God was cautioning me against depending on money, gifts, or talents of human beings, operating under human power and abilities, to do supernatural work. Such a system cannot successfully challenge Satan and cannot strike fear in the Enemy, much less drive the devil out. Only a person filled with the Holy Ghost and operating in His power can have the influence on society that God wants us to have.

I still have much to learn, and there remains much that I don't understand. But one thing I can say with absolute confidence is that God has been faithful to me. At our son Josh's memorial service, Jasmine led the large crowd in singing "Goodness of God." With hands raised to God, we sang, "All my life You have been faithful. All my life You have been so, so good; with every breath that I am able, I will sing of the goodness of God."[12]

That was my prayer then, and it remains my prayer today.

While speaking at Regeneration Nashville in 2022, I heard familiar words coming out of my mouth: "One day you will come and you won't be able to find an empty seat. There will come a day when you will have to get here early if you hope to find a seat. Cars will be lined up and down the road in front of the church."

Some people rolled their eyes in skepticism when I spoke those words. Others who know our story—and more importantly, understand the goodness of God—are looking forward, as I am, to getting to church early!

More than thirty-five years ago, the Lord declared to Candy that I would be a prophet to the nations. I could not have imagined how that word would come to pass, but it did.

My prayer is that what He has done in and through my life will be an encouragement to you to trust Him to fulfill what He has promised to do in yours.

Afterword

ON SUNDAY, APRIL 16, 2023, Regeneration Nashville celebrated the groundbreaking of our new home at 709 Rivergate Parkway in Goodlettsville, Tennessee. We named the project Destination Miracle because God had miraculously provided the location and the resources we needed. We know He will continue to do so in the future as our church family serves the community and we continue to point people to Jesus. It will forever be known as a place where people can freely experience the healing power of the Lord.

For more information, contact us at:

Regeneration Nashville
P.O. Box 448
Goodlettsville, TN 37070-0448
615-606-1635
contact@regenerationnashville.org

Endnotes

1   Candy Christmas, *On the Other Side: Life Changing Stories from under the Bridge* (Abilene, TX: Leafwood, 2010), 20–21.

2   Christmas, *On the Other Side*, 22.

3   The Bridge Ministry continues to expand, now feeding more than 1,500 people face-to-face each week in six weekly outreaches in Nashville and one in Chapel Hill, TN. We also serve nearly 7,000 students through our Bridge to Kids ministry, providing bags of food and snacks to the children. The Bridge to Kids bags are distributed through 95 local schools and aftercare programs.

4   Joshua Christmas, "Joshua Christmas Deliverance from Homosexuality," YouTube, July 6, 2015, https://www.youtube.com/watch?v=wnTY8szGcVE.

5   Some people may have assumed that I misspoke when I prophesied that the president would be reelected. I did not. I spoke what God gave me to say. Millions of voters remain convinced that President Donald J. Trump was reelected, even though, through various machinations, another person occupied the White House in 2021.

6   Rock Church, "Kent Christmas—Rock Church—'Prophetic Word for 2020,'" YouTube, January 2, 2020, https://www.youtube.com/watch?v=DN68DvCIzss.

7   The Urim and Thummim were gems or stones in the breastplate of the Jewish high priest, which were consulted when God's people needed simple yes, no, or wait types of answers. Some scholars believe these stones were cast similar to lots or dice. See *The Revell Bible Dictionary*, ed. Lawrence O. Richards (Old Tappan, NJ: Fleming H. Revell, 1990), 1002.

8   This entire incident is readily available for viewing online or at Regeneration Nashville's website: www.regenerationnashville.org/miracles.

9   Roberts Liardon, "Kathryn Kuhlman: 'The Woman Who Believed in Miracles,'" in God's Generals: Why They Succeeded and Why Some Failed (Tulsa, OK: Albury, 1996), 271.

10 The person who experienced this healing continues to attend Regeneration Nashville and has medical records to attest to being cancer-free.

11 Norman Grubb, C. T. Studd, Athlete and Pioneer (Grand Rapids: Zondervan, 1946), 129.

12 "Goodness of God," written by Ed Cash, Brian Johnson, Ben Fielding, Jason Ingram, © 2018 Alletrop Music, SHOUT! Music Publishing (Australia), Fellow Ships Music, So Essential Tunes, Bethel Music Publishing (Admin. Bethel Music Publishing Capitol CMG Publishing, Essential Music Publishing LLC, Hillsong Music Publishing). Used by permission.

I had presented the biblical message for more than fifty years, but in 2020, something unusual happened.

Photo Credit: Frederick Breedon, IV

As I approached the podium in front of the huge crowd, I had nothing to say, no leading from God about what to share.

When I began to speak, God gave me the message; I lifted my gaze and saw thousands of people praising God.

A small portion of the more than one hundred thirty-thousand people on the National Mall for The Return, 2020.

I knew the words I was speaking did not originate in my own thoughts.

"I'm going to cause the church," sayeth the Lord, "to rise to her feet. There is a roar of the Lion of Judah!"

Some of our dear friends in ministry: "The Isaacs" and Danny Gokey.

Photo Credit: Frederick Breedon, IV

With Kevin Jessip, founder of The Return, and
Rabbi Jonathan Cahn, a true prophet.

Photo Credit: Frederick Breedon, IV

Seeking God in prayer has been central to my life, as well as my ministry.

Photo Credit: Frederick Breedon, IV

When speaking for God, I speak forcefully, sometimes loudly, and always passionately.

Photo Credit: Frederick Breedon, IV

*Candy and I have fun together. We are best friends, as
well as marriage and ministry partners.*

*A Candy tradition: taking the
first bite out of a delicious cake.*

Photo Credit: Frederick Breedon, IV

*Visiting Alaska together with God's
handiwork on display all around us.*

*With son, Josh, backstage at the Grand Ole Opry House,
where we held our 2021 July 4th Let Freedom Ring service.*

Photo Credit: Frederick Breedon, IV

Our son, Nicholas, has a heart for God and a love for people.

Big Kent and "Little Kent."

Photo Credit: Frederick Breedon, IV

Jasmine and JonMichael's family

Photo Credit: Meshali Mitchell

The grandkids were doing their best not to laugh by this point.

Photo Credit: Frederick Breedon, IV

His eyes often welled with tears as Josh talked about the blood of Jesus.

Photo Credit: Frederick Breedon, IV

"If you can't have faith for your healing," Josh said,
"I'll have faith for you." His license plate read: HEAL SICK.

Photo Credit: Frederick Breedon, IV

None of us imagined this would be our last Christmas photo with Josh.

When Josh went to heaven, he left behind his wife, Carrie, and sons, Charlie and Cash. We miss him, but we know we will see him in heaven.

Photo Credit: Kim Lancaster

Spending time fishing with JonMichael, Nick, and Burton Gaar became even more important after Josh's passing.

Enjoying God's creation in Alaska. I like to walk outdoors when I pray.

Christmas 2022 with the grandkids.

Photo Credit: Frederick Breedon, IV

Candy and I continue to believe for God's best.

Photo Credit: Adrian Payne

*From left to right: Nicholas, Cash, Carrie, Charlie, Candy, Kent,
Adele, Jasmine, JonMichael, Mavis Bleue, and Cooper.
Our family has been through many challenges,
but God's goodness remains.*

Photo Credit: Meshali Mitchell

Jasmine leading worship at Regeneration Nashville.

Photo Credit: Frederick Breedon, IV

Our daughter Jasmine and our son Nick both have a special anointing of God on their lives.

Nick's winsome personality makes everyone feel welcome.

Photo Credit: Frederick Breedon, IV

Candy and I work well together, and we believe God together.

Photo Credit: Frederick Breedon, IV

I want to focus on things that are eternal.

Photo Credit: Frederick Breedon, IV